PAGANS IN THE
EARLY MODERN BALTIC

FOUNDATIONS

Further Information and Publications
www.arc-humanities.org/search-results-list/?series=foundations

PAGANS IN THE EARLY MODERN BALTIC

SIXTEENTH-CENTURY ETHNOGRAPHIC ACCOUNTS OF BALTIC PAGANISM

Edited and translated
from Latin by

FRANCIS YOUNG

ARCHUMANITIES PRESS

The publication of this book was supported by a Book Publication Subvention from the Association for the Advancement of Baltic Studies.

British Library Cataloguing in Publication Data

A catalogue record for this book is available from the British Library.

ISBN (PB): 9781802700220

www.arc-humanities.org

Printed and bound in the UK (by CPI Group [UK] Ltd), USA (by Bookmasters), and elsewhere using print-on-demand technology.

CONTENTS

Woodcut showing Lithuanian pagans worshipping trees, snakes and fire, from Olaus Magnus, *On the Northern Peoples* (reproduced with the permission of The History Collection / Alamy Stock Photo)

PREFACE AND ACKNOWLEDGEMENTS

As their citizens will often tell visitors with pride, the Baltic nations were among the last in Europe to accept the Christian faith and lay aside their ancestral religions. In spite of considerable academic and popular interest in the persistence of pagan beliefs and practices in medieval Europe, the writings of late medieval and early modern ethnographical commentators on Prussia and Lithuania (which constitute an important body of evidence for the beliefs and practices of European pagans) have remained inaccessible to most scholars. While the pagan Balts attracted attention during the Northern Crusades of the thirteenth and fourteenth centuries, in the fifteenth century curiosity partially overcame abhorrence. Humanist scholars began to write about pagans in new ways, informed by new methods of historiography and ethnography. The resulting commentary is the subject of this book.

This project emerged from the convergence of two things: a research agenda that was increasingly focussed on expressions of popular Christianity and the question of "pagan survivals," and a longstanding personal fascination with the history of Lithuania. The book started from the thought that a good way to gain a better understanding of what was and was not "pagan" in medieval Europe might be to look at the documentary evidence for Baltic paganism, where paganism was truly a force to be reckoned with. From the start, therefore, this project has never been narrowly focussed on the Baltic, and the research questions underpinning the book pertain to European (and indeed global) history: how did early modern European scholars make sense of alien ancestral belief systems? And to what extent can we rely on their reports as a reliable account of pagan beliefs? It is these questions of interpretation that the present volume seeks to address.

I have incurred many debts of gratitude in the course of preparing this book. I thank my wife Rachel and daughters Abigail and Talitha for their forebearance with—and support for—all my historical research. The staff of the British Library and Cambridge University Library were, as usual, unfailingly helpful, and it is also appropriate for me to record my appreciation of the University of Valladolid for its digitization of the *Cosmographia* of Enea Silvio Piccolomini, the "Polona" project (Projekt Patrimonium) for its digitization of Filippo Buonacorssi's *Vita et mores Sbignei cardinalis*, and the University of Vilnius for its digitization of the *Catechismusa* of Martynas Mažvydas. I acknowledge with gratitude the generous award of a book subvention to support the publication of this book by the Association for the Advancement of Baltic Studies. I thank Peter Lorimer for preparing the map of the Baltic region, Sarah Clark for her expert transcriptions of many of the Latin texts, Anna Henderson of Arc Humanities Press for her support for the project, and Saulė Kubiliūtė for not only reading and commenting on the manuscript but also translating the Lithuanian summary of the book's introduction. I am also grateful to all those who, over the years, deepened my understanding of the richness of Baltic culture— Jolanta Coverdale, Jūratė Terleckaitė, and Mantas Adomėnas, to name but a few. Above all, however, I am grateful to Vaida Balsevičiūtė for first introducing me to the culture, language, and people of Lithuania. This book is dedicated to her.

F. Y., Peterborough, England

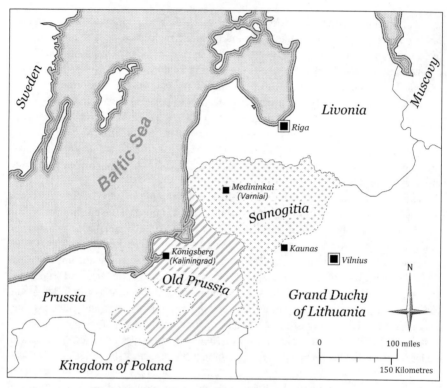

The southeastern Baltic region in the early modern period.
(Drawn by Peter Lorimer.)

INTRODUCTION

THE PEOPLES OF the southeastern shore of the Baltic Sea were among the last in Europe to accept baptism and abandon their ancestral religions. Indeed, in the twelfth century the persistence of ancestral religion in the Baltic region when the rest of northern Europe had been brought within Catholic or Orthodox Christendom inspired the Northern Crusades, a series of campaigns against the unconverted Slavs and Balts which eventually resulted in the establishment of the crusader states of Prussia and Livonia. While the Baltic peoples under the rule of crusading orders were forcibly (albeit often unsuccessfully) converted to Christianity, the Lithuanians and Samogitians not only remained ostentatiously pagan, but also expanded their rule over Orthodox principalities in today's Belarus and Ukraine until the Grand Duchy of Lithuania grew into one of the largest polities in Europe. Finally, between 1387 and 1417 Lithuania was formally (yet superficially) converted to Catholic Christianity. In the fifteenth and sixteenth centuries, the apparent continued existence of paganism in the Baltic fascinated a new generation of humanist historians and ethnographers in Poland, German Prussia, and elsewhere, who applied novel methods of historiography and ethnography to some of Europe's last pagan societies.

The Latin writings of humanist writers about Baltic religion constitute one of the most detailed collections of records of a non-literate ancestral religion in northern Europe. While there is no shortage of evidence from many European countries of "pagan" beliefs and practices deemed unacceptable by the church, the evidence for Baltic paganism stands apart because it was recorded by historians and ethnographers whose curiosity about paganism often went beyond the desire to condemn it. While attempts to suppress paganism were well underway in fifteenth-century Lithuania, there was also a new climate of secular scholarly curiosity in and about the Baltic region. The arrival of humanist learning in Poland and Prussia, along with the newly Christianized Lithuanian nobility's desire for a distinguished pedigree, produced intense curiosity about the origin of the Baltic peoples and their religion. As Lithuania took its place not only as one of the nations of Christendom, but also as a major Catholic power, Lithuania's history became a matter of European importance.

The transition from medieval anti-pagan polemic to humanist proto-ethnography in early modern writing on the Baltic peoples anticipated the far better-known development of sympathetic scholarly attitudes to the indigenous peoples of the New World. Catholic Europe's engagement with the "barbarian" Balts invites comparison with Catholic Europe's imminent encounter with indigenous peoples across the Atlantic who had no knowledge of the Christian faith.[1] The ethnographic discourse developed by writers on the non-Christian peoples of Europe, whether Baltic pagans or Muslim Tatars and Turks, created the space for positive evaluations of indigenous cultures in the aftermath of European contact with the Americas, and provided a language, conceptual framework, and range of imagery for scholars seeking to describe beliefs very different from

---

1 On the term "barbarian" and its equation with "pagan" in medieval discourse see Surekha Davies, *Renaissance Ethnography*, 40–42.

their own. Far from being a subject of narrow national interest only to the Baltic states, the ethnographic literature on Baltic paganism is of European and, indeed, global importance for understanding how Europeans perceived and interacted with alien belief systems in the so-called "age of discovery."

The purpose of this book is to provide English translations of Latin accounts of the origins and religion of the Prussians and Lithuanians written in the "long" sixteenth century, with the earliest account written in around 1458 and the last in around 1582. While some authors speculated briefly about the origins of the Balts before the middle of the fifteenth century, Piccolomini was the first humanist author to contribute an entirely new perspective to the study of Baltic religion by recording an eyewitness account of mission in Lithuania. The purpose of the introduction is to set these "humanistic" accounts of Baltic religion in their religious, historiographical, ethnographic, and literary contexts. The scope of this volume does not permit extensive interpretation or reconstruction of Baltic religion itself, a debate that has sometimes been a source of friction between historians primarily concerned with understanding the Christianization of Baltic lands and ethnographers primarily interested in reconstructing Baltic mythology and religion. Rather than the faithfulness or otherwise of the texts' portrayals of Baltic religion (which can be very difficult to assess), this book is concerned primarily with the uses to which discourses about Baltic paganism were put by humanist scholars. Such uses included the formation of a newly Christianized Lithuanian national identity, the formation of a common Polish-Lithuanian identity before and after the Union of Lublin, and Reformation-era debates over the religious future of Prussia and Lithuania.

This introduction sets the early modern Baltic region in its historical context before examining the phenomenon of "Baltic paganism" and the difficulties of defining it. The introduction sets the texts within the context of the extended Christianization of the Baltic region, critically assessing approaches to reconstructing Baltic religion, and considers the impact of the Reformation and rising interest in vernacular languages on discourses about ancestral beliefs and practices. The introduction then sets the texts within the context of the development of early modern ethnography, analyzing the various purposes to which these texts were put and the interpretative traditions on which their authors drew. Finally, the introduction analyzes the relationship between the different texts included in the volume and the textual traditions they represent, and considers their broader importance. A summary of the introduction in Lithuanian is included below for the benefit of Lithuanian readers.

The Historical Context:
The Late Medieval and Early Modern Baltic Region

In the late Middle Ages the Baltic peoples inhabited not only the territory of the modern states of Lithuania, Latvia, and Estonia but also parts of modern Belarus, Poland, and the exclave of the Russian Federation now known as Kaliningrad Oblast.[2] The names of

---

2 The term "Baltic peoples" is here used in its inclusive sense to cover the indigenous inhabitants of the Baltic region, rather than in its more specific sense of speakers of Baltic languages (which

many Baltic tribes, such as the Sudovians and Yotvingians, have long since disappeared from the map, while the name of the Prussians was co-opted by their German-speaking conquerors as the "Old Prussians" themselves were gradually assimilated into the new German Prussia. By the mid-fourteenth century modern-day Latvia and Estonia, known together as Livonia, were under the rule of the Teutonic Knights, a German crusading order originally founded to convert the pagan Balts that developed into a powerful monastic-military polity. The core territory of the Teutonic Knights, however, was Prussia, traditionally the entire coastal territory lying between the rivers Vistula and Nemunas on the southeastern Baltic littoral. South and east of the Teutonic Knights lay Samogitia and Lithuania, the two pagan territories never successfully conquered or assimilated in the Northern Crusades.

The name "Lithuania" was used in at least three different ways in the late Middle Ages. The strictest use of the term was confined to what are today the ethnographic regions of Aukštaitija and Dzūkija in the Republic of Lithuania—roughly the eastern two-thirds of the modern country. Samogitia (Žemaitija) was sometimes included within this restricted meaning of Lithuania, and sometimes considered a separate territory with its own language and customs. However, "Lithuania" also had an extraordinarily broad geographical meaning: the entire territory controlled by the grand dukes of Lithuania. The late medieval Grand Duchy of Lithuania was the largest polity in Europe, stretching from the Baltic to the Black Sea. "Lithuania" in this broadest sense referred to western Rus' (modern Belarus and Ukraine), along with the ethnic Lithuanians in the far north of the Grand Duchy. To further complicate matters, some ethnic Lithuanians lived under the rule of the Teutonic Order in "Lithuania Minor" (the coastal territory south and west of Klaipėda) so "ethnic Lithuania" did not neatly correspond to a territory within the Grand Duchy of Lithuania, in spite of the latter's vast size.

The Grand Duchy of Lithuania was a remarkable composite state that developed as a result of the gradual conquest of Rus'ian principalities by pagan Lithuanians from the thirteenth century onwards, at a time when the princes of Rus' were weakened by Tatar invasion.[3] Although they were themselves the target of periodic territorial incursions by the Teutonic Knights, the Lithuanians were protected by the thick forests of their homeland from both German and Tatar invaders, and used this position to their advantage to dominate western Rus'. After Grand Duke Mindaugas's failed experiment with Catholicism in 1251–1263 (for which he received papal recognition as Lithuania's first and only king), the grand dukes reverted to their pagan traditions.[4] However, while the Grand Duchy was controlled by a pagan Lithuanian military elite, it was from the start an inclusive, multilingual, and multiconfessional polity where pagans lived alongside Catholics, Orthodox Ruthenians, Muslim Tatars, and Jews.

---

would exclude the Uralic-speaking Estonians). Kaliningrad is also referred to in historiographical literature in its German and Polish forms, Königsberg and Królewiec.

3 Rowell, *Lithuania Ascending*, 17–25.

4 On the conversion of Mindaugas see Rowell, *Lithuania Ascending*, 51–52; Baronas and Rowell, *The Conversion of Lithuania*, 55–118.

While the Grand Duchy remained officially pagan, Lithuanian paganism in no way challenged the Orthodox Christianity of the Rus'ian principalities it controlled. Indeed, the Gediminid rulers of Lithuania actively protected Orthodoxy in order to command the loyalty of their Ruthenian subjects, while the Ruthenian language (the ancestor of modern Belarusian) became the Grand Duchy's administrative language.[5] The complex religious policy of Grand Duke Gediminas (ca. 1275–1341) upheld paganism as the Grand Duchy's state religion, while at the same time Gediminas supported Orthodoxy and invited Franciscan friars to establish a religious house in Vilnius on condition they did not engage in proselytism; he was prepared to execute them if they did.[6] On one interpretation, Gediminas's religious policy was designed to play off Lithuania's rivals—and the Roman Catholic and Orthodox faiths—against one another, as Gediminas gave periodic tantalizing indications that he might convert to Christianity, but never did.[7]

On this reading, the state paganism of the Grand Duchy of Lithuania—which was a set of ancestral traditions rather than a proselytizing faith—was first and foremost a political device designed to keep Lithuania independent of the influence of its Catholic, Orthodox, and Muslim neighbours. It constituted a politically-motivated refusal to accept one of the great monotheistic religions rather than a coherently formulated alternative to them; Lithuanian paganism was certainly not a rival to Europe's monotheistic faiths, and is better understood as a collection of ancestral practices that filled the void left by an absence of confessional commitment to any one of them.[8] When their refusal to commit to a religion ceased to confer a political advantage on the grand dukes, as Lithuania found itself squeezed between the Teutonic Order and the ever-present threat of Orthodox defections to Muscovy, a tactical conversion became the best policy.[9]

That policy came to fruition with Jogaila (d. 1434), the son of Grand Duke Algirdas (ca. 1296–1377) and grandson of Gediminas, who succeeded his father as grand duke but shared power first with his uncle Kęstutis and then his cousin Vytautas. In return for Samogitia and a promise to accept Catholic baptism, in 1382 the Teutonic Order helped Jogaila overthrow Kęstutis, but gave safe haven to the rebellious Vytautas after Jogaila failed to ratify the treaty. Faced with the prospect of the Order taking revenge, in 1383–1384 Jogaila's stepmother Yuliana of Tver reputedly signed a treaty with the grand prince of Muscovy, Dmitrii Donskoy, agreeing that Jogaila would receive Orthodox

---

5 Frost, *Oxford History of Poland-Lithuania*, 26.

6 Rowell, *Lithuania Ascending*, 275–77. On the Franciscan missions see also Baronas and Rowell, *The Conversion of Lithuania*, 175–220.

7 Rowell, *Lithuania Ascending*, 195–98.

8 On the state cult in medieval Lithuania see Rowell, *Lithuania Ascending*, 118–48; Vaitkevičius, "The Main Features of the State Religion." For a skeptical assessment of the idea of Lithuanian paganism as state policy see Baronas, "Christians in Late Pagan, and Pagans in Early Christian Lithuania."

9 Frost, *Oxford History of Poland-Lithuania*, 28. On Jogaila's road to Catholicism and the crown of Poland see Baronas and Rowell, *The Conversion of Lithuania*, 221–60.

baptism,[10] but in the end Jogaila decided his best option was to marry the young queen of Poland, Jadwiga. By a treaty signed at Krewo (in present-day Belarus) Jogaila promised "to apply his lands of Lithuania and Rus' to the crown of Poland forever" (*terras suas Lithuaniae et Rusiae coronae regni Poloniae perpetuo applicare*) in return for recognition as king of Poland.[11] Accordingly, Jogaila finally received Catholic baptism in Wawel Cathedral on February 14, 1385.[12]

The exact meaning of the dynastic union into which Jogaila entered with Poland continues to be debated to this day, but Jogaila reinvented himself as King Władysław II Jagiełło and set about bringing the Christian faith to Lithuania. The conversion of Lithuania formally occurred in Vilnius in February 1387, and marked the nominal acceptance of Catholicism by Lithuania's noble elite (apart from those who were already Orthodox) and the superficial conversion of the people of Aukštaitija and Dzūkija. However, the majority of the Grand Duchy's people were Orthodox Ruthenians, and the Duchy of Samogitia remained pagan, and formally in the hands of the Teutonic Order. It was only after Władysław's decisive defeat of the Order at the Battle of Grunwald (or Žalgiris) in 1410 that he was able to assert his authority over Samogitia by going there to formally convert the region to the Christian faith in October 1413.[13] When the Teutonic Order continued to contest Samogitia, Władysław arranged for a Samogitian delegation to arrive at the Council of Constance in December 1415, as a demonstration of the success of his Christianization of the region in contrast to the methods of the Order, whose violence had done nothing to bring the Samogitians to the faith.[14] In reality, as will be discussed further below, the "conversion" of Samogitia was not the resounding success Władysław liked to portray.

While the "personal union" between Poland and Lithuania remained complex and unstable over the next century and a half, the Jagiellonian dynasty continued to rule both countries and Christianity was—at least officially—triumphant in Lithuania after the final Samogitian rebellion against Lithuanian rule in 1441.[15] Although the Grand Duchy faced major challenges from the Muscovites and Ottomans, Casimir IV Jagiełło managed to annexe the western part of Prussia ("Royal Prussia") to the crown of Poland by the Second Peace of Thorn in 1466, while eastern Prussia (later known as "Ducal Prussia") remained under the control of the Teutonic Order, albeit feudally subject to Poland.[16] The

---

10 Frost, *Oxford History of Poland-Lithuania*, 28–35. Baronas and Rowell, *The Conversion of Lithuania*, 251–56 dispute the authenticity of the treaty and argue that Jogaila's conversion to Orthodoxy was never contemplated.

11 Frost, *Oxford History of Poland-Lithuania*, 47.

12 Frost, *Oxford History of Poland-Lithuania*, 30–33.

13 On the conversion of Samogitia see Baronas and Rowell, *The Conversion of Lithuania*, 342–47.

14 Frost, *Oxford History of Poland-Lithuania*, 125; Baronas and Rowell, *The Conversion of Lithuania*, 347–53.

15 Frost, *Oxford History of Poland-Lithuania*, 299.

16 Frost, *Oxford History of Poland-Lithuania*, 228, 230

canonization of Casimir's second son Casimir (1458–84), whose body was enshrined in Vilnius Cathedral, lent the once pagan Jagiellonians the aura of royal sanctity.[17]

Sigismund I "the Old" (1467–1548) lost Lithuanian territory to both the Muscovites and Ottomans, but also managed to bring eastern Prussia under the Polish crown. Sigismund's nephew Albert von Hohenzollern (1490–1568) was elected Grand Master of the struggling Teutonic Order in 1511. Convinced by Martin Luther that the Order had no future after Albert's confrontations with Poland resulted in defeat, Albert formally submitted to Poland on April 1525 on condition that the *Ordenstaat* of the Teutonic Knights become a secular duchy with him as duke.[18] Albert also became a Lutheran, and founded the Albertina (University of Königsberg), the first university in the Baltic region, in 1544.

Sigismund resisted the Reformation, but by the 1550s Lithuania was increasingly controlled by the Radziwiłł family in the name of the grand duke, who, in spite of being polonized themselves, opposed closer union with Poland.[19] Mikołaj Czarny ("the Black") Radziwiłł (1515–1565), grand chancellor of Lithuania, was a Calvinist who took advantage of the weakness of the Catholic church in Lithuania to promote Calvinism,[20] while Lutheran missionaries sought the souls of still "pagan" Prussians and Lithuanians in the territories of Ducal Prussia. While it may be too simplistic to say that Lithuanians turned to Protestantism because they resented Polish dominance of the Catholic church,[21] the small number of Catholic bishops in Lithuania and the weakness of parochial structures meant that Catholicism had shallow roots in the country even a century and a half after formal conversion.

The Union of Lublin in July 1569, whereby Poland-Lithuania became a federal commonwealth with an elected monarchy, resulted in the more intensive polonization of Lithuania and a resurgence of Catholicism led by the Jesuits, who founded a Jesuit academy in Vilnius in 1579 that would become Vilnius University.[22] On the death of Grand Duchess Anna Jagiellon in 1596 the Jagiellonian dynasty, which had ruled Lithuania since around 1289 and expanded its rule to most of Eastern Europe, came to an end. The grand dukes of Lithuania would thenceforth be elected monarchs, and always one and the same individual as the king of Poland.

In the space of less than a century the Jagiellonians had transformed themselves from pagan warrior rulers into Renaissance monarchs who rivalled the Habsburgs as the greatest European dynasty of the fifteenth century. However, the success of the transformation of Lithuania's people into faithful Christians in the same period is more questionable. Even in Prussia, under the watchful eye of the Teutonic Order and its Lutheran successors, paganism in some form seems to have survived into the sixteenth

---

17 Frost, *Oxford History of Poland-Lithuania*, 280.

18 Frost, *Oxford History of Poland-Lithuania*, 392–93.

19 Frost, *Oxford History of Poland-Lithuania*, 323.

20 Frost, *Oxford History of Poland-Lithuania*, 443.

21 Mullett, *Historical Dictionary of the Reformation and Counter-Reformation*, 300–301.

22 On the Union of Lublin see Frost, *Oxford History of Poland-Lithuania*, 477–94.

century. Exactly how that Baltic "paganism" should be defined and understood is the question to which we now turn.

Baltic Paganism

The vocabulary we choose to use to discuss Baltic religion is fraught with difficulty. In the first place, "Baltic religion" should not be understood as a single religion of Baltic peoples, each of whom had their own distinct religious practices; it is, rather a conventional term used for the pre-Christian ancestral religious beliefs and practices of the various Baltic peoples.[23] The definition of "pagan," a term developed by early Christians to describe the followers of the old, local faith of the *pagus* (countryside) rather than the universal faith of the one God, is notoriously problematic.[24] Paganism is hard to define because Christian authors were in the habit of labelling as "pagan" any belief or practice they disapproved of, particularly in the Reformation period. "Pagan" is not only an etic term (bestowed by outsiders), but also a pejorative one.

There is no sign that ancestral ritual practices in the Baltic admitted any sort of clear distinction between "religious" and "secular" ritual, and if we choose to define paganism negatively as "non-Christian (or pre-Christian) religious practices," that begs the question of what counts as religious practice to begin with. For example, Christian writers often dwelt on funeral, burial, and nuptial rites as part of descriptions of the "pagan" Balts. Such rites can be interpreted as part of a "religiously neutral" festive culture which, while it clearly had religious implications (such as equipping the dead for a materialistic afterlife), was only "pagan" if critics chose to interpret it that way.[25] Sources produced in the ferment of the Reformation—as several of the texts translated in this volume were—are especially problematic, since it was a standard trope of Protestant anti-Catholic discourse to accuse Catholics (and, in the case of Jan Łasicki, Orthodox Christians too) of being pagans.[26] Teasing out the "real" pagan practices denounced in an anti-Catholic text from the popular Christianity imagined to be pagan by Protestants and Counter-Reformation Catholics is not straightforward.

The example of sacred trees provides one illustration of the interpretative pitfalls of "paganism" as a concept. As late as the 1760s Stanisław Rostowski wrote of "the gods of the Couronians, still secretly worshipped secretly in groves by the people today, from their oaks and altars ...."[27] Jesuit missionaries in Lithuania periodically cut down sacred trees well into the eighteenth century, but it is unclear why these trees were more idolatrous than the sacred trees of other long since Christianized European nations, such as

---

23 Ališauskas, ed., *Baltų Religijos ir Mitologijos Reliktai*, 14 (hereafter abbreviated to *BRMR*).

24 On the definition of paganism see Chauvin, *A Chronicle of the Last Pagans*, 7–9; Owen Davies, *Paganism*, 1–6; for a discussion of the definition of paganism within the context of medieval northern Europe see Palmer, "Defining Paganism in the Carolingian World."

25 Baronas and Rowell, *The Conversion of Lithuania*, 261.

26 Cameron, *Enchanted Europe*, 208–10.

27 *BRMR*, 432: "Curonum deos, in lucis adhuc furtim a plebe cultos, e quercubus suis et aris ...."

the fairy trees of Ireland or the "Ladies' Tree" of Domrémy described by Joan of Arc.[28] One difference was that Jesuit missionaries in eighteenth-century Lithuania knew that Lithuania was one of the last European nations to accept baptism. Did they therefore conclude, following a circular pattern of reasoning, that Lithuania's sacred trees were pagan because the survival of customs such as the veneration of trees confirmed that Lithuanians were inclined to paganism? In the absence of detailed information about the rites performed at sacred trees, we cannot be certain; but it is possible that practices little different from the popular religion practised all over Catholic Europe were met with particularly intense opprobrium in Baltic lands because those areas had a pagan reputation.

"Paganness" was not and is not an objective category, and the legacy of nineteenth-century folklorists determined to see "pagan survivals" in folk cultures all over Europe has distorted perceptions just as much as the religious paranoia of post-Reformation clergy. One approach that may mitigate the danger of mislabelling "pagan" practices is to adopt a minimal definition of pagans: unbaptized adults adhering to pre-Christian beliefs and practices, or people who may or may not have been baptized who sacrificed to ancestral gods. The act of sacrifice to a named deity arguably set someone apart as definitively pagan in a way less ambiguous than inhumation practices, for example. Yet even here the definition is not without difficulty, since a minor ritual act such as a libation could be classed as a sacrifice as well as the formal ritual slaughter of an animal—and, as we shall see below, there are questions about what constituted a deity in Baltic belief.[29] This book broadly adopts Ronald Hutton's "minimalist" approach to the category of paganism, defining paganism in contradistinction to Christianity as "the pre-Christian religions of Europe and the Near East," understood as "active worship of the deities associated with those old religious traditions."[30]

Recent scholarship on Baltic paganism has been cautious in accepting contemporary descriptions of pagan beliefs and practices at face value. S. C. Rowell has argued both that Lithuania before 1387 was more Christianized than it seemed, and that the Slavs were less Christianized than they seemed,[31] while Endre Bojtár put forward a pessimistic assessment of the extent to which the reality of Baltic religious belief can be retrieved from Christian sources that are essentially literary in nature.[32] Likewise, Baronas and Rowell evince skepticism regarding the existence of pagan temples and priests in late fourteenth-century Lithuania, arguing that the countryside was inhabited by a mixed population of pagan Lithuanians and more or less Christianized Orthodox Ruthenians; and, while various forms of divination were practised by the Lithuanians, accounts of a pagan temple on the site of Vilnius Cathedral are unreliable, and organized paganism was essentially extinct in Lithuania by 1387. The idea of pagan Lithuania was, rather, a

---

28 Meltzer, "Reviving the Fairy Tree."

29 Offerings to fairies remained common in the modern Balkans and other parts of southeastern Europe into the twentieth century, for example (Pócs, "Small Gods, Small Demons," 263).

30 Hutton, *Pagan Britain*, viii.

31 Rowell, *Lithuania Ascending*, 296–300.

32 Bojtár, *Foreword to the Past*, 278–356.

rhetorical *topos* necessary to establish Władysław's credentials as a Christian monarch; if Lithuania was portrayed as completely pagan it brought more glory to Władysław for converting the nation.[33]

While the evidence base for Baltic paganism in the medieval and early modern periods is greater than for most other non-literate northern European paganisms, it remains a slender body of evidence from which to attempt a reconstruction of Baltic paganism. It is beyond the scope of this book to attempt such a reconstruction; rather, the purpose of this volume is to contextualize the key sources for Baltic pagan religion and their authors (thereby providing a crucial foundation for any future attempts at reconstruction other scholars may wish to undertake). It is worth noting, however, that attempts at reconstruction and systematization based on folkloric material and comparative mythology (such as the work of Norbertas Vėlius, Algirdas Greimas, Jonas Trinkūnas and Gintaras Beresnevičius) are historiographically problematic.[34] The merits of comparative mythology as a methodology continue to be debated,[35] while supplementing medieval and early modern historical evidence for Baltic paganism with folkloric material collected in the nineteenth century (such as the collections of Jonas Basanavičius), on the assumption that it encoded lingering pagan practices, can lead to significant problems of interpretation.

Pre-Christian religion cannot be reliably reconstructed from practices in a Christianized society assumed to derive from pre-Christian religion, since whether practices are deemed "pagan" or not will depend, in most cases, on little more than subjective intuition and personal prejudice. We can no longer speak with the same confidence as Marija Gimbutas of "the [Baltic] folk religion which still lives in folklore in surprisingly pure elements going back to earliest antiquity."[36] The excesses of nineteenth- and twentieth-century British folklorists in identifying "pagan survivals," inspired by the writings of Sir James Frazer, provide a cautionary example against these fallacious lines of reasoning,[37] which often involve the enthusiastic exploitation of sources for their content with scant regard for their chronological priority or literary context. The Lithuanian folklore of the nineteenth century is evidence for Lithuanian popular religion in the nineteenth century, but not in the fourteenth.

Similarly, the idea that Baltic religion (by analogy with the remarkably archaic Lithuanian and Samogitian languages) represents a "pure" inheritance of the earliest stratum of belief from a common Indo-European culture is attractive, yet entirely unverifiable. It is an idea that rests on ignoring the possibility that Baltic paganism, like every other religion, was subject to continual and ongoing outside influence and reinvention. In the

---

33 Baronas and Rowell, *The Conversion of Lithuania*, 266–76.

34 Vėlius, *The World Outlook of the Ancient Balts*; Greimas, *Of Gods and Men*; Trinkūnas, ed., *Of Gods and Holidays*; Beresnevičius, *Lietuvių Religija ir Mitologija*.

35 For discussions of the merits of comparative mythology see Belier, *Decayed Gods*, 15–20, 228–40; Allen, "Debating Dumézil"; Segal, ed., *Structuralism in Myth*; Miller, "Georges Dumézil."

36 Gimbutas, *The Balts*, 204.

37 For a discussion of reading "paganism" back on Christianized societies see Hutton, "How Pagan Were Medieval English Peasants?"

aftermath of conversion, "pagan-seeming" practices can arise in a number of different ways, including complex processes of religious syncretism in popular Christianity, so that assertions of pagan survival can only truly be justified by historical rather than folkloric evidence. As Baronas and Rowell have observed, studies of Baltic mythology, characterized by a "headlong rush to catch glimpses of a lost mythical world," have not been accompanied by much critical analysis of the sources. Instead, they have generally focussed on "holistic" approaches to interpreting a very diverse range of material.[38]

None of this is to say that reconstructing Baltic ancestral beliefs is impossible, but it should be undertaken with the utmost caution. It is easy to forget that we have no account of Baltic paganism from a Baltic pagan, nor even from a former pagan. All of our sources were written by classically educated Christian authors who, even if they did not write for the express purpose of condemning paganism, viewed Baltic religion through the twin lenses of Christian theology and classical literature. At the very least, their views on what constituted the important elements of Baltic religion were influenced by their own faith and education. These authors did not write as dispassionate witnesses but as individuals with political, cultural, and religious agendas; they also wrote in a long tradition of interpretation of northern paganism. Disentangling the reality of Baltic religion from all of this is, evidently, a task of immense difficulty.

The paganism of the Balts was often mentioned in medieval Latin sources such as chronicles, papal letters, treaties, and geographical works. These sources usually describe warfare between Christians and pagans and comment on the unusual beliefs and practices of the Balts, but contain little detail about the deities worshipped by Baltic pagans. Medieval Christian accounts of Baltic religion generally emphasized the Balts' mistaking of the creature for the creator, ridiculed and expressed horror at the Balts' worship of animals, and wondered at Baltic funeral customs (such as the cremation of horses alongside their owners).[39] Christian authors often denied Baltic deities the title of "gods," but as time went on commentators on the Baltic wanted to understand more about Baltic paganism and therefore turned to Greece and Rome. Thus the fifteenth-century Greek chronicler Laonikas Chalkokondylas reported that the Prussians worshipped Apollo and Artemis,[40] adopting a tradition of *interpretatio Romana* (or, in this case, actually *interpretatio Graeca*) whose significance will be further discussed later in this introduction.

The Christianization of the Baltic

Several of the texts in this volume deal with the conversions of Lithuania in 1387 and Samogitia in 1413–1417, and all of them are preoccupied, to a greater or lesser degree, with the extent to which the Lithuanians of the fifteenth and sixteenth centuries could be said to be Christians. The formal moment of "conversion" (signified by elite accept-

---

38 Baronas and Rowell, *The Conversion of Lithuania*, 264.

39 For a comprehensive collection of medieval accounts of Baltic paganism see the first volume of Norbertas Vėlius, ed., *Baltų Religijos ir Mitologijos Šaltiniai* [hereafter *BRMŠ*].

40 *BRMŠ*, 1:541.

ance of Christianity and mass baptisms symbolic of the baptism of an entire nation) should not be confused with the process of Christianization, which in Lithuania was a long-drawn-out process, arguably continuing into the eighteenth century. Many of the texts included in this volume display an ambivalence towards the status of Christianity in the Baltic that is evident in the grammatical tenses used by the authors to describe pagan practices. While the imperfect tense predominates, with the sense of former practices that used to occur, the authors periodically switch to the present tense to describe ongoing pagan rites.[41] Martynas Mažvydas and Jan Łasicki lay a much greater stress on paganism as a present-day reality, but the other authors portray paganism as simultaneously a thing of the past and a feature of the now.

This apparent inconsistency in the portrayal of paganism reflects the rhetorical tensions at play in accounts of Christianization. On the one hand, portraying Christianization as a successful process brought glory to God and emphasized the political integration of the Lithuanians into Christendom; but on the other hand, it was necessary to portray paganism as a recrudescent threat in order to support and motivate continuing efforts to Christianize the nation. Assessing the extent and speed of a society's Christianization at any point in time is very difficult indeed, on account of the tendency of writers concerned about Christianization to exaggerate the surviving "pagan" elements of a society as a rhetorical and evangelistic strategy. Views of what constituted acceptable Christian behaviour changed over time, thereby casting those who failed to meet the required standards at any time as "pagan."[42] Christian literature on the pagan Baltic was often designed to shame Christians into doing more to bring pagans or semi-converted Christians to the fullness of faith. Furthermore, the prominence of outraged records of "pagan" practices in missionary literature such as the letters of the Jesuits can have the effect of concealing the extent of unremarkable religious compliance—which, by definition, was not worth reporting.

Hutton has astutely observed that debates about Christianization (and, by the same token, pagan survivalism) can lead into "endless, and irreconcilable, arguments over the extent of the survival of the essence of a religion when the people who professed it have been formally converted to another."[43] The Baltic region is unusual because the processes of conversion and Christianization happened there centuries later than in most of the rest of Europe, and the military role of the Teutonic Knights made the conversion

---

41 For example, see Johannes Stüler (Erasmus Stella), *De Borussiae antiquitatibus* (1518), 28–29: "Even now they are still buried in this fashion ..." (*Quo more usque nunc sepeliuntur*); Lituanus, *De moribus Tartarorum*, ed. Grasser (1615), 23: "The cult of Aesculapius still very greatly endures in certain places" (*adhuc in quibusdam locis durantibus maxime cultu Aesculapii ...*); Alessandro Guagnini, *Sarmatiae Europeae descriptio* (1581), fol. 60v: "Four miles from Vilnius is the royal village of Lavoriškės, in which many snakes are still worshipped" (*Est etiam quatuor a Vilna miliaribus Lauariiki villa Regia, in qua a multis adhuc serpentes coluntur*); Malecki, *Libellus de sacrificiis et idolatria*, ed. Schmidt-Lötzen, 185: "For many superstitious rites and idolatrous cults are still secretly preserved in these regions" (*Multi enim superstitiosi ritus, idolatricique cultis passim in his regionibus adhuc occulte servantur*).

42 Baronas, "Christians in Late Pagan, and Pagans in Early Christian Lithuania," 53.

43 Hutton, *Pagan Britain*, viii.

of Prussia and Livonia different from that of nations who accepted Christianity under an indigenous leadership. However, in spite of their late date the conversions of Lithuania and Samogitia were not significantly structurally dissimilar from other European conversions, involving a "top-down" conversion of the ruler and the elite followed by the baptism of ordinary people.[44]

The "stages of conversion" identified by the Norwegian scholar Fridjof Birkeli in the 1970s have proved influential in framing interpretation of the Christianization of medieval European societies. Birkeli argued that an "infiltration" phase (in which a pagan society has extensive passive contact with Christianity) is followed by mission, when missionaries actively introduce Christianity and a formal conversion event may occur. The third phase of "institution" involves the erection of diocesan and parochial structures and the establishment of the Christian church as an organization.[45] Timothy Insoll adds a phase of "identification," whereby a population begins to assimilate Christianity into its worldview and to align itself with the new faith, followed by a final displacement of the old religion.[46]

If we take the sources at face value, these stages of identification and displacement seem to have taken a very long time in the Baltic territories. The medieval rulers of Prussia and Estonia faced significant pagan rebellions against their rule and against the Christian faith—most seriously in 1260–1274 in Prussia and in 1343–1345 in Estonia. In Lithuania, the Samogitians reverted to paganism after their first "conversion" in 1413, requiring a "relaunch" of the conversion in 1417 (including the establishment of the bishopric of Medininkai),[47] but the Samogitians rose against Christian Lithuanian rule in 1418 and 1441,[48] on the last occasion led by Daumantas, who has been portrayed as the last Samogitian nobleman to openly espouse paganism.[49] At a local level there is much evidence for the persistence of old customs and a lukewarm attitude towards Catholicism in rural Lithuania in the sixteenth, seventeenth and even eighteenth centuries.[50]

Baronas and Rowell have argued that, while the conversion of Lithuania in 1387 was not inevitable, the decay of Lithuania's pagan official religion was already far advanced, and Christianity was already well entrenched in the Grand Duchy.[51] On this interpretation, a religious vacuum needed filling, and the choice facing Jogaila before his marriage to Jadwiga was not so much whether to convert at all, but whether Lithuania's future lay with the Orthodox or Catholic worlds. Baronas has portrayed the conversion process as the assumption of ever more Christian elements into fourteenth-century Lithuanian

44 For studies of other national conversions in Northern and Eastern Europe see the individual chapters in Carver, ed., *The Cross goes North* and Berend, ed., *Christianization and the Rise of Christian Monarchy.*

45 For a summary of Birkeli's scheme see Hoggett, *The Archaeology of the East Anglian Conversion*, 15.

46 Insoll, "Introduction" in Insoll, ed., *Archaeology and World Religion.*

47 Frost, *Oxford History of Poland-Lithuania*, 125.

48 Frost, *Oxford History of Poland-Lithuania*, 299.

49 Baronas, "Christians in Late Pagan, and Pagans in Early Christian Lithuania," 70–71.

50 See the primary sources collated by Vytautas Ališauskas in *BRMR.*

51 Baronas and Rowell, *The Conversion of Lithuania*, 266.

society, "which gradually combined and won the day,"[52] largely as a result of the lifestyle preferences of individual grand dukes.

In contrast to the late yet incremental (and relatively peaceful) Christianization of Lithuania, in Estonia paganism continued to be a site of resistance to foreign rule well into the seventeenth century. In the 1630s and '40s Lutheran clergy reported that people continued to gather on hilltops for sacrifices and elderly people refused to learn about Christianity, come to church, or receive communion.[53] Some rural Estonians saw Christianity as "an alien form of magic" and ridiculed neighbours who went to church. In many areas, pre-Christian burial mounds remained in use,[54] and as late as 1698 the authorities threatened people with dispersal by cavalry if they did not cease gathering for sacrifices on a hill at Lääne-Nigula.[55] At the same time, however, these Estonian practices were not unconnected with Christianity at this date, with sacrifices sometimes celebrated at chapels and on specific saints' days (although whether Estonians were sacrificing to saints or to traditional gods is sometimes unclear). In both Lithuania and Estonia, Christianization was accompanied by an alien language—German or Danish in Estonia, Polish in ethnic Lithuania—and it is not always easy to disentangle hostility to Christianity from hostility to foreigners.

Popular religion in early modern Estonia comes across as an entirely syncretistic mixed faith, perhaps comparable to Haitian Vodou's syncretism of Yoruba religion and Catholicism.[56] The assumption that what we encounter in accounts of Baltic paganism is "pristine" pagan religion hides from sight the possibility that the Lithuanian religion being described in fifteenth- and sixteenth-century sources was really a syncretistic faith based partly on badly understood and half-assimilated Christianity. As Baronas has pointed out, the missionary John-Jerome of Prague told lurid tales of Lithuanian paganism but made no mention of baptizing anyone, suggesting the people he encountered had already been formally converted. Furthermore, when a group of women approached Grand Duke Vytautas asking him to put an end to John-Jerome's activities, they complained that cutting down sacred trees was driving God from his abode—suggesting that they now associated holy trees with the Christian deity, or some version of him.[57]

The Christianization debate hinges, ultimately, on how the religion of a people is defined. If that religion is defined from the top down (a people adheres to the religion expected by its ruler) then the Lithuanians were essentially Christian from at least 1417, in spite of any wavering or deviant forms of popular religion. If, however, a people's religion is reconstructed from the evidence for worship "on the ground," a different picture may emerge. Yet while this latter approach may be desirable, since it takes seriously the

---

52 Baronas, "Christians in Late Pagan, and Pagans in Early Christian Lithuania," 53.

53 Kahk, "Estonia II," 278–79.

54 Kahk, "Estonia II," 280–81.

55 Kahk, "Estonia II," 283.

56 On the Christianization of Estonia see also Valk, "Christianisation in Estonia."

57 Baronas, "Christians in Late Pagan, and Pagans in Early Christian Lithuania," 72–73. Piccolomini's Latin is ambiguous, however, and it is unclear whether he is referring to some god of a polytheistic pantheon or to the Christian God.

actual beliefs of ordinary people, it is questionable whether sufficient evidence survives to attempt a reconstruction of the religious status of a people at any point in time. In the absence of self-conscious articulations of belief of the kind encouraged within Christianity and other monotheistic religions—but often absent from ancestral religions—the essence of the faith and religious beliefs of past people remains frustratingly opaque.

Gods or Spirits?

When it comes to belief systems that are only faintly understood, apparently insignificant choices in vocabulary can have major consequences for the conceptual framework adopted. For example, while many medieval commentators on Baltic religion identified the beings worshipped by the Balts as *numina* ("spirits"), the decision to name these entities as *dii* ("gods") by Jan Łasicki and other authors implicitly invited comparisons between the "gods" of the Balts and the gods known to all educated people in early modern Europe—the deities of ancient Greece and Rome. Combined with the desire to trace the origins of the Lithuanians to Rome (discussed further below), the temptation to discern a "Lithuanian pantheon" became overpowering—even before the rise of Indo-European comparative mythology created yet another motive to link Lithuanian deities with their supposed Greek, Roman, or Indic counterparts.

Norbertas Vėlius believed that medieval accounts of Baltic religion provided sufficient evidence to assert that the Balts had "personified gods, sharing some of them with other Indo-Europeans,"[58] but it is important to remember that the idea of "Indo-Europeans" as a group of people (other than the speakers of languages belonging to the Indo-European language groups) is a contentious construct, and there is no substantive evidence (setting aside hypothetical reconstructions derived from comparative mythology) for the nature of "Indo-European gods" or "Indo-European religion." Algirdas Greimas displayed some caution in this respect, arguing that comparative mythology might be used to identify divine functions but ought not to be used to identify individual gods.[59]

In his commentary on the "Samogitian gods," Łasicki was describing the beliefs of a people that had been formally Christian for almost a century and a half, not an unconverted pagan population untouched by Christian belief. It is possible (though unlikely) that Christianity in Samogitia was in full retreat by the sixteenth century. But it is also possible that Łasicki saw what he wanted to see, taking beliefs in spirits of nature that were current in many Christianized European cultures and treating them as evidence of pagan worship, because Samogitia (as the last well-defined European territory to formally receive Christianity) had a pagan reputation. But Łasicki would have been wrong to assume that whatever pre-Christian beliefs the Samogitians cherished made them pagans, unless we designate as pagans anyone in early modern Europe who held pre-Christian beliefs (such as belief in fairies or other minor spirits of nature) as part of their worldview.

---

58 *BRMŠ*, 1:74.

59 Greimas, *Of Gods and Men*, 193.

Some of the beings Łasicki described, such as the Kaukai and Barstukai, should probably be placed in the category of what Michael Ostling terms "small gods," tentatively defined as "animistic 'survivals' problematically present within a Christianity that attempts to exclude them."[60] The anthropologist Joel Robbins has pointed to the "ontological preservation" of local spiritual entities within a universalizing Christian framework in post-conversion contexts,[61] and this may be one way of interpreting the evidence of pagan survivals in early modern Prussia and Lithuania. While some Baltic gods seem to have exercised celestial sovereignty—most notably Perkūnas—the gods and goddesses of the earth, of the forests, and of plants and trees described by several of the authors included in this volume are hardly comparable with the deities of the Olympian pantheon. Writing to authorize a crusade in 1199, Pope Innocent III emphasized the Balts' worship of the natural world above their veneration of "unclean spirits,"[62] and Oliver of Paderborn (writing in around 1220) reported that the Livonians, Estonians, and Prussians worshipped "the spirits of the Gentiles" (*numina gentilium*), listing an array of mythical creatures: *Dryades, Amadryades, Oreades, Napeas, Humides [Naides?], Satyros et Faunos*.[63] Thomas of Cantimpré, writing in 1263, identified the forest gods of the Prussians with the Dusii of the Gauls, a group of nature spirits mentioned by Augustine.[64] A minority of medieval authors used the terms *deus* or *dii* for the objects of Baltic worship.

The idea proposed by Lewis Spence in *British Fairy Origins* (1946) that folkloric nature spirits are the remnants of degenerated gods, while not entirely abandoned by folklorists and anthropologists, has generally been succeeded by a greater recognition that "small gods" exist in pagan as well as post-pagan cultures.[65] The near-universal belief in these beings (under many names) across European cultures into the very recent past suggests that "small gods" often played an indispensable role in people's experience of reality in pre-industrial rural societies. Such spirits were not always the recipients of a formal cult, and they therefore survived in popular religion with little difficulty alongside the adoption of Christianity as an overarching framework of spiritual understanding. However, there were moments in the Middle Ages when the "fairy faith" that most ordinary people saw as compatible with a broad commitment to Christianity was elaborated to such an extent that inquisitors perceived it as a challenge to the Christian faith.[66]

Models of conversion and Christianity as the straightforward replacement of one faith by another fail to do justice to the complexity and endurance of popular belief. In a study of Rus'ian folk belief (which coexisted alongside Lithuanian ancestral beliefs in

---

60 Ostling, "Introduction," 10.

61 Robbins, "Crypto-Religion and the Study of Cultural Mixtures."

62 *BRMŠ*, 1:201.

63 *BRMŠ*, 1:224–25.

64 *BRMŠ*, 1:249. On Augustine's Dusii see Green, *Elf Queens*, 3.

65 Nevertheless, "demotion" of entities from the higher to the lower ranks of spiritual beings still occurs in some converted societies (Ostling, "Introduction," 20–22).

66 Green, *Elf Queens*, 16–18.

the Grand Duchy) Dmitriy Antonov has shown that the Orthodox church elided nature spirits with the realm of the demonic, yet people continued to offer prayers to *Leshii* ("masters of the forest") and *Vodyanye* ("masters of the water") at forest margins and bodies of water. "Vernacular Orthodoxy" increasingly influenced official portrayals of demons in the seventeenth century, who became progressively less spiritual and more fleshly.[67] The persistence of "small gods" in nominally Christian Lithuania can perhaps be discerned in John-Jerome of Prague's report that, even after he had cut down the sacred groves, "lesser groves" (*minores lucos*) still remained where women made offerings.[68]

In recent decades, historians of magic and supernatural belief have emphasized the slow and incremental progress of a Weberian "disenchantment" in early modern and modern Europe, which can no longer be linked unproblematically to any single process—be it Christianization, Reformation, Enlightenment or industrialization.[69] While nineteenth- and twentieth-century commentators on popular belief often saw "superstitions" as shadows that vanished instantaneously when the light of education was thrown upon them, the effect of modernity on traditional belief might be better compared with the slow peeling of the layers of an onion, where the outermost layers correspond to abstract assertions about divine sovereignty and the origins of the universe, while the inner layers represent supernatural beliefs associated with the mundane, everyday experiences of rural subsistence common to the majority of early modern Europeans.

The persistence of pagan practices in early modern Lithuania need not be perceived as a rejection of Christianity. A syncretistic response to conversion in late medieval Lithuania is altogether more plausible than the kind of decisive turning away from ancestral belief sometimes portrayed in evangelistic propaganda, and would explain the recrudescence of beliefs and practices deemed unacceptable by the missionaries. Nevertheless, Christianity's association with earthly power and with ultimate accounts of the origin of reality seems to have led, over time, to popular adoption of a broadly Christian framework for understanding the universe—the replacement of the outer layer of the onion, in other words, with abstract presuppositions coloured by Christianity. It may be no accident that the first sermon preached to the Samogitians by the Dominican friar Nicholas Vazik focussed on the creation of the world and the fall of Adam and Eve,[70] suggesting that the priority of conversion was to correct the Samogitians' cosmology and install the Christian God above all.

Yet the installation of the Christian God above all afforded no guarantee against the flourishing of a rich ecosystem of "small gods" at lower levels of the cosmos. A belief in spirits that might have been described as "superstition" (or, at worst, "heresy") in Western Europe was "pagan" if detected in Prussia or Lithuania. But the late Christianization of the Baltic did not necessarily mean there was any greater risk of folk belief

---

67 Antonov, "Between Fallen Angels and Nature Spirits," 136–39.

68 Piccolomini, *Cosmographia Pii Papae* (1509), fol. 111v.

69 Ostling, "Introduction," 13. For an overview of critical responses to Max Weber's "disenchantment" thesis, see Mishima, "The 'Disenchantment of the World'."

70 Długosz, *Historiae Polonicae* (1711–1712), 1:345–46.

overpowering Christianity there than in Western Europe. In the end, whether we choose to interpret post-conversion Baltic folk religion as full-blown paganism, pagan survivalism, syncretism or an eccentric form of popular Christianity depends on the story we wish to tell about it.

The Reformation and Vernacular Culture

Several of the texts in this volume were influenced by the Reformation and Catholic Counter-Reformation, and their authors wrote in the shadow of the religious upheavals of the sixteenth century even if they did not address them directly in their comments on Baltic paganism and its origins. Martynas Mažvydas's 1547 preface to his Lithuanian catechism (the first book published in the Lithuanian language) is the text in this collection most overtly concerned with evangelism, but both the Maleckis' *Libellus* and Łasicki's *De diis Samagitarum* bear the hallmarks of Protestant preoccupation with unacceptable popular beliefs and practices.

The tide of religious reform overtook the Grand Duchy of Lithuania at a time when the Christianization of the Lithuanians and Samogitians was still an ongoing process. For Protestants such as Hieronim Malecki, the Catholics' failure to stamp out paganism in the decades since the Teutonic Order's conquest of Prussia and the conversion of Lithuania was evidence of the inadequacy of Catholicism as an idolatrous parody of the true Christian faith, little better than paganism itself. The Protestant tendency to accuse Catholics and Orthodox Christians of being pagans makes it difficult to distinguish those who may actually have been pagans from those whose Christianity was deemed unacceptable. The Calvinist Łasicki, for example, directly attacked the faith of the Orthodox Ruthenians as idolatrous in his treatise on the gods of the Samogitians, making clear his belief that Ruthenians simply worshipped pagan gods under the guise of saints.[71]

The equation of Catholicism (and Orthodoxy) with paganism was a central plank of Reformation polemic against the Catholic church,[72] but it depended on the earlier critique of the Catholic humanist Desiderius Erasmus (1466–1536). In colloquys such as *The Shipwreck* (where mariners in a storm in the English Channel debate who they should invoke), Erasmus inveighed against mercenary, mechanical, and self-serving late medieval religion, although he stopped short of the later Protestant claim that saints were nothing more than reconditioned pagan gods.[73] While a discourse of unacceptable religious practice as superstition stretched far back into Christian antiquity, Erasmus "broadened the literary critique of popular religious practices outwards from the obviously and profanely magical to include the most materialistic and apparently 'mechanical' cults found in traditional religion."[74] Erasmus extended the meaning of "superstition"—a term usually applied quite narrowly to magical practices in the Middle Ages—to cover a very flexible range of deviant and unacceptable religiosity.

---

71 Łasicki, *De diis Samagitarum* (1615), 51–53.

72 Cameron, *Enchanted Europe*, 208–10.

73 Cameron, *Enchanted Europe*, 151.

74 Cameron, *Enchanted Europe*, 155.

Erasmus enjoyed immense popularity in Poland-Lithuania during his lifetime—to a greater extent, perhaps, than in any other country.[75] For Protestants, the fact that Erasmus was a Catholic gave them a rhetorical advantage, since it showed that even some Catholics agreed with them about the parlous state of Catholic popular religion. Thus Łasicki was able to quote the *Shipwreck* of Erasmus, "not at all a Lutheran," with approval.[76] However, Łasicki also quoted the Reformer Heinrich Bullinger, who took Erasmus's thought a stage further and openly denounced the saints as substitutes for gods.[77] One of the more skeptical interpreters of Łasicki dismissed *De diis Samagitarum* as not directed against paganism at all; the book was simply an attack on Catholicism and Orthodoxy as religions derived from paganism.[78]

It is certainly true that a paranoid Reformation theology sometimes saw pagans around every corner, but one of the paradoxes of the Reformation was that Protestantism actually drove renewed interest in folk culture. Where the medieval church had interacted with the people largely through the medium of more or less tolerated forms of popular religion, the reformers were adamant that the people would interact directly with the Bible as the Word of God—and that required the translation of the Bible and catechetical texts into vernacular languages, including Prussian and Lithuanian. This task was facilitated by Königsberg's Albertina, the centre of Protestant learning in the Baltic. Translations of Lutheran catechisms into Prussian were printed at Königsberg [Kaliningrad] in 1540, 1545, and 1561,[79] and the Lithuanian catechism of Mažvydas (whose Latin preface is translated in this volume) was printed in 1547.

The Reformation simultaneously attacked vernacular popular religion as idolatrous paganism and precipitated a revival of interest in the cultures and languages of hitherto marginalized nationalities. Dorothy Noyes has argued that, even before the Reformation, Renaissance interest in "popular antiquities" such as folk beliefs and customs emerged from interest in vernacular languages.[80] Communicating with people in their own language entailed encountering their conceptual world, just as Władysław II managed to communicate the Christian faith in a form they could understand to the Lithuanians and Samogitians. Conversely, Łasicki's *De diis Samagitarum* reveals the perils of trying to understand a conceptual world in the absence of proper knowledge of a people's language.

The Counter-Reformation in Lithuania, led by the Jesuits, portrayed the confusion sown by Calvinist and Lutheran missionaries as the cause of a resurgence of paganism.[81] Whether such a resurgence was real is unclear, but the same factors that enabled the spread of Protestantism in mid-sixteenth-century Lithuania could also have allowed the

---

75 On Poland's love affair with Erasmus see Louthan, "A Model of Christendom."

76 Łasicki, *De diis Samagitarum* (1615), 53.

77 Łasicki, *De diis Samagitarum* (1615), 52.

78 Jaskiewicz, "A Study in Lithuanian Mythology," 65.

79 Klussis, ed., *Old Prussian Written Monuments*, 8–9.

80 Noyes, "The Social Base of Folklore," 16.

81 Rostowski, *Lituanicarum Societatis Iesu historiarum*, 118.

reappearance of pre-Christian practices—namely the weakness of church structures in Lithuania, the large size of dioceses, and the lack of many clergy who spoke the Lithuanian language. It seems unlikely that the Reformation increased the speed of Lithuania's Christianization—it may even have slowed it down—but the Reformation played a crucial role in the appearance of Lithuanian at long last as a written language (and therefore, in the long run, to the awakening of Lithuanian national identity).

Early Modern Ethnography

In addition to describing the religion of the Baltic peoples, the texts in this volume are concerned with their origin and customs—in other words, with ethnography. The ancient Greek writer Herodotus, often considered the "father of history," was also an ethnographer who was interested in the customs, location, and character of alien peoples. Herodotus inaugurated a classical ethnographic tradition that persisted into the Middle Ages, albeit overlaid with new Christian evangelistic imperatives. Recent scholarship has challenged an older view of medieval Europe as insular and uninterested in foreign peoples, and drawn attention to a rich ethnographic tradition.[82] Above all, what made a people alien to medieval Christians was the absence of the Christian faith, or even a faith familiar to the medieval Christian world such as Judaism or Islam. The religion of a pagan people was a key element of any ethnographic description, to the extent that ethnography cannot be meaningfully separated from medieval discussions of "barbarian" paganism.

Paganism (or any kind of infidelism) rendered foreigners monstrous to Christian eyes, and medieval Lithuanians were sometimes portrayed as *cynocephali* (dog-headed people).[83] Baltic peoples did not live as far away from the civilized world as the peoples of the New World encountered at the close of the fifteenth century—and their customs were not as radically different—but they nevertheless lived in regions unknown to the authors of antiquity, and therefore encounters with Lithuanian paganism raised similar questions about the relationship between textual authority and empirical experience.[84] When Enea Silvio Piccolomini first heard the missionary John-Jerome of Prague describe the religion of the Lithuanians at Basel he was incredulous, and felt the need to seek out the old man to hear his story again.[85] The rediscovery and printing of Tacitus's *Germania* in the 1470s, one of the most important ethnographical texts of the Roman world, introduced a richer language for talking about the customs of non-literate "barbarian"

---

82 On ancient ethnography see Almagor and Skinner, eds., *Ancient Ethnography*. On medieval ethnography see Classen, ed., *Meeting the Foreign in the Middle Ages*; Khanmohamadi, *In Light of Another's Word*.

83 Rowell, "Unexpected Contacts," 558–59. On the portrayal of foreign peoples as monsters see Davies, *Renaissance Ethnography*, 14–15.

84 On the epistemological tensions thrown up by fifteenth-century encounters with the other see Davies, *Renaissance Ethnography*, 23–24.

85 Piccolomini, *Cosmographia Pii Papae* (1509), fol. 110r.

peoples.[86] It seems likely that John-Jerome's account would have been more plausible to Piccolomini if the latter had had the opportunity to read the *Germania*.

While paganism was of course abhorrent to Christian writers, the Christian world faced the paradox that, in order to eradicate idolatry, pagans had to be brought to faith, and that required a recognition of their capacity for rationality—which in turn implied that some degree of rationality subsisted within pagan religion in the first place.[87] Medieval Christian horror at paganism was tempered by curiosity, and even admiration. The "virtuous pagan" narrative of Sir John Mandeville, for example, acted as a mirror to the vices of European Christians by showing that even those who did not know Christ could behave better than they did.[88] Similarly, Rowell has argued that Peter of Dusburg's elaborate fictitious account of a Baltic religion led by a "pope" in a pagan "Rome" was a literary device designed to shame Christians.[89]

As European Christians increasingly came into contact with adherents of ancestral religions in the fourteenth century—such as the Mongols and the Guanches of the Canary Islands—a strand of sympathetic commentary on paganism developed.[90] When Portuguese sailors found an idol on the Canary Islands in 1341 they brought it back to Lisbon as a curiosity, while the Christianized Guanches were encouraged to venerate the Virgin Mary where once they had worshipped idols.[91] The Franciscans of Vilnius seem to have had a similar attitude, keeping an idol of Perkūnas in their dormitory as a trophy of the conversion of Lithuania for centuries thereafter.[92] In the sixteenth century, the proto-ethnographer Sebastian Münster, who briefly surveyed the pagans of the Baltic,[93] was prepared to regard pagans in a sympathetic light "who conducted themselves with simple virtue" and had never heard the Gospel preached.[94]

This rather relaxed attitude towards the conversion of pagans may have owed something to a perception that peoples at the European margins such as the Lithuanians and Guanches of Gran Canaria were unthreatening "pagan remnants" to be assimilated into European Christianity. The pagan peoples of the New World, on the other hand, represented a threatening and apocalyptic prospect whose conversion signalled the likely end of the world.[95] Yet the fourteenth-century pagan Lithuanians, the masters of a great European empire who were in possession of cannon by the 1380s, were hardly the unthreat-

---

86 Davies, *Renaissance Ethnography*, 42.

87 Khanmohamadi, *In Light of Another's Word*, 29; Davies, *Renaissance Ethnography*, 32–33.

88 Khanmohamadi, *In Light of Another's Word*, 113–44.

89 Rowell, *Lithuania Ascending*, 125–28.

90 Cervantes, *The Devil in the New World*, 12. On Christian encounters with Mongolia see Khanmohamadi, *In Light of Another's Word*, 57–87.

91 Young, *A History of Exorcism*, 142.

92 *BRMR*, 438.

93 Sebastian Münster, *Cosmographiae universalis* (1554), 906.

94 McLean, *The Cosmographia of Sebastian Münster*, 194.

95 Weber, "Conquistadores of the Spirit," 129.

ening Guanches of Gran Canaria.[96] They were, rather, the "Saracens of the north," and the implacable opponents of a centuries-long crusade.[97] Nevertheless, the accession to the Polish throne of a recently pagan king still ruling over a largely pagan people produced an unusual set of circumstances where Polish intellectuals had a motive to defend the rights of pagans—most notably Paweł Włodkowic (Paulus Vladimiri), who in 1410 advanced a strikingly bold argument for the sovereignty of pagan peoples in the context of Władysław II's struggle to regain Samogitia from the Teutonic Order.[98]

Along with Władysław's political agenda against the Teutonic Knights, the seemingly inexplicable rise of the Ottoman Turks in Asia Minor (leading eventually to the traumatic fall of Constantinople in 1453) led medieval Christians to become increasingly fascinated by non-Christians.[99] Margaret Meserve has argued that authors such as Piccolomini displayed a "compulsion to look to the past in order to make sense of a messy and disturbing present."[100] The sudden arrival of the Turks exposed the ethnically fluid character of the Eurasian steppe, and fuelled a renewed interest in the Scythians, Sarmatians, Cimbrians, and other peoples mentioned by classical authors.[101] While their scholarship was often not as original as humanist authors claimed,[102] the humanist historians of the fifteenth century were asking new questions and developing a new historiography. Meserve identified four characteristics of the "historiographical revolution" of the fifteenth century: adherence to classical models of history writing; skepticism towards earlier authorities; a strong interest in rhetoric (including the use of history for rhetorical purposes); and an approach to historical causation that eschewed overt religious claims such as a reliance on divine providence.[103]

"Secular" humanist historiography presented historians with the problem that they were less able to critique infidel religion—whether Islam, Judaism, or paganism.[104] Yet unlike the threatening Islam of the Ottomans, the paganism of the Lithuanians had been politically neutralized (albeit not eradicated) by the time humanist historians came to write about it. The imperative for writers such as Jan Długosz was to explain to Poles and other Christian Europeans who the Lithuanians were, since this formerly pagan and "barbarian" people had been suddenly thrust to the centre of European affairs with the marriage of Jogaila to Jadwiga and the extraordinary success of the Jagiellonian dynasty. Lithuania could no longer be without a history—and therefore its religion and customs were crucial for understanding its origins, and no longer primarily objects of Christian opprobrium.

---

96 Kaushik, *Military Transition in Early Modern Asia*, 20.

97 On western European perceptions of Lithuanians see Murray, "The Saracens of the Baltic."

98 Frost, *Oxford History of Poland-Lithuania*, 123–24.

99 Meserve, *Empires of Islam*, 3.

100 Meserve, *Empires of Islam*, 2.

101 Meserve, *Empires of Islam*, 152–53.

102 Meserve, *Empires of Islam*, 4.

103 Meserve, *Empires of Islam*, 8.

104 Meserve, *Empires of Islam*, 9.

Cultural interest in Lithuania that went beyond an agenda of converting the Lithuanians to the Christian faith was not entirely new in the fifteenth century.[105] Rowell has argued that there was already a vogue for Lithuanian "pagan chic" at western European royal courts in the fourteenth century.[106] In his personal copy of Virgil's *Aeneid*, Petrarch (1304–1374) annotated the line "they stood and made a treaty over the slaughtered pig" with a reference to a treaty sworn between the Lithuanians and Hungarians in 1351, when Gediminas's son Kęstutis slaughtered an ox, cut off its head, and walked three times through the blood between the animal's body and severed head while pronouncing a ritual formula.[107] While many Christians in medieval Europe might have dismissed Kęstutis's ritual as nothing more than pagan barbarism, Petrarch drew on a tradition that saw all paganism as essentially the same, meaning that the practices of contemporary Lithuanians could elucidate the *Aeneid*, at the time perhaps the single most valued literary product of the Graeco-Roman world.

Fifteenth-century ethnography was dominated by "The idea of nations as homogenetic groups, each enjoying direct and unbroken descent from a primordial race of founding fathers and marked by inborn and unchanging traits of character," and early ethnographical accounts of Lithuanians were no different.[108] Rather than the *Germania* of Tacitus, however, Jakub Niedźwiedź has shown that the most important ancient literary influence on portrayals of Lithuania was Virgil's *Aeneid*.[109] It was Długosz who first claimed that the Lithuanians were the descendants of Romans fleeing the civil war between Caesar and Pompey, a narrative of flight and settlement recalling the flight of Aeneas from Troy. The name "Lithuania," according to Długosz, was a corruption of "Lithalia," from "La Italia."[110] While Buonacorssi was critical of the Italian hypothesis, linking the Lithuanians instead to the Bosphorus and comparing their rites to those of the Gauls, subsequent authors enthusiastically elaborated the "Virgilian" Roman origin myth.[111] Michalo the Lithuanian, most notably, argued that the Lithuanians were descended from Roman soldiers lost at sea during Caesar's departure from Britain, along with their British captives—an idea also taken up by Łasicki.[112]

Meanwhile, in the Ruthenian chronicle tradition the name Palemon was given to a mythical leader of the Romans who colonized Lithuania in the principate of Nero, although the imaginary Palemon did not make his way into Latin writings on Lithuania until Alessandro Guagnini.[113] Christine Watson has argued that Długosz probably docu-

---

105 Rowell, *Lithuania Ascending*, 32–33.

106 Rowell, "Unexpected Contacts," 557–77.

107 Virgil, *Aeneid*, bk. 8, line 641: "stabant et caesa iungebant foedera porca." On Petrarch's annotation see Rowell, *Lithuania Ascending*, 145n128.

108 Meserve, *Empires of Islam*, 243.

109 Niedźwiedź, "How Did Virgil Help Forge Lithuanian Identity," 36–40.

110 Długosz, *Historiae Polonicae* (1711–1712), 1:113.

111 Buonaccorsi, *Vita et mores Sbignei cardinalis*, ed. Finkel, 28.

112 Lituanus, *De moribus Tartarorum*, ed. Grasser (1615), 24; Łasicki, *De diis Samagitarum* (1615), 43.

113 Rowell, *Lithuania Ascending*, 41; Watson, *Tradition and Translation*, 42–43; Guagnini, *Sarmatiae Europeae descriptio* (1581), fol. 45r.

mented a story that was genuinely current at the time, since he did not usually display a great deal of interest in Lithuania.[114] In Robert Frost's view the second recension of the *Chronicle of the Grand Duchy of Lithuania and Samogitia*, where Palemon made his first appearance, was compiled between 1510 and 1517, partly in response to a Polish historiographical tradition that portrayed the Lithuanians as barbarous, and partly to match Muscovite claims of Roman ancestry.[115] In 1555 Martin Kromer identified the Palemon of the Ruthenian chronicles with a certain Publius Libo.[116]

Frost has argued that Albertas Goštautas (ca. 1480–1522), grand chancellor of Lithuania from 1522, was responsible for an alternative Lithuanian origin myth in the Bychowiec Chronicle (ca. 1525). In this narrative, five hundred families accompanied a Roman prince, Apolonus, to Lithuania in order to escape Attila the Hun's depredations in Italy. The Bychowiec Chronicle was specifically designed to counter Maciej z Miechowa's portrayal of Lithuania as a subordinate partner in a personal union with Poland, and presented Poland and Lithuania as equals. Długosz was a protégé of Cardinal Zbigniew Oleśnicki (1389–1455) whose agenda for Lithuania was the assimilation of the Grand Duchy in an unequal union with Poland,[117] and subsequent authors in the "Dlugossian" tradition, such as Buonacorssi and Miechowa, reflected this attitude.

There was a tension in the writings of Polish authors like Długosz and Miechowa between a nationalistic desire to portray the Lithuanians as barbarians brought to civilization by the Polish nation and the need to give an illustrious history to the land that produced the Jagiellonian dynasty. Lithuanian religion was generally treated as evidence of the Lithuanians' Roman origin. With the exception of Buonacorssi, who thought Lithuanian religion resembled Gaulish Druidism,[118] ethnographic commentators linked Lithuanian worship to Roman religion, comparing the cult of snakes to the worship of Aesculapius and the perpetual fire to the flame guarded by the Vestal Virgins.[119] However barbarian the Lithuanians were said to be, seeking to understand Lithuanian religion through the lens of Roman paganism was still a world away from the ecclesiastical denunciations of the thirteenth and fourteenth centuries.

In addition to the supposed similarity between Lithuanian and Roman rites, according to some authors the Roman origin of the Lithuanians was also proved by the similarity of the Lithuanian language to Latin.[120] Michalo was the most vocal advocate of Lithuanian as a "semi-Latin speech,"[121] at a time when some Lithuanians were so convinced

---

114 Watson, *Tradition and Translation*, 42.

115 Frost, *Oxford History of Poland-Lithuania*, 413–14.

116 Kromer, *De origine et rebus gestis Polonorum* (1555), 61.

117 Frost, *Oxford History of Poland-Lithuania*, 414–15.

118 Buonaccorsi, *Vita et mores Sbignei cardinalis*, ed. Finkel, 28.

119 Długosz, *Historiae Polonicae* (1711–1712), 1:113; Lituanus, *De moribus Tartarorum*, ed. Grasser (1615), 23; Malecki, *Libellus de sacrificiis et idolatria*, ed. Schmidt-Lötzen, 187.

120 Długosz, *Historiae Polonicae* (1711–1712), 1:113; Miechowa, *Tractatus de duabus Sarmatiis* (1518), sig. (e vr); Guagnini, *Sarmatiae Europeae descriptio* (1581), fol. 45r; Łasicki, *De diis Samagitarum* (1615), 43.

121 Lituanus, *De moribus Tartarorum*, ed. Grasser (1615), 23–24.

Lithuanian was a degraded form of Latin that they argued Latin should be adopted as the Grand Duchy's official language.[122] Just as the development of Renaissance ethnography allowed new questions to be asked about the origins of peoples hitherto without a history, so the development of Renaissance linguistics and emerging awareness of vernaculars allowed new questions to be asked about hitherto overlooked languages such as Lithuanian.[123] As it turned out, the Lithuanian Latinizers were wrong about the relationship between Lithuanian and Latin, but their recognition of the similarities between two Indo-European languages laid the foundation for the later exploration of Lithuanian as an archaic representative of the Indo-European family.[124]

Interpretative Traditions: *interpretatio Christiana* and *interpretatio Romana*

The two hermeneutical pillars of late medieval and early modern religious ethnography were the traditions of *interpretatio Christiana* and *interpretatio Romana*, the former stretching back to the Church Fathers of late antiquity while the latter can be traced even further into the writings of classical authors. While *interpretatio Christiana* furnished a framework for Christians to understand paganism, *interpretatio Romana* provided the resources to understand alien, barbarian religion by assimilating it to the well-understood Graeco-Roman pantheon. While *paganus* was a word derived from early Christian anti-pagan polemic, and *gentilis* (Gentile) derived from Scripture, the word *superstitio* (superstition) derived from *interpretatio Romana*. In ancient Rome, *superstitio* signified unacceptable or barbarian religious and magical practices, but the early Christians adopted the word to refer to paganism as well as unsanctioned popular beliefs and practices among Christians.[125] All three terms were deployed to describe Baltic pagans.

While many of the Church Fathers wrote about paganism, it was above all Augustine of Hippo (354–430) who established the conceptual parameters for *interpretatio Christiana* recognized by the authors included in this volume.[126] Within a medieval Christian worldview, where Scholastic theologians proclaimed that the reality of God was evident from nature, the existence of pagan "error" required an explanation. Building on St. Paul's denunciation of the foolishness of pagans for worshipping "an image made like to corruptible man, and ... birds, and fourfooted beasts, and creeping things" (Romans 1:22–25), as well as many other Biblical condemnations of idolatry, early Christian authors portrayed paganism as a consequence of both the fall of human beings and

---

122 On sixteenth-century Lithuanian Latinism see Zinkevičius, *The History of the Lithuanian Language*, 73; Dini, *Prelude to Baltic Linguistics*, 45–82; Narbutas, "Latinitas in the Grand Duchy of Lithuania"; Young, "Lingua semilatina."

123 For an overview of early modern linguistics see Lepschy, ed., *History of Linguistics, Volume III*.

124 Zinkevičius, *The History of the Lithuanian Language*, 277–79.

125 On the meaning of *superstitio* in ancient Rome see Beard, North, and Price, *Religions of Rome*, 1:215–19. On changing definitions of *superstitio* in medieval Europe see Cameron, *Enchanted Europe*, 4–7.

126 On Augustine's views on paganism and *superstitio* see Cameron, *Enchanted Europe*, 81–84.

demonic deceit, since demons tricked humans into worshipping them under the guise of gods. Even when the authors in this volume did not directly quote Augustine, his thinking permeates their approach to paganism. For instance, Jan Łasicki's ever-lengthening list of Samogitian deities with ever more specialist tasks can be traced back to a well-known example of anti-pagan rhetoric in Augustine's *City of God* (4.9), where Augustine mocks the proliferation of Roman deities presiding over every aspect of agriculture, and even over the doors of houses—such as Forculus the god of doors, Cardea the goddess of hinges, and Limentinus the god of threshholds.[127]

Christian authors who wrote on Baltic paganism were convinced that the Prussians and Lithuanians worshipped demons who actively deceived their devotees. This explained the Balts' fear of extinguishing perpetual fires or profaning sacred groves. John-Jerome of Prague gave Piccolomini a vivid description of how he believed a demon had deceived the people by an illusion in which a man trying to cut down a sacred tree seemed to have struck and injured himself.[128] On the other hand, the confidence with which John-Jerome and, indeed, the Polish soldiers of Władysław II cut down the sacred groves suggests they believed the demons had no power to harm Christians. This was consistent with an early Christian tradition that viewed demonic power primarily as deceit, in contrast to the more fearful attitude to the demonic that developed from the early fourteenth century onwards (which emphasized the reality of demonic power and demons' collaboration with sects of sorcerers).[129]

If *interpretatio Christiana* established that pagans were deluded worshippers of demons, *interpretatio Romana* assimilated alien barbarian religions to the familiar pagan religion of Greece and Rome. Authors routinely identified the thunder god Perkūnas with Jupiter, compared the Baltic worship of snakes with the cult of Aesculapius, and used terms such as *lares* and *penates* (the Roman household and domestic gods) to describe household spirits. Similarly, Malecki and Łasicki directly identified the Baltic festival of communing with the dead, Ilgės or Vėlinės, with the Roman Parentalia.

Perhaps the most famous (or notorious) exponents of *interpretatio Romana* in the Roman world were Julius Caesar in his accounts of Gaul and Britain and Tacitus in his account of Germanic tribes. Caesar and Tacitus presumed that the "pantheons" of barbarians could usually be slotted into the Roman pantheon, with barbarian gods taking on the classic functions of deities such as Jupiter, Mars, Apollo, and Ceres. So great was Caesar's confidence in his interpretation that he did not even bother to record the names of the deities of the Gauls and Britons—leaving scholars to guess at the correct identification of Gaulish Mercury, for example.[130] Comparative mythology has the potential to do much the same as *interpretatio Romana*, deploying a kind of *interpretatio Indoeuropeana* that forces the fragmentary mythology of every Indo-European culture into patterns derived from well-attested textual traditions from India, Iran, Greece, and Rome.

---

127 Augustine, *The City of God*, ed. Dyson, 153.

128 Piccolomini, *Cosmographia Pii Papae* (1509), fol. 110v.

129 Boureau, *Satan the Heretic*, 22–27.

130 On *interpretatio Romana* see Ando, "Interpretatio Romana."

The attempt to understand a culture by assimilating it to the familiar patterns of another, whether by *interpretatio Romana* or the slightly more sophisticated process of *interpretatio Indoeuropeana*, rests on large assumptions about the similarity of cultures and ignores the possibility that one ancestral religion might differ very greatly from another in form as well as in substance. Classicizing assumptions, such as the existence of an Olympian-style pantheon led by a thunder god and gendered deities with distinct personalities and functions, risk obscuring the distinctiveness of indigenous belief systems and determining subsequent patterns of research. The listing of gods in Łasicki's *De diis Samagitarum*, along with their supposed functions, is an approach rooted in *interpretatio Romana* and presupposes a single religion shared by the Samogitians with a uniform texture and an established pantheon. By contrast, John-Jerome of Prague portrayed Lithuanian cults as highly localized, with one people group worshipping snakes and another the Sun. The shift from John-Jerome's emphasis on worship of natural phenomena to Łasicki's complex pantheon is a striking one that has no adequate explanation, although the influence of *interpretatio Romana* and Łasicki's possible confusion between senior gods and local nature spirits may partly account for it.

W. C. Jaskiewicz, one of the more extreme skeptics about the possibility of reconstructing Baltic religion, argued that Łasicki or his informant essentially made up the content of *De diis Samagitarum*—even arguing there was insufficient evidence the Lithuanians ever worshipped snakes,[131] a practice alluded to in virtually every later medieval and early modern account of Lithuanian religion. Decades before Jaskiewicz had produced his withering assessment of Łasicki, however, Christian Krollmann had already argued persuasively for the improbability of Simon Grunau simply making up a list of Prussian gods to match a Nordic scheme—a proposition that, in Gregory Nagy's words, "strains credulity."[132] Although Endre Bojtár continued to uphold the view that Grunau invented the Prussian pantheon entirely,[133] there is a point when a skeptical position, taken to extremes, becomes less plausible than the shaky hypotheses it originally set out to challenge.

The most recent commentator on Łasicki, Vytautas Ališauskas, is adamant that Łasicki must be considered an unreliable source, because he writes with a specific polemical purpose and wants to surprise and entertain his readers.[134] Furthermore, neither Łasicki nor his informants knew the Lithuanian language; nor did they know the country they were living in very well.[135] Łasicki lists "an incredible number of deities," many of them not attested in other sources, while some of Łasicki's theonyms are not really the names of gods at all, but rather place names or the names of things.[136] Łasicki

---

131 Jaskiewicz, "A Study in Lithuanian Mythology," 105.

132 Krollmann, *Das Religionswesen der alten Preußen*, 14–17; Nagy, *Greek Mythology and Poetics*, 184n21.

133 Bojtár, *Foreword to the Past*, 314–15.

134 Łasicki, *Pasakojimas apie Žemaičių Dievus*, ed. Ališauskas, 23–29.

135 Łasicki, *Pasakojimas apie Žemaičių Dievus*, ed. Ališauskas, 29–40.

136 Łasicki, *Pasakojimas apie Žemaičių Dievus*, ed. Ališauskas, 40–47.

did not properly understand the material he was collecting, and he therefore misidenti-fied deified forces of nature as personal beings, turned spirits into gods, and did not know the functions of mythological beings.[137]

Nevertheless, in spite of all these flaws, Ališauskas insists that by paying careful attention to correspondences with other sources for Balto-Slavic mythology, the Samo-gitian gods can be reconstructed (albeit tentatively) from Łasicki's text. Correspon-dences between Łasicki's material and later records of folklore, ritual, and belief are sufficient argument, in Ališauskas's view, against skeptics who deny the authenticity of Łasicki's gods altogether.[138] Understanding the literary and rhetorical context of texts like Łasicki's *De diis Samagitarum* is a crucial precondition of any attempt to separate genuine ethnographic information from a soup of rhetorical *topoi*, religious polemic and inherited stereotypes.

The Texts

The texts translated in this volume are Latin accounts by authors educated within the humanist milieu of the fifteenth and sixteenth centuries who were, for a variety of dif-ferent reasons, interested in the origins and religious beliefs and practices of the Baltic peoples of Prussia and Lithuania. Five of the authors were Polish (Jan Długosz, Maciej z Miechowa, Jan and Hieronim Malecki, and Jan Łasicki), three Italian (Enea Silvio Piccolomini, Filippo Buonacorssi, and Alessandro Guagnini), two Lithuanian (Martynas Mažvydas and the mysterious "Michalo the Lithuanian"), and one German (Johannes Stüler). What united these disparate authors was the language they wrote in: Latin, western Christendom's universal language of learning—which several of them also believed was the ancient language of Lithuania itself. The writings of Simon Grunau (ca. 1470–ca. 1530) and Maciej Stryjkowski (ca. 1547–ca. 1593), authors of the period who wrote about Baltic paganism in German and Polish respectively,[139] are not included in this edition, which focusses on Latin texts that had the potential to be read widely in the transnational intellectual culture of early modern humanism.

Just as the authors included in this volume were diverse in nationality, so they wrote in a variety of genres. The extracts from Długosz, Miechowa, and Guagnini are digressions discussing ethnography and religion within annalistic histories. Piccolo-mini's account of his interview with a former missionary to Lithuania takes the form of autobiographical personal reminiscence, while Buonacorssi included an ethnographic digression in a work of biography. Stüler's account of Prussian paganism is an aside in a larger work on Prussian history, while Mažvydas's preface is evangelistic and exhorta-tory. Michalo, meanwhile, was writing political and social polemic. Only the works by

---

137 Łasicki, *Pasakojimas apie Žemaičių Dievus*, ed. Ališauskas, 72–80.

138 Łasicki, *Pasakojimas apie Žemaičių Dievus*, ed. Ališauskas, 47.

139 Simon Grunau, *Preussische Chronik*, ed. Perlbach; Maciej Stryjkowski, *Kronika Polska*. For discussions of Grunau's and Stryjkowski's accounts of Baltic paganism see Beresnevičius, "Ricko-yotto šventykla"; Usačiovaitė, "Motiejus Strijkovskis apie lietuvių pagonybę." On Stryjkowski's reliance on Malecki's *Libellus* see Pompeo, "Etnografia umanistica," 64.

Malecki and Łasicki were focussed exclusively on Baltic religion. In several cases the works of these authors were published decades after the authors first wrote, with the result that the religious and cultural landscape of the era of publication bore little relation to the circumstances in which the author originally wrote. This temporal distortion no doubt contributed to the confusion of some early modern writers about the extent to which the Lithuanians and Samogitians had been converted or were still pagans.

Not every chronicler of Lithuanian history displayed an interest in the religion of the Lithuanians. Augustine Rotundus, the chronicler of the grand dukes of Lithuania, declined to describe the conversion of Lithuania in his "Summary of the princes of Lithuania" (1576) because it was adequately dealt with by Polish chroniclers,[140] while Stanisław Sarnicki similar skimmed over the conversion of Lithuania and did not even mention the conversion of Samogitia in his *Annales* (1587).[141] My selection of texts for inclusion in this volume was largely determined by their authors' level of interest in Baltic religion, the origins of the Baltic peoples, and the Christianization of the pagan Balts. Chroniclers with little interest in these matters are excluded. Furthermore, with the exception of the Maleckis' *Libellus* and Łasicki's *De diis Samagitarum* (which are given in full), the texts presented here are extracts from larger works.

In all cases, these translations are the first time the texts have appeared in English.[142] When English-speaking scholarship has paid attention to Baltic paganism in Prussia and Livonia, it has generally been as part of studies of the Northern Crusades.[143] S. C. Rowell (latterly in collaboration with Darius Baronas) has focussed specifically on the history of medieval pagan Lithuania,[144] but interest in the early modern sources for Baltic paganism has hitherto been confined largely to Lithuanian-language scholarship. In particular, the work of Norbertas Vėlius, Vytautas Ališauskas, and Pranas Vildžiūnas in comprehensively collating and interpreting the medieval and early modern sources for Baltic religion and translating them into Lithuanian stands out as an immense achievement.[145]

---

140 Augustine Rotundus, *Epitome principum Lituaniae*, ed. Jakubowski, 102.

141 Stanisław Sarnicki, *Annales* (1587), 337–38.

142 A comprehensive collection of Lithuanian translations of sixteenth-century texts about Baltic religion and mythology can be found in the second volume of *BRMŠ*. The sole English translation of Jan Długosz is a translation from an abridged Polish edition, not from the original Latin (*The Annals of Jan Długosz*, trans. Michael). One Latin text featuring ethnographical and religious commentary on the Lithuanians that has recently appeared in translation is Nicolaus Hussovianus, *Song of the Bison*, ed. Booth; for that reason Hussovianus is not included in this volume.

143 Recent studies on the Northern Crusades include Murray, ed., *Crusade and Conversion on the Baltic*; Fonnesberg-Schmidt, *The Popes and the Baltic Crusades*; Murray, ed., *The Clash of Cultures*; Tamm, Kaljundi, and Jensen, eds., *Crusading and Chronicle Writing on the Medieval Baltic Frontier*; Gładysz, *The Forgotten Crusaders*; Pluskowski, *The Archaeology of the Prussian Crusade*; Selart, *Livonia, Rus' and the Baltic Crusades*; Reynold, *The Prehistory of the Crusades*; Mänd and Tamm, eds., *Making Livonia*.

144 Rowell, *Lithuania Ascending*, 118–48, 189–228; Baronas and Rowell, *The Conversion of Lithuania*.

145 See the four volumes of *BRMŠ*; *BRMR*; Łasicki, *Pasakojimas apie Žemaičių Dievus*, ed. Ališauskas; Ališauskas and Vildžiūnas, *Dingęs Šventybės Pasaulis*.

The texts in this volume are not isolated documents, but rather the chief representatives of a textual tradition of ethnographic and historical commentary on Baltic peoples and their religion that began in the fifteenth century. While it is not altogether clear whether Enea Silvio Piccolomini wrote his reminiscences of a meeting with a former missionary to Lithuania before Długosz wrote his accounts of the conversions of Lithuania and Samogitia, it seems likely that the future Pope Pius II's recollections mark the beginning of humanist historiography's engagement with Baltic culture.[146] Piccolomini's account of the Lithuanians in his *Cosmographia* subsequently found its way (largely unaltered) into Marcus Antonius Sabellicus's *Enneades* (1498),[147] but although it contains similar elements (such as the emphasis on the worship of snakes and fire), it is not obvious that Długosz's "annalistic" account of Lithuanian religion was derived from Piccolomini.

Ališauskas declined to include Długosz's accounts of Lithuanian paganism in his collection of sources for Baltic mythology on the grounds that they were "retrospective or reconstructive presentations of the old religion" written after the conversion,[148] while Frost is critical of Długosz's reliability as a historian owing to Długosz's dislike of the "foreign" Jagiellonian dynasty ruling his native Poland.[149] However, it is unclear how a "reconstructive" account of Lithuanian paganism can be distinguished from an account based on firsthand testimonies at this early date, when it is likely almost all of the practices described by Długosz were still part of life in barely Christianized Lithuania and Samogitia. In Długosz's favour, the content and themes of his account of Lithuanian religion correlate closely with Piccolomini's, in the absence of indications that Długosz knew of or borrowed from Piccolomini's recollections of the missionary memoirs of John-Jerome of Prague—suggesting both men relied on different sources reporting the same genuine religion.

Unlike Piccolomini, Długosz never specified the source of his information on Lithuanian paganism, and Baronas and Rowell are skeptical that, writing around eighty years after the events he described, Długosz could have had a living informant.[150] It does not follow from this, however, that Długosz simply made everything up. The broad consistency between Długosz's account and Piccolomini's has already been noted, and while no living person may have remembered the events of 1387 by 1455 (when Długosz began his chronicle), the final conversion of Samogitia had occurred less than forty years earlier. Lithuanians routinely attended the university in Kraków after 1387,[151] and many would surely have heard stories about the ongoing pagan practices of their countrymen.

---

146 On John-Jerome of Prague see Hyland, "John-Jerome of Prague"; Baronas and Rowell, *The Conversion of Lithuania*, 309–15.

147 *BRMŠ*, 1:607–8.

148 *BRMR*, 9.

149 Frost, *Oxford History of Poland-Lithuania*, 75. On Długosz's dislike of the Jagiellonians see Koczerska, "L'amour de la patrie et l'aversion pour la dynastie," 171–80.

150 Baronas and Rowell, *The Conversion of Lithuania*, 272–73.

151 Frost, *Oxford History of Poland-Lithuania*, 318.

Although Długosz's chronicles remained unpublished until the early eighteenth century, his account would prove very influential, and parts of it were copied almost verbatim by Maciej z Miechowa, Alessandro Guagnini, and Jan Łasicki. These authors added their own elements to the "annalistic" tradition, with Miechowa (alone among Latin humanist authors) referencing the fourteenth-century Dutch chronicler Peter of Dusburg's myth of Romowe, the legendary pagan city ruled by the "pagan pope" called the Krivė.[152] Miechowa also brought his own distinctive theory of the Baltic languages as a single "quadripartite" language, which led him to see speakers of Baltic languages as a unified culture in some sense.[153] Guagnini produced a synthesis largely based on Długosz's account, although a few elements in his narrative (such as his striking account of a man punished with mutilation for forsaking paganism) were new.[154] Guagnini relied heavily on Stryjkowski to the point of plagiarism.[155] For Łasicki, Długosz continued to provide a basic template for the description of Baltic religion which Łasicki elaborated.

Alongside the Dlugossian or "annalistic" tradition, quite different textual traditions were represented by the German Prussian Johannes Stüler (known in Latin as Erasmus Stella) and the father and son Polish-Prussian authors Jan and Hieronim Malecki. Stüler largely drew on unflattering descriptions of the customs and beliefs of the Old Prussians in medieval chronicles of the Teutonic Knights, and portrayed the Prussians as little better than beasts. This was characteristic of much German commentary on the Prussians, since there was no *prima facie* political incentive for settler colonialists to portray the people they sought to replace in a positive light. Nevertheless, as Rasa Mažeika has argued, extended proximity and interaction between German Christians and Baltic pagans produced a kind of grudging and sullen respect between enemies.[156] This phenomenon, as well as traces of humanist ethnographic interest, can perhaps be discerned even in Stüler's writing on the Prussians. Stüler is keen to explain how the Prussians acquired their customs from a legendary leader, Widewuto. Thus the beginnings of German Prussians' later fascination with their Baltic Prussian forebears can be discerned in Stüler's *De Borussiae antiquitatibus*.

Stüler's commentary pre-dated the Prussian Reformation and the secularization of the duchy, which sharpened the importance of converting any still pagan Prussians and Sudovians. Jan Malecki and his son Hieronim, although they were Poles, lived and worked as printers and translators in Königsberg, the capital of Ducal Prussia. They published Latin and German versions of a text known as the Sudovian (or Yotvingian) Book, which described the customs of the pagan Sudovians in Prussia. Whether Jan Malecki was actually responsible for writing the Sudovian Book remains unclear, but he sent it to George Sabinus in the form of a letter around 1545. This letter was published in

---

152 Miechowa, *Tractatus de duabus Sarmatiis* (1518), sigs f ıIJv–(f vr). Rowell, *Lithuania Ascending*, 125–28 has shown that Peter of Dusburg's narrative is a literary excursus and moral lesson rather than an attempt to describe the actual organisation of Baltic paganism.

153 On Miechowa see Bonda, *History of Lithuanian Historiography*, 86–87.

154 Guagnini, *Sarmatiae Europeae descriptio* (1581), fol. 60v.

155 Bonda, *History of Lithuanian Historiography*, 89.

156 Mažeika, "Granting Power to Enemy Gods," 157–58.

1551 but subsequently augmented by Jan Malecki's son Hieronim in 1561.[157] The Maleckis' *Libellus* portrayed the Catholicism of the Teutonic Knights as the direct successor of the paganism of the Prussians: "[Prussia] was submerged in the horrible furies of the popes, from which men fell into such confusion of opinions that they considered that God might be placated and propitiated by whatever sacrifices and rites were brought in by the audacity of human invention."[158] The justification for a book about pagan practices, therefore, was to show those in the duchy who still hankered after Catholicism that their rites were scarcely different from those of the pagans. Malecki's *Libellus* went on to be a key source for Łasicki, who copied a significant portion of it verbatim into his *De diis Samagitarum*.

The two Lithuanian authors included in this volume were a Lutheran catechist and an obscure figure whose true identity remains unclear. While the purpose of Mažvydas's Latin preface to the first book published in the Lithuanian language was to explain the need for a vernacular Lutheran catechism, Michalo's *De moribus* is a secular social and political jeremiad against what the author perceives as a decadent and degenerate Lithuania that has declined from its former glory and is now weak in the sight of its neighbours.[159] Mažvydas offers a snapshot of how a Lutheran missionary—himself a native Lithuanian—saw the state of his country in the late 1540s. Mažvydas denounces the worship of the Kaukai, Žemėpatis, Laukasargis, and the Aitvarai in his preface, a theme he returns to in the Lithuanian text of the catechism itself.[160] Both Mažvydas and Michalo, for different reasons, were motivated by embarassment on their nation's behalf—Mažvydas because Lithuania was "before other nations ... ignorant, unsophisticated and lacking in all piety and the Christian religion,"[161] and Michalo because Lithuania was weakened by luxury.

While Michalo writes as a Catholic and makes few direct references to pre-Christian Lithuanian religion, a striking feature of his commentary is the unfavourable comparisons he makes between the Lithuanians and the Muslim Tatars. Meserve has argued that the fifteenth-century Christian project of discrediting the Ottoman Turks as illegitimate interlopers who destabilized Europe caused Christian scholars to portray other Muslim states in a positive light as potential allies against the Ottomans.[162] Michalo's positive evaluation of the Tatars should perhaps be seen as part of this anti-Ottoman tradition (although Michalo does not actually discuss the Ottomans).[163]

157 For a detailed source analysis of the Sudovian Book see Kregždys, "Sūduvių knygelės nuorašų formalioji analizė." On Malecki see Pompeo, "Etnografia umanistica."

158 Malecki, *Libellus de sacrificiis et idolatria*, ed. Schmidt-Lötzen, 180.

159 On Michalo see Bonda, *History of Lithuanian Historiography*, 81–83.

160 Mažvydas, *Catechismusa prasty szadei* (1547), sigs A vr–A vv.

161 Mažvydas, *Catechismusa prasty szadei* (1547), sig. A iijr.

162 Meserve, *Empires of Islam*, 5.

163 On Christian views of Muslims in the late fifteenth and sixteenth centuries see Malcolm, *Useful Enemies*, 30–56. For examples of positive approaches to Muslims by European Christians see Brummett, "The Myth of Shah Ismail Safavi"; Meserve, *Empires of Islam*, 3.

Conclusion: Baltic Pagans in Global Context

A late medieval growth of interest in Baltic religion and ethnography was motivated, first and foremost, by political considerations. The rise of the Jagiellonian dynasty and the conversion of Lithuania at the end of the fourteenth century meant that Lithuania was no longer a territory to be forcibly converted by the agents of Christendom, but a power within Christendom to be reckoned with. Accordingly, the Lithuanian people required a history, and the distinctiveness of their beliefs and customs required explanation. The continued presence of adherents of ancestral religions in the Baltic region, even after formal Christianization, both fascinated and appalled literary commentators, and the rhetorical tropes developed by Erasmus and the Protestant reformers opened up new ways of making sense of Baltic infidels. Yet even the most overtly evangelistic texts displayed a desire to understand Baltic vernacular culture, as Protestants were faced with the paradox that "irrational," "barbarian" pagans had to be brought to faith by persuasion. Above all, humanist engagement with Baltic religion was characterized by a triumph of curiosity over condemnation; while the authors had multiple agendas, several of them also found Baltic paganism interesting in and of itself.

The body of humanist writing on Baltic paganism is unique, since other pagan peoples (such as the Sámi of northern Scandinavia) were of insufficient political importance to attract much attention,[164] while aberrant religiosity among nominally Christian peoples might be viewed through a lens of sorcery and witchcraft rather than paganism.[165] The open paganism of the Prussians and Lithuanians may have largely spared them accusations of witchcraft, a crime that often implied the existence of a secret Satanic conspiracy. If pagans unabashedly worshipped "demons" in the form of their gods, there was hardly any need for the devil to deceive them in the form of witchcraft, and sorcery is little discussed in the fifteenth- and sixteenth-century literature on Lithuanian paganism.[166]

While the Catholic Michalo never went so far as to openly commend the ancient religion of his people, the implications of his claims of the Lithuanians' Roman ancestry, their former fierceness, and his scathing critique of the Catholic church, were quite clear: the pagan past could not be recovered, but it was nothing to be ashamed of. The cocktail of curiosity and repulsion that characterized Renaissance engagement with European paganism would be carried to the New World, where the earliest portrayals of indigenous peoples drew on imagined accounts of "wild" European ancestors such as the German tribes described by Tacitus.[167] Many writers on the peoples of the New World reflected Stüler's attitude to the Prussians as little better than wild animals. However,

---

164 The religion of the pagan Sámi people of northern Scandinavia was not the subject of a book until 1613 (Rasmussen, "The Protracted Sámi Reformation," 172).

165 For a text aimed at the semi-converted peoples of Scandinavia see Hemming/Hemmingsen, *Admonitio de superstitonibus magicis vitandis.*

166 On witchcraft in the Grand Duchy of Lithuania see my forthcoming chapter "Authorities and Control," in *A Cultural History of Magic in the Age of Enlightenment.*

167 Brienen, *Visions of Savage Paradise*, 77; Davies, *Renaissance Ethnography*, 42.

the writings of Bartolomeo de las Casas on indigenous peoples were tinged with anxieties about lingering paganism in Europe, and he accused colonizers of hypocrisy for suspecting indigenous people of syncretism and hidden paganism when they failed to discern their own failure to suppress pagan practices in the Old World.[168] In Mexico, just as in the pagan Baltic, *interpretatio Romana* was applied to indigenous deities,[169] while in Peru the gods and origin myths of the Incas were interpreted according to Roman models.[170] Similarly, the historical contextualization of pagan belief in the Baltic provided a precedent for "the increasing historicization of human political and religious diversity" that led Catholic missionaries in the Indian Subcontinent to go beyond mere condemnation of Hindu idolatry to express curiosity about Indian religion,[171] and the peasants of Lithuania were a point of reference for the Jesuit Giovanni Botero when describing the lives of people in the Vijayanagara Empire of South India.[172]

Perhaps because German Prussians and Poles were rarely directly involved with the early colonization of the New World, the possibility that their writings on the pagans of Eastern Europe had some influence on European perceptions of native American peoples has not received much consideration. While scholars no longer argue that Paweł Włodkowic's arguments in favour of the rights of the pagan Samogitians had a direct influence on New World debates about indigenous peoples,[173] Eastern European scholars interacted with their western counterparts, and the products of printing presses in Königsberg and Kraków were accessible to humanists throughout Europe.

In 1531 the prince-bishop of Warmia, Jan Dantyszek (Danticus), wrote to Esteban Gabriel Merino (who held the title of Patriarch of the West Indies) that Poland's recent victory over the Moldavians "should incite Christian princes by a similar example against the enemies of our religion," referring specifically to "all your most fortunate Spanish part of the Christian globe."[174] Anna Skolimowska has argued that Dantyszek saw Jagiellonian Poland's struggle against the enemies of Christianity in Eastern Europe as part of the global struggle for the assertion of the Christian faith led by Spain.[175] Although it was fighting the Ottomans in the sixteenth century, Poland's credentials as a champion of Christianity historically depended on Władysław II Jagiełło's conversion of Lithuania. An interaction like this suggests that the question of whether humanists interested in the New World read texts about the Baltic peoples is one that merits further investigation.[176]

---

168 Lupher, *Romans in a New World*, 315.

169 Torres, *Military Ethos and Visual Culture*, 70.

170 MacCormack, *On the Wings of Time*, 53–54.

171 Rubiés, *Travel and Ethnology*, 311.

172 Rubiés, *Travel and Ethnology*, 296.

173 Russell, "Paulus Vladimiri's Attack on the Just War," 253; Knoll, "*A Pearl of Powerful Learning*", 460–61.

174 Dantyszek, *Victoria serenissimi Poloniae regis*.

175 Dantyszek, *Ioannes Danticus' Correspondence with Alfonso de Valdés*, 60.

176 On Eastern European interest in the New World see Tasbir, "La conquête de l'Amérique."

The Polish-Lithuanian author Nicolaus Hussovianus, who elsewhere denounced Baltic paganism, reported with horror that the citizens of Rome—the centre of Christendom—sacrificed a black bull in the Colosseum to ward off plague in 1522.[177] Paganism was a lingering presence in early modern literature, whether as the religion of indigenous peoples in the New World, the preoccupation of artists and writers with pagan antiquity, the recrudescent deviance of popular European Christianity, or the polemic of Protestant reformers against a Catholic church they saw as pagan. In comparison with these "paganisms," the paganism of the Baltic peoples has received little attention, but as the texts in this volume show, the past and present beliefs and practices of the Prussians and Lithuanians were an object of fascination to humanist scholars. Those scholars, applying new historiographical and ethnographical methods, preserved a remarkable body of evidence at a time when Baltic ancestral religion was still, to some extent, a living reality. In spite of the considerable difficulties attendant on interpreting that evidence, it remains a unique witness to one of Europe's last pagan cultures.

---

177 Hussovianus, *Song of the Bison*, 4–5.

EDITOR'S NOTE

The original Latin texts reproduced in this volume are taken from early modern printed books, with some standardization of spelling, orthography, and layout for the sake of this edition.

Capitalization

The first word of a sentence is capitalized in all cases. Where nouns are capitalized within the original text, capitalization has been retained, and where proper nouns are uncapitalized in the original, they are left without capitalization.

Spelling and Orthography

Except in proper nouns taken from languages other than Latin, in all cases *i* is substituted for *j*, *i* for *y*, and *u* for *v* (and vice versa) where appropriate. Where the diphthong *ae* is rendered by *e* or *æ* in the original texts, in all cases it is given as *ae* in this edition. Early modern typesetters often lacked a letter *w*, and where the letters *uu* or *vv* clearly represent the letter *w*, a *w* is substituted in this text. However, if there is any doubt or ambiguity about the letters represented (especially in words from languages other than Latin), the original letters are retained.

Abbreviations and Punctuation

Standard Latin abbreviations are expanded without comment. Where an abbreviation is not standard, or there is any ambiguity, the expansion is given in square brackets. Except where it marks an abbreviation, the punctuation of the original texts is retained, apart from the addition of single quotation marks to distinguish quotations from the rest of the text.

Subheadings and Paragraph Breaks

Marginal annotations functioning as subheadings (summarizing the content of the text and breaking it into thematic sections) in the original books are here given as subheadings in italics in order to aid the contemporary reader (who will be more familiar with subheadings than marginal annotations). However, in Guagnini's *Sarmatiae Europeae descriptio* the marginal annotations function as an epitome of the text rather than as subheadings to guide the reader or break up the text into thematic sections, and so are omitted from this edition. While the original paragraph breaks are retained in the Latin text, it should be noted that I have introduced my own paragraph breaks to the translations where I judge they should fall in the English translation. In those texts where selected extracts only are given, text omitted is indicated thus: ...

Pagination, Foliation, and Signatures

The original pagination of the edition used for each of the Latin texts is given in square brackets **[thus]**—although, for ease of reading, where a word was split over two pages by the original typesetter, the page division is given before the split word. Where the source was foliated rather than paginated, folio numbers are given instead of page numbers. Where the original source is foliated by signatures rather than sequential folio numbers, the signatures are given as they appear in the text and "implicit" signatures following on from the printed signatures are inserted in brackets, in order to avoid leaving any pages unpaginated. Thus a printed sig. f IIIjv is followed by an "implicit" [sig. (Vr)] in order to mark the unpaginated folio that immediately follows.

Errors in the Texts

Small misprints in the texts are corrected without comment; more significant errors (or errors giving rise to any ambiguity in translation) are noted in the footnotes.

TRANSLATOR'S NOTE

The early modern Baltic region was a complex multilinguistic society. Most of today's national borders in the region did not exist, and the Baltic languages (of which only Lithuanian and Latvian now survive) were in their infancy as written languages in the sixteenth century. In translating latinized versions of vernacular names it is necessary for the translator to make decisions about which vernacular language those names should revert to when included in a modern English translation.

Personal and Place Names

Personal and place names are generally given, where known, in their standard modern forms in the language in which they originate (unless there are well-established anglicized forms). Thus, names of Polish individuals are given in their standard Polish forms, and names of German individuals in their standard German forms, etc. An exceptional case is Jogaila, to whom I refer by his Lithuanian name before his conversion to Christianity, but by his Polish regnal name Władysław II Jagiełło after his baptism.

Place names are given in their modern forms in the language of the country in which the place is now located (Lithuania, Poland, Belarus, or Ukraine), with the exception of Prussian place names (now located largely in the Kaliningrad Oblast of the Russian Federation or in Poland), where I use the German versions of place names that were current in the early modern era. Transliterations from the Cyrillic alphabet follow a modified form of the Library of Congress System, omitting diacritics, and I use the terms Rus' and Rus'ian (as opposed to Russia and Russian) to refer to Slavonic-speaking territories and peoples (including modern Russia, Belarus, and Ukraine) in order to avoid confusion with the later Russian Empire; I use the terms "Muscovy" and "Muscovite" to refer to the predecessor state of the Russian Empire and modern Russia.

Quotations

Quotations in languages without standard modern forms, such as Old Prussian and Samogitian, as well as blundered quotations by authors not proficient in the language they were attempting to record are given unaltered. Individual Old Prussian, Lithuanian, and Belarusian (Ruthenian) and German words quoted in the text are given in their standard modern forms in the translation.

Theonyms

For ease of identification, the names of all Baltic deities are given in the Lithuanian forms reconstructed by Norbertas Vėlius in *Baltų Religijos ir Mitologijos Šaltiniai*. If a theonym is reconstructed from any other source, it is given in a footnote.

Scriptural Quotations

All Scriptural quotations (given in the original texts from the Latin Vulgate) are rendered in translation according to the Authorized (King James) Version.

I

COSMOGRAPHIA PII PAPAE IN ASIAE ET EUROPAE ELEGANTI DESCRIPTIONE

[Extract]

[fol. 110r] **Hieronymus Pragensis heremita Lituanos ad Christi fidem convertit.**

Novi ego Hieronymum Pragensem sacris literis apprime eruditum: vitae mundicia et facundia singulari clarum: qui annos supra viginti in heremo Camalduensi in Apennino etrusco poenitentiam egit. Hic oriente apud Bohemos Hussitarum haeresi fugiens pestiferum virus in Polonia transivit. Ubi acceptis literis ab Vladislao rege commendaciis predicaturus evangelium Christi ad Vitoldum principem in Lituaniam penetravit: multosque populos Vitoldi favore fretus ad salutiferam dei Christi fidem convertit. Venitque tandem ad synodum Basiliensem. Vocatus a Iuliano sancti Angeli Cardinali cum de rebus Bohemicis agerent: narrabat hic multa de Lituanis: quae paene incredibilia videbantur. Audiebam ego ex aliis eius dicta. Nec movebat ut crederem: libuit adire hominem atque ab eius ore lata cognoscere: comites mei fuerunt Nicolaus Castellanus (qui tum cardinalis Iuliani domum regebat); Bartholomeus Lutimanus Archiepiscopi Mediolanensis scriba; et Petrus Noxetanus Cardinalis Firmiani secretarius: viri graves et docti hominem in cella sua trans Rhenum apud Carthusienses convenimus. Cuius haec narratio fuit.

Narratio de Lituanis per Hieronymum Pragensis heremitam. Serpentes colebant. Ignem alii colebant.

Primi quos adii ex Lituanis serpenteis colebant. Paterfamilias suum quisque in angulo domus serpentem habuit: cui cibum dedit: ac sacrificium fecit in foeni iacenti. Hos Hieronymus iussit omnes interfici. Et in foro adductos publice cremari. Inter quos unus inventus maior caeteris: quae saepe admotus ignis consumere nullo pacto valuit. Post hos gentem reperit: qui sacrum colebat ignem. Eumque perpetuum appellabat. Sacerdotes templi materiam ne deficerat ministrabat: hos super vita aegrotantium amici consulebant. Illi noctu ad ignem accedebat: mane vero consulentibus responsa. Dantes umbram aegroti apud ignem sacrum se vidisse aiebant.

THE COSMOGRAPHY OF POPE PIUS II IN AN ELEGANT DESCRIPTION OF EUROPE AND ASIA (1458)

ENEA SILVIO PICCOLOMINI (POPE PIUS II)[1]

The hermit Jerome of Prague converts the Lithuanians to the faith of Christ

I knew Jerome of Prague—erudite to the highest degree in sacred learning, famous for the purity of his life and singular eloquence—who did penance for over twenty years in the hermitage of Camaldoli in the Tuscan Appenines. This man, fleeing east from the pestiferous virus, the heresy of the Hussites among the Bohemians, crossed into Poland. Having accepted letters of commendation from King Władysław to preach the Gospel of Christ, he penetrated to Vytautas, prince in Lithuania; and supported by Vytautas's favour he converted many people to the salvation-bearing God of the faith of Christ. And at last he came to the Synod of Basel.[2] Having been called by Cardinal Giuliano of Sant'Angelo since he dealt with Bohemian affairs,[3] this man spoke much about the Lithuanians which seemed scarcely credible. I heard his words from others. It did not move me to believe; it pleased me to go to the man and know it as told from his own mouth. My companions were Niccolò Castellano (who then governed Cardinal Giuliano's household), Bartolomeo Lusimano (a scribe of the archbishop of Milan), and Pietro Nossetano (Cardinal Firmiano's secretary). We grave and learned men met the man in his cell across the Rhine with the Carthusians. This was his narrative.

Narrative about the Lithuanians by the hermit Jerome of Prague. They worshipped serpents. Others worshipped fire.

First of all, the Lithuanians to whom I went used to worship snakes. Their head of the household had a snake in a certain corner of the house, to whom he gave food, and made sacrifices to it lying in the straw. Jerome ordered them all to be killed and, having been brought into the marketplaces, to be publicly burnt. One among them was found to be larger than the others, and having been frequently moved would not be consumed by the fire by any means. After these things he found a people who worshipped a sacred fire, and they called it perpetual. The priests of the temple supplied material lest it should run out, and the friends of sick people consulted them about their life. They used to come to the fire at night, and in the morning there was a response for those consulting them.

---

1 This text is based on Piccolomini, *Cosmographia Pii Papae* (1509), fols 110r–111r.

2 A reference to the Council of Constance, at the time when it was convened at Basel between 1431 and 1438.

3 Cardinal Giuliano Cesarini (1398–1444), cardinal deacon of Sant'Angelo from 1430, who was president of the Council of Constance convened at Basel.

Quae cum se calefaceret signa vel mortis vel vitae ostentasset: moriturum portendit. Testari igitur et rebus suis consulere suadebant: delusionem hanc esse Hieronymus ostendit: [fol. 110v] persuaso populo deleto templo ignem dissipavit. Christianos mores induxit.

Solem et malleum alii.

Profectus introrsus aliam gentem reperit: quae solem colebat et malleum ferreum rarae magnitudinis singulari cultu venerabantur. Interrogati sacerdotes quid ea sibi veneratio vellet, responderunt olim pluribus mensibus non fuisse visum solem. Quem rex potentissimus captum reclusisset in carcere munitissime turris. Signa zodiaci deinde opem tulisse Soli: ingentique malleo perfregisse turrim: Solemque liberatum hominibus restituisse. Dignum itaque veneratu instrumentum esse: quo mortales lucem recaepissent. Risit eorum simplicitatem Hieronymus, inanemque fabulam esse ostendit. Solem vero et Lunam et stellas creatas esse ostendit. Quibus maxime deus ornavit caelos: et ad utilitatem hominum perpetuo iussit igne lucere.

Silvam alii venerabant.

Postremo alios populos adiit qui silvas daemonibus consecratas venerabantur: et inter alias unam cultum digniorem putavere. Praedicavit huic genti pluribus diebus fidei nostrae aperiens sacramenta. Denique ut silvam succenderet imperavit: ubi populus cum securibus affuit: nemo erat qui sacrum lignum ferro contingere auderet. Prior itaque Hieronymus assumpta bipenni excellentem quandam arborem detruncavit. Tum secuta multitudo alacri certamine alii ferris, alii dolabris, alii securibus silvam deiiciebant. Ventum erat ad medium nemoris: ubi quercum vetustissimam: et ante omneis arbores religione sacram: et quam potissime sedem esse putabant: percutere aliquamdiu nullus praesumpsit. Postremo ut est alter altero audacior: increpans quidam socios: qui lignum rem insensatam percuture formidarent. Elevata bipenni magno ictu cum arborem caedere arbitraretur: tibiam suam percussit: atque in terram semianimis cecidit. Attonita circum turba flere, conqueri, Hieronymum accusare, qui sacrum dei domum violari suasisset, neque iam quisquam erat qui ferrum exercere auderet.

They said they could see the sick people casting a shadow in the sacred fire; and that when it grew hotter it displayed a sign either of life or death, and portended that someone was about to die. Thus they persuaded people to confess and consult them on their business. Jerome showed this to be a delusion, and having persuaded the people, with the temple destroyed, he put out the fire. He led them into Christian customs.

Others [worship] the sun and a hammer

Having set out into the interior he found another people who worshipped the Sun, and venerated an iron hammer of rare size in a singular cult. Asking the priests why it wanted such veneration, they replied that once, for many months, the Sun had not been seen. A most powerful king, having captured her, had shut her in prison in a very well defended tower.[4] The signs of the zodiac then helped the Sun, and with a huge hammer broke down the tower, and restored the liberated Sun to men. Therefore this tool which had brought back light for mortals was worthy of veneration. Jerome laughed at their simplicity, and showed it to be an empty fable. He showed, indeed, that the Sun and Moon and stars were created, that God greatly adorned the heavens with them, and that he ordered them to shine with fire forever for the use of men.

Others worshipped a forest

Afterwards he went to another people who worshipped forests consecrated to demons. And among others they thought one cult more worthy. He preached for many days to this people, opening the sacraments of our faith. Finally he ordered the forest to be set on fire, since the people were plentiful in axes but there was no-one who dared touch the sacred wood with iron. Therefore Jerome, having taken up a double-edged axe first of all, cut branches from a certain excellent tree. Then the crowd following, in a quick contest, cut down the forest—some with iron tools, some with pick-axes, some with axes. They had come to the middle of the grove, where for some time no-one presumed to cut a very ancient oak, and sacred above all trees in their religion, which they thought to be a most powerful habitation. At last, one was more daring than the others, rebuking his fellows who feared to cut wood, an inanimate thing. Lifting up his double-edged axe, he decided to cut down the tree with a great blow; he hit his shin and fell down on the ground half dead. The surrounding crowd, astonished, wept and were overcome, accusing Jerome who had persuaded them to violate the sacred house of a god, and there was now no-one who dared make use of iron.

---

4 In Latin *sol* is a masculine noun; I use the feminine pronoun in the translation because *saulė* is a feminine noun in Lithuanian (the language in which John-Jerome heard the story) and we should therefore expect any personification of the sun in Lithuanian culture to be female.

Attentatum illusionem.

Tum Hieronymus illusiones daemonum esse affirmans, qui deceptae plebis oculos fasci-
narent. Surgere quem cecidisse vulneratum diximus imperavit. Et nulla in parte laesum
ostendit: et mox ad arborem adacto ferro adiuvante multitudine ingens onus cum magno
fragore prostravit, totumque nemus succidit. Erant in ea regione plures silvae pari religione sacrae: ad quas dum Hieronymus amputandas pergit mulierum ingens numerus
plorans atque eiulans. Vitoldum adit. Sacrum lucum succisum queritur: et domum dei
ademptam. In qua divinam opem petere consuessent. Inde pluvias, inde soles obtinuisse.
Nescire iam quo in loco deum quaerat: cui domicilium abstulerit: esse aliquos minores
lucos in quis dii coli soleant. Eos quoque delere Hieronymus velle [fol. 111r] qui nova
quaedam sacra introducens partium more extirpet: rogare igitur atque obtestari: ne
maiorum religionum loca: et caerimonias auferre sinat. Sequuntur et viri mulieres: nec
se ferre posse novum cultum asserunt. Relinquere potius terram et patrios lares quam
religionem a maioribus acceptum dicunt. Motus ea re Vitoldus veritusque populorum
tumultum: Christo potius quam sibi deesse plebem voluit. Revocatisque literis: quas
praesidibus provinciarum declarat iubens parere Hieronymo: hominem ex provincia
decedere iussit. Haec nobis Hieronymus constanti vultu nihil haesitans: ac per iuramen-
tum affirmavit: dignum fidei et gravitas sermonis et doctrina ostendit: et viri religio. Nos
quam accepimus imutata retulimus: veri periculum non assumimus: persuasi tunc et
nos et comites ab eo recessimus.

The illusion tested

Then Jerome affirmed these things to be illusions of demons, who enchanted and deceived the eyes of the people. He commanded the man whom we have said fell wounded to rise up. And he showed no injury in any part. And soon, having put iron to the tree, with the crowd helping, its great burden brought it down with a great crack, and he cut down the whole grove. There were in that region many forests equally sacred in their religion. A great number of women were begging and weeping at this while Jerome proceeded to cutting them down. They went to Vytautas. They complained that the sacred grove had been cut down, and the house of God[5] taken away in which they had been accustomed to beseech divine aid—and from which they had obtained rain and sunlight. They did not know where to find God, whose dwelling he would take away; there were other lesser groves in which they were accustomed to worship the gods. They also said that Jerome wanted to destroy them, who extirpated them when he introduced certain new rites in a partial manner.

They bore witness and asked, therefore, that the places of the religion of their ancestors and their ceremonies should not be taken away. And men followed the women, and asserted they were not able to bear the new cult. They said they would rather abandon their land and the household gods of their fatherland than the religion received from their ancestors. Vytautas, moved by this matter—and fearing an uprising of the people—wanted Christ to be removed from the people rather than himself. He revoked the letters ordering the prefects of the provinces to obey Jerome, and he ordered the man to depart the province.

Jerome affirmed this to us with an unchanging expression, not hesitating at all, and upon oath. The graveness and learning of his speech—and the religion of the man—showed him to be worthy of trust. We report unchanged what we heard; we have not suffered the danger of truth. Then, having been persuaded, both we and our companions withdrew from him.

---

5 Here, as elsewhere in John-Jerome's account as reported by Piccolomini, it is unclear from the Latin whether the Lithuanians are speaking of their understanding of the Christian God or of a god of their own. However, since the women are addressing the nominally Christian Vytautas, a reference to the Christian God seems most probable.

HISTORIAE POLONICAE

[Extracts from Book 10: the conversion of Lithuania, 1387]

[p. 109] Cum Hedvigi Regina in Lithuaniam vadit, et idolis effractis

Cum autem in Lithuaniam perventum esset, conventum pro die Cinerum apud Vilnam agit. Quo cum fratres Regii, Skirgallus Throcensis, Vithawdus Grodnensis, Wlodimirus Kiiovensis, Coributh Novogrodensis, Duces, et militum populariumque frequens nume-rus, regio iussu, convenisset, pluribus diebus a Wladislao Poloniae Rege, adiuvantibus illum Catholicis Ducibus, qui convenerant, apud milites et populares laboratum est, ut falsis diis, quo hactenus, vano gentilium errore decepti, colebant, abiectis, unum verum Deum, eisque Christianam religionem venerari, credere, et colere consentirent. Reluctantibus barbaris, et se suaque numina (erant autem haec praecipua, Ignis quem credebant perpetuum, qui per sacerdotes, subiectis lignis, nocte atque interdiu ado-lebatur; silvae, quas putabant sacrosanctas, et aspides serpentesque, in quibus Deos habitare et latere credebant) impium et temerarium contra maiorum instituta dese-rere et pessundare asserentibus; Wladislaus Rex ignem, qui perpetuus ab illis putaba-tur, in Vilnensi civitate, quae caput et metropolis gentis erat, sernatum, et a sacerdote eorum, qui Zincz appellabatur, et qui supplicantibus, ac de futuro rerum eventu Numen consulentibus, falsa edebant (quasi haec a Numine accepisset) responsa, custoditum, et sedula lignorum adiectione nutritum, barbaris inspectantibus, extingui, et templum aramque, in quibus hostiarum fiebat immolatio, disrumpi, silvas insuper quae sacro-sanctae putabantur, succidi, et lucos eorum confringi, aspides etiam et serpentes, quae et qui in singulis domibus veluti penates Dii reperiebantur, interfici et necari (barbari fletibus tantummodo et lamentis, falsorum suorum Deorum et Numinum, ruinam et cladem, ac exterminium, cum mussitare contra Regis imperium non auderent) **[p. 110]** prosequentibus disposuit. Confractis autem et exterminatis Idolis, dum Deorum suorum falsitatem, a quibus hactenus se ludificatos intellexerant, oculis pervidissent, universa Lithuanorum gens et natio, fidem Christianam suscipere, et vetusto errore renunciare, prona et obedienti devotione consensit.

POLISH HISTORIES (1455–1480)

JAN DŁUGOSZ[1]

[Jogaila] goes to Lithuania with Queen Jadwiga, and breaks the idols

... But when he had come to Lithuania, he urged a gathering at Vilnius on Ash Wednesday. The brothers of the king had gathered there by the king's order—Skirgaila, duke of Trakai, Vytautas, duke of Grodno, Vladimir, duke of Kyiv, and Kaributas, duke of Novhorod, and a great many of the knights and people. Władysław Jagiełło, king of Poland, laboured for many days so that they would cast aside the false gods by whom they had been deceived up to now (in empty pagan error) and so that they would worship the one true God, and agree to venerate, worship, and believe the Christian religion. The barbarians were reluctant, asserting it was impious to desert and do away with their gods, and presumptuous against those things instituted by their ancestors.

Foremost among these were the fire they believed to be perpetual (by the priests putting on timbers), which was worshipped night and day; the forests which they thought sacred; and the snakes and serpents in which they believed the gods lived and lay hidden. With the barbarians looking on, King Władysław arranged for the fire to be extinguished which was lit in the city of Vilnius (which was the chief and capital city of the people), and thought by them to be perpetual. They devoured false responses from their priest (as if he had received them from a god) who kept it and fed it by diligently throwing on timbers, who was called *žinis* ["knowledge"],[2] consulting the god about the course of future events. And he arranged for the temples and altars, in which there had been sacrifice of victims, to be broken; and, furthermore, for the forests which they thought sacred to be cut down, and their groves to be destroyed; and for the snakes and serpents (which were found in individual houses like domestic spirits) to be slaughtered and killed.

The barbarians lamented the ruin, destruction and extermination of their false gods and spirits with so many tears, since they did not dare mutter against the king. But when they had seen with their eyes the idols broken and destroyed, they understood the falseness of their gods, by whom they had so long been made sport. The whole Lithuanian people and nation received the Christian faith, renounced their ancient error, and consented with prostrate and obedient devotion.

---

1 This text is based on Jan Długosz, *Historiae Polonicae* (1711–1712), 1:109–10, 1:113–17, 1:342–46.

2 *Žinis* is one possible interpretation of the Lithuanian word signified by Długosz's *Znicz*, whose meaning is obscure; for a discussion of the word see Mierzyński, "Jan Łasicki. Źródła do mytologii litewskiej," 66–67.

Omnes gentes baptizat, donans illis pannum ex Poloniae adductum.

Per dies autem aliquot, de articulis fidei, quos credere oportet, et oratione dominica, atque Symbolo per Sacerdotes Polonorum, magis tamen per Wladislai Regis, qui linguam gentis noverat, et cui facilius assentiebat, edocta, sacri baptismatis unda renata est, largiente Wladislao Rege singulis ex popularium numero, post susceptum baptisma, de panno ex Polonia adducto, novas vestes, tunicas, et indumenta. Qua quidem provida liberalitate et largitione effecit, ut rudis illa natio et pannosa, lineis in eam diem contenta, fama huiusmodi liberalitatis vulgata, pro consequendis laneis vestibus, catervatim ad suscipiendum baptisma, ex omni regione accurreret. Et quoniam labor immensus erat, unumquemque credentium baptisare singillatim, concurrentis ad baptisma populi Lithuanici utriusque sexus multitudo mandante Rege, sequestrebatur in turmas, et cuneos, et universis de qualibet turmarum, benedicta aqua sufficienter conspersis, cuilibet etiam turmae et universis, qui in ea constituti erant,[1] nomen Christianum et usitatum, abrogatis barbaricis, videlicet primae turmae Petrus, secundae Paulus, tertiae Ioannes, quartae Jacobus, quintae Stanislaus etc. Foeminis vero, quae et ipse proprias faciebant turmas, competentia nomina videlicet Catharina, Margaretha, Dorothea, etc. iuxta numerum et quantitatem turmarum, imponebatur. ...

Lituani ortum, nomen, et mores ab Italis habent.

[p. 113] Quamvis autem parum constet, cum id nemo Scriptorum reliquerit, qualiter, quomodo, et quando gens Lithuanica et Samogithica in has, quas modo incolit, Septemtrionales regiones venerit, aut a qua stirpe gentem et genus ducat; verisimilis tamen praesumptio, et idiomatis et linguae earum sonus et proportio, ex variis circumstantiis et rerum qualificationibus sumpta, ostendit, Lithuanos et Samogithas Latini generis esse, etsi non a Romanis, saltem ab aliqua gente Latini nominis descendisse, et sub tempore bellorum civilium, quae primum inter Marium et Syllam, deinde inter Iulium Caesarem et magnum Pompeium, eorumque successores efferbuerant, sedibus veteribus, et solo patrio, credentes omnem Italiae oram clade civili perituram, derelictis, in regiones vastas et solitudines, solis feris pervias, quae assiduis fere uruntur frigoribus, quaeque a scriptoribus titulantur indagines, ad plagam septentrionalem cum coniugibus, pecore, et familias venisse, et regioni ex patrio et vetusto nomine Lithalia, genti vero Lithali, quae hodie Lithuania ex Ruthenorum et Polonorum immutatione appellatur, unam tantummodo literam L, quam etiam nunc Italici homines suae adiiciunt vulgari locutione, praeponendo, indidisse. Eadem quoque sacra, eosdem Deos, eosdem sacrorum ritus, easdem caerimonias, quae et qui Romanis gentilibus erant, ante susceptam fidem, coluisse, videlicet sacrum ignem, qui et credulitate ab illis perpetuus habitus est, et in illo Iovem tonantem, per Virgines Vestales Romae custoditum, cuius neglectam extinctionem capite expiabant. Item silvas quas vocabant sacrosanctas, et quas ferro contingere profanum atque mortiferum erat;

I *Constierant* in the text.

He baptizes all the people, giving them a robe brought from Poland

The people were taught for several days by Polish priests about the articles of faith which they ought to believe, and the Lord's Prayer and the Creed—as well as by King Władysław, who knew the language of the people. They agreed more easily with him. Reborn by the water of holy baptism, King Władysław bestowed on a number of the people, after they received baptism, new robes, tunics and clothes brought from Poland. By this generous liberality and largesse, he ensured that this primitive and ragged nation (at that time content with linen) ran from every region in large numbers to receive baptism after the rumour of liberality of this kind spread abroad—on account of the woollen clothes.

And since it was an immense labour to individually baptize every one of the believers, the Lithuanian people running to baptism, of either sex, were divided into squadrons and battalions by the king's order. When all of the squadrons had been sufficiently sprinkled with holy water, each squadron and everyone in it was established with a common Christian name, their barbarian names being taken away—for example, Peter for the first squadron, Paul for the second, John for the third, James for the fourth, Stanislaus for the fifth, etc. The women, who made up their own squadrons, were assigned adequate names, such as Catharine, Margaret, Dorothy, etc. according to the number and size of the squadrons. ...

The Lithuanians have their origin, their name, and their customs from the Italians

But, however, it remains uncertain, since no-one has left any of these writings, how, in what way, and when the Lithuanian and Samogitian peoples came to these northern regions, how they settled them, or from what line of people and race they descend. However, their identical stubbornness and the sound and proportion of their language (assumed on account of various circumstances and peculiarities of events) shows the Lithuanians and Samogitians to be of the Latin people. If not from the Romans, then by a leap they descended from some other people of Latin name. In time of civil war (which first boiled up between Marius and Sulla, and then between Julius Caesar and Pompey Magnus and their successors) they left their ancient seats, believing that all Italy was about to perish from civil war. They came with their families and cattle through vast and lonely regions, traversed only by wild beasts (they are named as hunters by some writers) to a northern tract of land; to a region anciently named from the ancestors Lithalia, and its people the Lithalians, which is now called Lithuania by the alteration of the Ruthenians and Poles, by placing a single letter "l" before it (which even now Italian people add in their common speech).

They worshipped according to the same rites, and had the same gods, and the same rites, and the same ceremonies as were among the Roman people before they received the faith; that is to say, the sacred fire, which on account of their credulity their custom was to keep perpetually alight for that thunderer Jove, guarded by the Vestal Virgins at Rome (for neglect of which they atoned with their heads). Similarly, they had forests they used to call sacred, in which it was sacrilegious and carried the penalty of death to touch them with iron.

omnes siquidem illas ferro contingentes et violantes, Satanae dolositas et versutia, in manu, oculo, pede, aut aliquo membrorum, ut cultores suos in fide sacrilega contineret, Deo permittente, offendebat, et non nisi arietum et vitulorum holocausti placatum, simulatam reddebat sanitatem. In silvisque huiusmodi, Deum silvarum, caeterosque Deos, iuxta illud Poëticum Habitarunt dii quoque silvas: consistere putans. In aspidibus vero et serpentibus, Deum Aesculapium in forma anguis, pro peste [p. 114] epidimiae graviter grassante, sedanda, Romam et Graecia et Epidauro navi advectum. Talibusque et simulibus sacris, etsi non ad liquidum Romanos et Italos exprimebant, pro magna tamen parte imitabantur. Erat insuper Lithuanis ex patrio ritu consuetudinarium et caerimoniale, dum illos gentilitatis detineret caligo, ad silvas, quas sanctas putaverant, collectis frugibus, sub principio mensis Octobris, cum coniugibus, pignoribus, et familiis venire, et Diis patriis, boves, vitulos, arietes, et caetera animalia, per triduum in holocausta et victimas, offerre. Et oblatis, sacrificatisque, sub eodem triduo, vacando comessationibus, ludis, et choreis epulari, convivari, et vesci libaminibus. Id inter omnia praecipuum et solenne sacrificium, quod nemini negligere licebatur, habebatur. Ex hostilibus quoque terris, triumphum aut praedas referentes, reversi, congerie de lignis et pyra extructa, ad cuius extructionem unusquisque lignum iaciebat, praestantiorem et insigniorem ex captivis iniicere, et conflagrare, existimantes Deos suos huiusmodi incenso prophano, quam maxime et gratificari, et placari. Idne a maioribus suis acceperint, an, ut solet, delusa gentilitas in errore passim grassari, hunc ritum per se quaesierit, incertum habemus. Mortuos insuper suos, quod non Italiae et Latinis tantummodo, sed et caeteris nationibus legimus fuisse solenne, comburebant. Lithuani tamen, cum silvarum et nemorum abundarent multitudine, habebant speciales silvas, in quibus singulae villae, et quaelibet domus atque familia, speciales focos obtinentes, decendentium cadavera solebant conflagrare. Adiungebantur autem cremando corpori quaeque potiora, equus, bos, vacca, sella, arma, vestes, cingulus, torques, annulus, et simul una cum cadavere, non habito respectu quod aurea vel argentea forent, cremabantur. In hunc quoque morem Olygerdus filius Gedimini, Magnus Dux Lithuaniae, et Wladislai Poloniae Regis genitor, in gentilitatis errore satis absumptus silva Kokiweyzus, prope castrum et villam Mischoli, cum equo optimo, iopula margaritis et gemmis intexta, veste ostro et auro superba, baltheo argenteo deaurato amictus, exustus est.

Accordingly, everyone who touched and violated them with iron offended, and the deceit and cunning of Satan did not restore them to simulated health in their hand, eye, foot or other member (with God permitting it) without an atoning sacrifice of calves or rams.

They think that the god of the forests, and the other gods, are in the woods in this way, as the poet has it, "The gods also have dwelt in the woods."[3] They also placate snakes and serpents—the god Aesculapius in serpent form, who was borne in a ship from Greece and Epidaurus to Rome when the plague was gravely increasing there. In these and similar rites, even if they do not purely express the Romans and Italians, they imitate them to a great extent. There is, moreover, a custom among the Lithuanians, received from the ancestors as a rite and ceremony when darkness still held that people. Having gathered in the harvest, they come with their wives, relatives, and victims to the forests they think holy, and they offer sacrifice and victims of cattle, calves, rams, and other animals to their ancestral gods for three days. And having offered and sacrificed for the same three days, in the interval they feast, celebrate, and eat, with feasts, games, dancing, and libations. In the midst of all this is held an important and solemn sacrifice, which no-one is allowed to neglect.

And also, when they are returning from hostilities to their lands, bringing back triumph or booty, they build a construction of logs and a pyre. For its construction each one lays a log, and they throw on the most important and outstanding of their captives and set them alight, considering that their gods are greatly gratified and pleased by this profane conflagration. Whether they received this from their ancestors or, as is accustomed, this people grew steadily in deluded error, we are uncertain

Furthermore, they used to burn their dead, which the Latins and Italians did not, but as we have read that other nations solemnly did. The Lithuanians, however, since they abound in a multitude of forests and groves, have special forests, in which there are individual houses for whichever house or family, having special hearths, where they were accustomed to burn the bodies of the deceased. Several things to drink, horses, cattle, chairs, shirts, cinctures, and rings were added to the body, and burnt together as one with the body—without regard for the things made of gold and silver. And in this way Algirdas,[4] the son of Grand Duke Gediminas of Lithuania,[5] and the father of King Władysław of Poland, was caught up sufficiently in superstitious error that he was consumed by fire in the forest of Maišiagala (near the town and castle of Kukaveitis) with an excellent horse, a jopula[6] woven with pearls and gems, a splendid golden and purple shirt, and a silver belt chased with gold.

---

3 The reference is to Virgil, *Eclogues* II, lines 60–61: "Quem fugis, a! demens? habitarunt di quoque silvas Dardaniusque Paris" (Ah, madman, whom do you flee? The gods also have dwelt in the woods, and Dardanian Paris).

4 Algirdas, Grand Duke of Lithuania (ca. 1296–1377).

5 Gediminas, Grand Duke of Lithuania (ca. 1275–1341).

6 *Jopula*: a close-fitting outer garment with a wide knee-length skirt, popular in the late Middle Ages.

Et situs naturaque Lithuaniae describitur.

Tam Lithuanicae autem quam Samogithicae gentes, gelidissimum septemtrionis axem magna ex parte spectant, adeoque imbre et frigore rigescunt, ut plerosque vis algoris extinguat, multos nasis, quod illic maior videtur inesse humor, in quem agat, mutilet. Duobus tantummodo mensibus in utraque regione sentitur magis quam habetur aestas, reliqua anni tempora frigore rigent. Coguntur proinde male matura frumenta igne torrere, et artificioso calore illis maturitatem conferre. Terrae autem quam inhabitant, et caeli, sub quo aluntur, proprietas, gentis quoque Ruthenica convictus et commixtio, p. 115 veterem illorum et priscam commutavit in plerisque, non tamen in totum sustulit, indolem. Qui a peregrinis voluptatibus excepti, contagione et alimento degenerant, populationibus incursionibusque, quam dimicatione, meliores. Lithuanica regio in annis superioribus, adeo contempta, obscura, et vilis fuerat, ut Kiiovienses Principes ab ea et eius incolis, ob egestatem, et soli nativi sterilitatem, sola perisomata et subera, in signum tantummodo subiectionis exigerent. Vithenen Dux Lithuanorum, rebellionem primus contra Ruthenos inducens, et se ipsum Ducem inter populares constituens, astu Principes Russiae aggressus conflixit. Sensim quoque adeo crevit viribus, ut iugo Principibus Russiae iniecto, etiam in tributa eos redigeret sibi pendenda, quae per plures aetates Ruthenis ipse penderat. Magnam partem servitorium Lithuani retinent. Ex quorum concubitu, caeteri in eandem sortem generati, nonnulli quoniam vel tributa, vel iudiciorum poenas, quae apud illos excessivae sunt, dependere nequeunt, ex liberis in servitutem redacti aut venundati, numerum servitorium in dies multiplicant: ministerisque et sudore servorum et suppellectilem congerunt et opes, arcana sua et Principum, veteri disciplina edocti, mira celant fide.

Lithuani, Samogitha, et Iaczwingi, licet appellationem diversam sortiti, et in familias plures divisi, unum tamen fuere corpus a Romanis et Italis ducentes genus, et natio longo et diuturno tempore ignobilis et obscura, tum primum erupit. Hi Romanorum et Italorum ferventibus bellis civilibus, inter Iulium Caesarem et Pompeium exules fuere. Qui sub tempore huiusmodi bellorum, partes Pompeianas secuti, victo primum in campis Pharsalicis, deinde apud Alexandriam in Aegypto occiso Pompeio, quoniam et proximi nonnulli ex eis erat cognitione Pompeio et partes Pompeii propensius quam caeteri Romani adiuvabant, victorem Iulium Caesarem perosi et veriti, ne in eos veluti sibi hostiliores, et magis invisos ac superstitiosos, crudelius saeviret; Roma cum omni substantia et servitiis, anno conditae Urbis septingentesimo quartodecimo, relicta, septemtrionales regiones, apud quas tute et impune latere possent, concesserunt.

And the situation and nature of Lithuania is described

The Lithuanian and Samogitian peoples are so numbed by cold and frost, since for the most part they look towards the North Pole, that the depth of the cold kills many, and mutilates many noses, since the humour on which it acts seems to be most greatly within them. In each of the two regions summer is felt to be no more than two months; the remaining time of the year is frozen with cold. Therefore the ill-matured fruits are gathered in order to char them with fire, and by the artificial heat bring them to maturity. But the character of the land they inhabit, and the skies beneath which they grow, and their association and mixing with the Ruthenian people has changed their old and ancient character in many ways, but has not, however, completely removed it. They become degenerate from luxuries received from travellers, by contact and by livelihood, and better by incursions of peoples, as well as by conflict.

In former years the Lithuanian region was so contemned, obscure, and worthless that the princes of Kyiv, on account of its poverty and the barrenness of the native soil, took only bark and the outer coverings of trees as a sign of subjugation. Vytenis, Duke of Lithuania, leading the first rebellion against the Ruthenians, and making himself duke among the people, fought the princes of Rus' by cunning.[7] He grew so gradually in strength that, having thrown a yoke on the Rus'ian princes, he had them pay what for many years he himself had paid to the Ruthenians. The Lithuanians retain [Ruthenians] as a great part of their servants. From their congress, other things of the same sort were generated, since there are many excessive tributes and excessive judicial penalties among them. If they cannot pay, having reduced their children to servitude, or sold them, the number of their servants multiplies day by day. And by the ministrations and sweat of their servants they accumulate both wealth and supplies, for their hidden places and those of their princes; and having been instructed in the old discipline, they hide them with wondrous trust.

The Lithuanians, Samogitians, and Yotvingians (different names may be chosen) are divided into many families; one family, however, was a band descended from the Romans and Italians. The nation was for a lengthy and extended time ignoble and obscure, but then at first it burst out. They were exiles from the raging civil wars of the Romans and Italians between Julius Caesar and Pompey. At the time of these wars they followed Pompey's party, which was first defeated on the field of Pharsalus. Then, when Pompey was killed at Alexandria, since they and many of those close to them were known to Pompey, they helped those on the side of Pompey more than other Romans. They dreaded and feared the victory of Julius Caesar, lest he should more cruelly rage against them, as people hostile to him. In the seven-hundred and fortieth year since the foundation of the city[8] they departed Rome with all their substance and slaves for the northern regions, where they could escape notice.

---

7 Vytenis, Grand Duke of Lithuania (fl. ca. 1295–ca. 1316) recaptured the Ruthenian principalities of Pinsk and Turaw (in present-day Belarus), which had been lost by the Lithuanians after the assassination of King Mindaugas (ca. 1203–63), but Długosz inaccurately implies that the Ruthenians took control of ethnic Lithuania itself (Rowell, *Lithuania Ascending*, 84).

8 13 BCE (Rome was traditionally founded in 753 BCE).

Hoc etiam ipsorum appellatione et vocabulo manifestatur. Omnes enim illae gentes Lithalos se vocabant, et ex veteri consuetudine Italici sermonis, qua et hactenus in suo vulgari, Itali ut communiter utuntur, L, addendo in praepositione pluribus verbis. Eisdem sacris, diisque, et cerimoniis, quibus et Romani in errore gentili usi; Vulcanum in igne, Iovem in fulmine, Dianam in sylvis, Aesculapium in viperis et serpentibus colunt; in civitatibus principalioribus tenendo ignem, quem vocabant et putabant aeternum, a Sacerdote custoditum, qui etiam a Daemone [p. 116] instructus, sacrificantibus et petentibus, ambigua dabat responsa. Iovem autem in fulmine venerando, vulgari suo illum Perkunum, quasi percussorum appellabant. Silvas etiam plerasque non secus quam sacrosanctas colebant, quas et intrare, et per detruncationem aut arboris aut frondis violare, capitale fuit. Detruncator enim frondium, aut silvae ingressor, aut iugulabatur a Daemone, aut in aliqua mutilabatur corporis parte. Viperas insuper et serpentes, fere singulorum hominum continebant domus, quibus et nutrimenta praebebant in lacte, et gallos illis velut hostias placationis immolabant. Lithuani enim, qui se primum Lithalos, processu vero temporis U. addita, et L mutata in N, ab aliis gentibus Lithuani appellati sunt, domesticis bellis et seditionibus Roma et Italia pulsi, solitudines vastas inter Poloniam, Russiam, Livoniam, et Prussiam sitas, furtim occupavere, quas ex magnitudine frigoris, pro maiori anni parte hibernale gelu premebat.

Lithuani oppido Vilno condito, illi, et fluminibus circa illud currentibus, Villia et Vilna, ex nomine Ducis sui Villi, nomen imposuerunt, et ob egestatem Ducibus Russiae in signum subiectionis nomine tributi perisomata pendebant.

Ibi primum oppidum Vilno, quod et in hanc diem caput genti est, ex nomine Villii Ducis, quo authore et Italiam deserverant, et regiones illas ingressi fuerant, condidere. Fluminibus quoque circa illud fluentibus, Villia et Vilna, ex eiusdem Ducis nomine, indidere nomina. Deinde non intercedentibus finitimis, primum pro libito suo iure usi viventes, dum germinando excrevissent, terram inferiorem versus Prussiam, quam ex proprietate sermonis sui Samogithiam, quod sonat terra inferior, ad extremum terram Poloniae contiguam, quam Iaraczones vocaverunt, populati sunt.

This is shown even in their name, and in their vocabulary; for all that people call themselves *Lithali*, and after the old custom of the Italian language (and up to now in their vulgar speech), as the Italians commonly use, they add an "l" before many words.

They used the same rites, gods, and ceremonies which the Romans used in their pagan error. They worship Vulcan in fire, Jove in thunder, Diana in the woods, and Aesculapius in snakes and serpents. In their principal towns they used to retain a fire, which they called (and considered to be) eternal, guarded by a priest who, instructed by a demon, gave ambivalent responses to suppliants and those offering sacrifice. They venerated Jove in thunder, calling him vulgarly Perkūnas, as if an assassin.[9] And they worshipped many forests as if they are nothing less than sacred; and to enter them, and violate them by cutting down trees and leaves, was a capital offence. The one who cut down trees, or entered forests, either had their throat slit by a demon, or was mutilated in some other part of the body. Furthermore, the houses of individual men generally used to contain snakes and serpents, to whom they offered milk as nourishment; and they used to sacrifice chickens as placatory victims.

The Lithuanians, who were at first *Lithali*, by the passage of time adding a "u," and changing "l" into "n," were called Lithuanians by other nations. Having been expelled from Rome and Italy by domestic wars and intrigues, they secretly occupied the vast solitudes located between Poland, Rus', Livonia, and Prussia. From the greatness of the cold, for the greater part of the year they are oppressed by winter ice.

The Lithuanians, having founded the town of Vilnius gave it its name from their Duke Vilius, and the rivers flowing around it, the Viliya and Vilnia; and on account of their poverty they paid bark to the dukes of Rus' as a sign of subjection under the name of tribute

Here the foremost town is Vilnius, which is in our day the capital of this people, from the name of Duke Vilius; it was founded after they had left Italy and come into these regions. They also named the two rivers flowing around it the Viliya[10] and Vilnia, from the name of the same duke.[11]

Then, when their neighbours did not intervene, they lived at first as they pleased according to their own law, and grew by multiplying; and the lowlands towards Prussia (which from the nature of their language they called Samogitia, which means lowland) to the furthest land contiguous to Poland (whose people are called the Yotvingians) were populated.

---

9 Długosz is proposing (incorrectly) that the Lithuanian theonym Perkūnas is a corruption of Latin *percussor* ("assassin," with the sense of one who kills with a blow).

10 Viliya: the Belarusian name for the River Neris.

11 There was no such duke; Długosz's legend of Duke Vilius may be a garbled version of some versions of the legend of Gediminas, in which the pagan priest Lizdeika (who interprets a dream of Gediminas and advises him to build a castle on the site of Vilnius) is given the name Radvila (Radziwiłł in Polish), meaning "the wolf advises" (*vilkas* means "wolf" in Lithuanian). The Radziwiłłs claimed descent from Lizdeika for this reason (Rowell, *Lithuania Ascending*, 125). Alternatively, the character of Vilius was simply invented to explain the name of Vilnius.

Principes Russiae et Kiiovienses, profectibus eorum permoti, ipsos, quoniam silvas eorum ditionis occupassent, vile tamen et modestum, in signum tantummodo ditionis et dominii, illos coegerunt. Pendebantque pro tributo annis multis ex quercinis frondibus perisomata, cum crassius ab his, ob terrae sterilitatem, exigi non posset. Sermo his latinus modica varietate distinctus. Qui etiam ex commercio gentium vicinarum, ad proprietatem vocabulorum Sclavonicorum defluxit, vestis et abscissio capillorum ac barbae, brevis olim moris fuit. Exercitus partem maiorem ex servis his conficiunt, quibus omnia aedificia et officia domestica explent, illaque pro dote generibus tribuunt. In quo nimiam austeritatem et parsimoniam plusquam barbaricam exercent. Nusquam vel raro manumittere soliti, ac per hoc omnibus servis nascentibus, crescit in dies eorum numerus. Frequenter insuper et liberi, debitis aut aere alieno nexi, aut iudiciis damnati, dum solutionem facere nequeunt, in servorum conditionem retruduntur. Quod et plerisque per violentiam, calumniam, aut iniuriam solet provenire, in nostrae praesertim aetatis tempestate; in qua Princeps Lithuaniae principalis (quem illae gentes more maiorum magnum vocare solent, qua etiam appellatione [p. 117] Pompeius vocitabatur) nullam pro oppressis et gravatis opponebat defensionem. Locupletissimus ut quisque est, ita plures in bellum Principi suo armatos praebet. Cibus genti parcus, castigatus, pascedis et ollis ex farina formatis coctus, igne magis quam aqua torritus. Inter Septemtrionales populos obscurissimi, Ruthenorum servituti et tributis vilibus obnoxii, ut cuius mirum videatur, ad tantam eos felicitatem, sive per finitorum ignaviam et desidiam provectos, ut imperent nunc Ruthenis, sub quorum imperio annis prope mille, veluti servile vulgus fuere. Funera illis gentilitatis tempore non alia fuere quam Italis: omnia enim cadavera cremabant igne, quibus equum, vestem, vas, quae viventi sciebant chariora, adiungebant, nunc illa terra obruunt. Ingenia genti tumida, seditiosa, fraudulenta, procacia, mendosa, et parca. Natura taciti, arcana sua et suorum Principum silentio tegunt. In liberos lascivi, in Rempublicam suam incensi et studiosi, in libidinem, ebrietatem, et assentationem proclivi, Sortilegiorum et divinationum studiosi, et rari sectatores. Parsimoniae dediti, et in cibum parci, nisi quoties coenarum apparatus et convivia instruunt pro hospitibus et advenis. In caerimoniis et ritibus ad curam rerum divinarum pertinentibus, Proceribus et Satrapis gentis praecipua cura, vulgo tenuis est. Foeminae eorum gubernatione et incremento rerum domesticarum, et in procuratione ciborum et victualium, ac omnifariorum staminum, quae ex lino texuntur, magno studio et cura callent, et in ebrietatem ipsae pronae. ...

The princes of Kyiv and Rus', stirred up by their successes, since they had occupied the forests of their dominion (however modest and contemptible), confined them as a sign of their sovereignty and dominion. And for many years they used to pay tribute in the form of the leaves and bark of oak trees; but they were unable to extract any more richly from them, on account of the barrenness of the land.

Their speech is Latin, a little different in kind. From commerce with neighbouring peoples, it slid into an idiom of Slavonic words. At one time, their custom was short shirts and the cutting of their beards and hair. They make up the greater part of their army from slaves, with whom they fill all their buildings and domestic offices, and whom they give to their children as dowries. Against them they exercise excessive severity and meanness, more than barbaric; never, or rarely, are they accustomed to free them, and with all their new slaves being born, their number grows day by day. Furthermore, children are often forced into the condition of slaves, owing debts contracted by another, or condemned in judgment while they are unable to make payment. Many are accustomed to prosper by violence, calumny, and harm, and especially in the tempest of this our age. In this, the principal prince of Lithuania (as this people are accustomed to call him after the custom of the ancestors—and by which name even Pompey was called) puts up no defence for those who are oppressed and accused. However richly provided he is, many offer their arms to the prince in battle.

Food for this people is frugal and restricted; they feed on grain from a jar, pressed together and cooked, and heated more by fire than water. Among the northern peoples, they are the most obscure, repugnant even to the servitude and mean tributes of the Ruthenians; and what seems extraordinary is that their good fortune is so great that they now command the Ruthenians (whether carried by their faintheartedness and idleness within their limits), beneath whose rule they have now been for nearly a thousand years,[12] like common slaves. Their funerals were no different from those of the Italians in pagan times. They cremated all bodies with fire, with whom they placed a horse, clothing, vessels, and whatever they knew was dearest to them in life; now the earth swallows up these things. The character of the people is puffed up with pride, seditious, deceitful, undisciplined, prone to mistakes, and frugal. They are by nature silent, and protect their secrets and those of their prince with silence. They are playful with children, and fierce and eager for their polity; given to lust, drunkenness, and flattery; eager in sorceries and divination, and infrequent followers. They are given to miserliness and frugal in food, unless it is whenever they hold or are preparing dinners and feasts for guests and new arrivals. Ceremonies and rites pertaining to the care of matters of the gods are the particular care of the first men and minor rulers[13] of the people, but unimportant to the common folk. Their women, by great eagerness and care, become skilled in the governance and increase of domestic affairs, and in obtaining food and supplies, and all kinds of weaving—but are themselves prone to drunkenness. ...

---

12 This was not historically true; Lithuanian expansion into Slavic territories began only in the twelfth century, three hundred years before Długosz was writing.

13 *Satrapis*, a term for the minor under-kings of the Persian Empire, here seems to refer to minor rulers of some kind, perhaps the *bajorai* of the Grand Duchy.

[from Book 11: the conversion of Samogitia, 1413]

[p. 342] Wladislaus Poloniae Rex in Lithuaniam, comitante eum Alexandro Magno Duce Lithuaniae, cum Anna Regina et filia Hedvigi processit. Ingenti autem cruciatus atque afflictus molestia, quod terrae suae naturales Samogithiae, caeco gentilitatis in eam diem errore detinerentur, non sine probro suo; omnes conatus suos, pro illustranda gente praedicta, fide et religione Christiana, intendit. Et id sibi primum agendum existimavit, ut a populis Samogithiae idolatriae spurcicias dispelleret. Assumptis itaque viris litera-tis et religiosis, zelum Dei habentibus, circa festum Sancti Martini, Samogithiam navali itinere, destinata animo executurus, ire pergit. Et Anna Regina cum impedimentis apud Kowno relicta, per flumen Nyemyen descendendo, usque ad fluvium Dubischa: abinde vero flumen Dubischa ascendendo, ad terram Samogitharum pervenit. Convocatoque utriusque [p. 343] universo Samogithico populo; docet foedum ac turpe esse univer-sis Lithuaniae tam Principibus et militaribus, quam popularibus, veri et universus Dei cultum agnoscentibus et tractantibus, Samogithas veteribus superstitionum erroribus detineri.

Wladislaus Rex ignem perpetuum a Samogithis pro Deo cultum extinguit; lucos succidit.

Aras deinde idolorum destruit, lucos succidit, et ad praecipuum Samogitharum Numen, ignem videlicet, quem sacrosanctum et perpetuum putabant, qui in montis altissimi iugo, super fluvium Nyewyasza sito, lignorum assidua appositione a sacrorum sacer-dote alebatur, accedens, turrim, in qua consistebat, incendit, et ignem disiicit et extin-guit. Succidit, deinde per milites suos Polonicos, silvas, quas non secus quam sanctas, et Deorum suorum habitacula Samogithae, iuxta illud Poeticum, "Habitarunt dii quoque silvas," venerabantur, in eam mentis caliginem prolapsi, quod et silvae praefatae, et aves feraeque in illis consistentes, sacrae essent, et quicquid in illas faceret ingressum, ut sanctum debet censeri. Non ergo Samogitharum aliquis in silvis praefatis ligna aude-bat concidere, aut alites vel feras venari: Violanti enim nemus, feras, vel alites, manus aut pedes daemonum arte curvabantur. Usu itaque longo, ferae et alites, apud silvas praefatas moratae, ad domesticarum instar, humanos neque horrebant neque vitabant conspectus. Maxima itaque barbaros tenebat admiratio, quod Polonorum milites nemus, ritu eorum sanctum, excidentes, nulla laesio, qualem ipsi in se frequentius experti erant, sequeretur. Habebant praeterea in silvis praefatis focos, in familias et domos distinctos, in quibus omnium charorum et familiarium cadavera cum equis, sellis, et vestimentis potioribus incendebant.

[from Book 11: the conversion of Samogitia, 1413]

King Władysław of Poland proceeded into Lithuania with Queen Anna and his daughter Jadwiga. But he was tormented and afflicted with trouble, since his natural lands of Samogitia were at that day held in blind paganism—not without disgrace to him. He extended the chance to all his relatives to illuminate this aforesaid people with the Christian faith and religion. And he considered that he himself had to act first of all to dispel the filthiness of idolatry from the people of Samogitia. Taking with him literate and religious men, having the zeal of God, he proceeded to go to Samogitia on a boat expedition, around St. Martin's Day,[14] and was about to perform this with a predestined soul. And having left Queen Anna indisposed at Kaunas, he went down the River Nemunas as far as the River Dubysa. Going up the River Dubysa from here, he came to the land of the Samogitians. And he summoned together the whole Samogitian people. He taught that it was filthy and disgraceful for the Samogitians to be held in the errors of ancient superstitions while the whole of Lithuania—princes, soldiers, and people—acknowledged and accepted the worship of the true and universal God.

King Władysław extinguishes the sacred fire, worshipped as a god by the Samogitians; he cuts down the groves

He then destroyed the idols and cut down the groves. And he came to the foremost god of the Samogitians—a fire they thought sacred and perpetual, which was situated on the high ridge of a hill near the River Nevėžis, and was kept going by the constant laying on of timbers by a priest of the rites.[15] He burnt the tower in which it was placed, and dismantled and extinguished the fire. Then, by his Polish soldiers, he cut down the forests which the Samogitians worshipped as nothing less than holy, and as the habitations of their gods—following that poet, "The gods also have dwelt in the woods."

They fell into that darkness of mind because they thought the aforesaid forests and the birds and wild animals living in them were holy, and that whoever made an entry into them ought to consider them sacred. No-one among the Samogitians dared hew wood in the aforesaid forests or hunt birds or wild animals. The hands or feet of those who violated the groves were made to curve over by art of the demons. Therefore, by long habit, the birds and wild animals living in the aforesaid forests, resembling domestic animals, were neither terrified at nor avoided human sight. Very great wonder seized the barbarians that no injury befell the Polish soldiers cutting down the groves—which they had frequently tested—that were sacred to their rite.

---

14 November 11.

15 A possible candidate for this sacred hill is Burveliai or Burve, on the east bank of the River Nevėžis near Krekenava, between Panevėžys and Kėdainiai. The River Nevėžis marked the traditional boundary between Samogitia and the rest of Lithuania.

Ritusque gentium qui late recensentur, abrogat.

Locabant etiam ad focos huiusmodi ex subere facta sedilia, in quibus escas, ex pasta in casei modum praeparatas, deponebant; medonem quoque focis infundebant: ea credulitate illusi, quod mortuorum suorum animae, quorum illic combusta fuerant corpora, nocte venirent, escaque se exsatiarent, ac medonem foco infusum, et dudum a cineribus absorptum, biberent; cum non animas, sed corvos, cornices, caeterasque silvestres aves et feras, ex assidua assuefactione, cibos depositos constabat absumpsisse. Prima insuper mensis Octobris die, maxima per Samogithas in silvis praefatis celebritas agebatur, et ex omni regione, universus utriusque sexus conveniens illic populus, cibos et potum, quilibet iuxta suae conditionis qualificationem, deferebat. Quibus diebus aliquot epulari, Diis suis falsis, praecipue Deo, lingua eorum appellato, Perkuno, id est, Tonitru, ad focos quisque suos, offerebant libamina, existimantes celebritate et epulatione illa, et placari Deos, et animas suorum necessariorum cibari. Est autem gens et regio Samogithica magna ex parte ad gelidum versa septentrionem, Prussiae, Lithuaniae, Livoniae **p. 344** contermina, silvis, montibus, et fluminibus circumsepta, foecundum habens solum, in hos districtus distincta, videlicet Iragola, Roszena, Medniki, Chrosze, Vidulky, Wyelunya, Colthim, Czetrae pro ea tempestate barbara, inculta,[2] atque ferox, et in omne facinus audax, procerae et altae staturae, parco et castigato victu, de pane aut carne, contenta, situm suam, raro medone aut cervisia, sed communius unda, sedare solita. Auri, argenti, ferri, aeris, vini, piscium et pulmentorum expers, et ignara. Apud quam licitum erat viro uni plures habere uxores, et patre mortuo, novercam, fratreque glotem in uxorem accipere. Nullius illi stubarum aut aedificiorum nobilium, sed tantummodo tugurii unius usus: Ventrem distentum et porrectum, extrema vero habens coarctata. Structura aedificii ex ligno et culmo, largius ab imo sensim operis incremento in acrius cogitur, in carinae maximae similitudinem elaborata, in cacumine fenestra una, superne lumen reddens. Subter quam focus et cibos parabiles coquens, et frigus, quo regio pro maiori anni parte constricta est, repellens. In ea domo se, uxores, pignora, servos, ancillas, pecus, armentum, frumentum, et omnem supellectilem condunt, nec alia aedificia, coenacula, palatia, promptuaria, aut cameras vel stabula norunt, sed iisdem habitationibus se, et pecus suum, armenta, atque alia omnia animalia domestica includunt. Gens agrestis, fera et inculta, et ad ritus prophanos, divinationes, et auguria, proclivis. ...

p. 345 Verbum Dei suscipiunt.

... ediditque consensum, paucis quidem verbis pronunciatis, sed facetis, per unum natu maiorem ad id delectum. "Ex quo," inquiunt, "Dei nostri, quorum culturum et sacra a maioribus acceperamus, a te tuisque miltibus, Rex Serenissime, deleti sunt,

---

2 *Inculcata* in the text.

And he abolishes the pagan rites which flared up again widely

Furthermore, they had fires in the aforesaid forests, for different families and households, in which they burnt the bodies of their family and loved ones with horses, chairs, and useful clothing. They even put at the fire little chairs of a kind, made of bark, on which they placed food prepared in the manner of cheese pastry cakes. And they also poured mead on the fires—deceived, in their credulity, that the souls of their dead whose bodies were burnt there would come at night and satisfy themselves with the food and drink the mead poured on the fire (long since absorbed by the ashes). Since it was not souls, but ravens, crows, and other forest birds and animals who, by continual custom, took away the food left behind.

Furthermore, on the first day of October there was a great celebration by the Samogitians in the aforesaid forests, and this people gathered together from every region (everyone of both sexes), and they brought food and drink, according to the ability of their condition. Feasting for several days, they offered libations to their false gods at their fires—especially to the god called in their language Perkūnas (that is, thunder). They think by this celebration and feasting to placate the gods, and that their spirits are thus fed with necessities.

But this region of Samogitia, a great part of which faces the frozen north, bordering Prussia, Lithuania, and Livonia, is surrounded by forests, hills, and rivers. It has fertile soil in these distinct regions, that is to say Ariogala, Raseiniai, Medininkai, Kražiai, Viduklė, Veliuona, Kaltinėnai, and Šėta. The people is barbarous on account of storms, unsophisticated, ferocious, and daring in every crime, noble and tall in stature, sparing and severe in a diet of bread or meat. They are content, and rarely accustomed to quench their thirst with mead or beer, but more often with water. They are ignorant and lacking in experience of gold, silver, iron, bronze, wine, fish, and poultry.

It was permitted among them for one man to have many wives, and, on the death of his father, to take his stepmother or his brother's wife as a wife. There are no rooms or noble buildings among them, but just a single hut is customary; it has a distended and stretched out middle, having a narrow top. The structure of the building is of wood and thatch, getting larger little by little from the ground, the work is then gathered together into a point. They are decorated much like a ship; at the top there is one window, admitting the light from above. Beneath is the hearth and materials for preparing food, and keeping off the cold by which that region is held for the larger part of the year. In this house they keep themselves, their wives, their hostages, their slaves, their slave-girls, their sheep, their cattle, and all their apparatus. And they are unacquainted with other buildings, upper storeys, palaces, storehouses, rooms, or stables, but enclose themselves and their sheep, cattle, and other domestic animals in the same homes. They are a rustic, wild and uncouth people, prone to profane rites, divinations, and auguries. ...

They receive the word of God

[The people of Samogitia] gave its consent, pronounced in few (but witty) words, by one of the eldest chosen for this: "On account of the fact that our gods, whose cults and rites we received from our ancestors, were destroyed by you and your soldiers, most serene king,

et velut inertes et languidi, a Polonorum Deo devicti, Deos nostros et sacra eorum deserrimus, et Deo Polonorum atque tuo, velut fortiori adhaeremus." Notabiliores itaque eorum in fide edocti, et de fidei articuli plene instructi, inspectante et procurante Wladislao Poloniae Rege, et Catholica nomina eis adaptante, baptizantur. Universus autem, qui fidem Christianam et Baptisma susceperunt, Wladislaus Rex pannos optimos, equos, vestimenta, pecunias, et alia munera, in fidei sanctae favorem, liberaliter largitus est: ut caeteri ad suscipiendam religionem Orthodoxam forent proniores. In districtu autem et loco insigniori terrae Samogithiae Medniki, Cathedralem Ecclesiam sub honore tituli Sanctorum, Alexandri, Theoduli[3] et Eventii Martyrum, item in aliis locis Parochiales Ecclesias Wladislaus Rex fundat et aedificat, atque erigit, et illis in dotem sufficientes redditus et introitus consignat, et literis suis inscribit. ...

[p. 346] De salute Samogitharum Rex solicitus.

Conversione Samogithicae gentis, solicito studio Rex Poloniae Wladislaus feliciter, propitia Divinitate, consumata, ex Samogithiae recessurus, sciens intellegensque Samogithas fluxae fidei homines esse, iamque nonnullos, eos praecipue, qui fidei et baptismatis charactere insigniri derectaverant, pro deletione falsorum Deorum suorum, et ignis, quem sanctum et perpetuum putabant, extinctione, ingenti amaritudine molestos, ad reaccendendum ignem perpetuum, propter ea, quod cineres loci aliqualem calorem spirabant, clandestinis consiliis et sermonibus, in hunc modum convenisse: "Recedente," inquiunt, "Rege, dummodo ex vetusto igne reaccendere focum poterrimus, Deum nostrum intelligamus deleri non potuisse': continuavit dies aliquot in superstitionum loco, intra quos omnibus militibus ex flumine Nyewyasza adferri aquam copiosam iussit, et focum locumque ignis prophani, aquarum multitudine usque ad os complui et inebriari.

Kinzgalum virum pietate insignem eis praeficiet.

Kinzgalonem insuper, virum unum ex Lithuaniae Baronibus timoratum et devotum, Samogithis et Capitaneum et Praefectum constituit: Cui districte imperat, quatenus exquisitam curam circa neophytos adhibeat, omni cura et conatu, ne ad veteres superstitiones relabantur, provisurus. Sed nec aliis fidei Sanctae iugum recusantibus, Diis suis offerre libamina, aut sacra et ceremonias frequentare permittat. Qui iussa Regis solicite exequens, et roborabat neophytos, et gentiles a superstitione veteri cohibebat. Quapropter gens Samogithica, sub brevi dierum spatio, plenarie ad fidem religionemque Catholicam accedens, Diis quoque suis falsis manus iniiciens, silvas, quas sanctas putaverat, in uberem culturam redegit.

---

3 *Theodori* in the text; the feast of the Roman martyrs Alexander, Theodulus and Eventius (d. 113 CE) was celebrated on May 3.

and were defeated by the God of the Poles as if they were inert and powerless, we desert our gods and their rites, and adhere to your God and that of the Poles as stronger." The more notable among them were therefore baptized, taking on Catholic names, having been taught the faith and fully instructed in the articles of faith, with King Władysław arranging it and looking on. But King Władysław liberally favoured everyone who received baptism and the Christian faith with excellent clothes, horses, robes, money, and other gifts, in honour of the holy faith—so that others would be more inclined to receive the orthodox religion. But in a well-known place and district of Samogitia, at Medininkai, King Władysław founded, built, and erected a cathedral church dedicated to St. Alexander, St. Theodulus, and St. Eventius, along with parish churches in other places. And having returned and entered [Poland], he assigned them sufficient endowments, and wrote it in his letters. ...

The king is concerned about the salvation of the Samogitians

When the conversion of the Samogitian people had been completed by divine providence and the concern and hard work of Władysław, fortunately king of Poland, he was about to leave Samogitia. But knowing and understanding that the Samogitians were a people unstable in faith, and that many (especially those who had lined up to be signed with the faith and character of baptism) were annoyed with great bitterness on account of the destruction of their false gods, and the extinction of the fire which they thought holy and perpetual. They gathered together in order to re-light the sacred fire, whose ashes they blew to heat in a certain place, by secret counsels and speeches, in this manner: "With the king returning," they said, "in the meantime we can re-light a fire from the old fire; we understand that our god could not be destroyed." The superstition continued for several days in that place; in the meantime, [Władysław] ordered all his soldiers to bring large amounts of water from the River Nevėžis, and to fill and saturate that fire and the place of the sacred fire with a great deal of water, up to the mouth.[16]

He puts Kęsgaila, a man of outstanding piety, in charge of them

Furthermore, he appointed Kęsgaila, one of the *bajorai* of Lithuania, a devout and God-fearing man, as Captain and Prefect of Samogitia. He strictly ordered him, as much as was his especial concern, to prevent the neophytes falling back into their old superstitions by every care and effort. Nor did he permit others who refused the yoke of the holy faith to offer libations to their gods, or to frequent the rites and ceremonies. Diligently executing the king's order, he both strengthened the neophytes and restrained the pagans from their old superstition. On account of this the Samogitian people, in the brief space of a few days, fully accepted the Catholic faith and religion. And raising violent hands against their false gods, they put the forests they had considered sacred to profitable cultivation.

---

16 The reference to the Nevėžis suggests that the sacred fire was re-lit in the same place as before, which may have been the hill of Burveliai.

VITA ET MORES SBIGNEI CARDINALIS

[Extract]

[p. 27] **XIV.** Res ipsa admonet, quia super eius gentis origine non consentitur, ut, quae a diversis dicuntur, in medium afferantur.

Gentem Lytifanam plerique ab **[p. 28]** Italia profectam dicunt, divinantium magis more, quam eorum, qui asseverationes suas certo aliquo argumento confirmandas putant. Probabiliusque coniectari videntur illi, qui a Gallis oriundam credunt. Nam quo tempore Celtarum pars in Italiam transcendit, partem etiam duce Lemonio cum liberis atque uxoribus in Boreum Oceanum profectam dicunt extrema Europae occupasse eamque regionem primo tenuisse. Quae mox Livonia, corrupto vocabulo, a Lemonio duce, ut credi par est, nominata. Cimbris postea expeditionem ducentibus versus Bosporum, qui ab illis Cimmericus, quasi Cimbricus nuncupatur. Celtas relictis sedibus, quas ceperant in mediterranea Sarmatia, ad ea, quae nunc obtinent loca, se recepisse. Indigenas vero, qui agricolationis propemodum ignari essent, cum viderent in eius studio illos plurimum occupatos, a fructibus terrae, quos generali nuncupatione lingua sua dicebant Litifa, Litifanos vocavisse. Licet sint, qui putent, quasi Lituanos a litore Oceani dictos, quod illinc oriundi arbitrentur. Sed utcumque id nominis acceptum sit, quamvis a Graecis minime ignaris verae originis composito vocabulo ex nominibus antiquae ac novae patriae Celtoscythae pridem dicerentur, usque ad haec tempora perseveravit. Rarissima enim aliarum gentium commercia prope necessariam occasionem praebuere Celtoscytharum nominis abrogandi; mansitque ea nuncupatio, quam retinere illi, quibuscum omnia humana semper habuere communia.

Ceterum Gallicae ac non Romanae originis argumentum adducitur idioma omnino ab Italo abhorrens, mos praeterea et religio consecrandorum nemorum sine ullis templis ritu Gallorum Druidarum, quae Romanis habentibus deorum aedes et ministeria sacrorum diuersa sunt. Sed nec caerimonia exurendorum corporum nec ergastula servorum in agris cum plerisque aliis institutis, quibus utebantur prisci Litifani, proficisci a Romanis potuerunt, ad quos sero admodum et cum iam gens illa in Sarmatia esset, pervenerunt. Nam et colendi agri per servos recentior est apud Romanos consuetudo, et regem Numam universamque gentem Corneliam et plerosque alios viros claros Romae humatos legimus. Quod facit argumentum omne aliud genus sepulturae, tum novum tum peregrinum esse. Ad extremum more ac consuetudine militandi minime cum Romana disciplina conveniunt.

THE LIFE AND MANNERS OF CARDINAL ZBIGNIEW (1480)

FILIPPO BUONACCORSI[1]

Chapter 14

The matter itself admonishes, since there is no agreement on the origin of this people, that what is said by different authors ought to be brought to some common consent.

And many say that the Lithuanian people set out from Italy, divining more from their customs than from those who think their assertions confirmed by some other argument. Those who believe them to come from the Gauls seem to conjecture more probably. For they say that at that time part of the Celts passed beyond Italy, and some of them (led by Lemonius) set off to the northern ocean with their wives and children, and first occupied the extremities of Europe and held that region. Soon Livonia, by corruption of words, was named from their leader Lemonius—which is equally to be believed. The Cimbrians afterwards mounted an expedition towards the Bosphorus, from whom it is called Cimmerian or Cimbrian. The Celts, having left their homes (which they had taken in the middle of Sarmatia), betook themselves to those places where they now obtained homes. But the native people, who were almost completely ignorant of agriculture, when they saw them much occupied in that work, called them *Litifani* from the fruits of the earth, generally called *litifa* in their language. Let it be allowed that there are those who judge that the Lithuanians are named from the shore (*litus*) of the ocean, from which they originate.

But no matter how the name was received, they were said by the Greeks to have been not ignorant for a long time of their true origin and their new Celto-Scythian homeland, having put together their speech from ancient words, and it persisted even up to the present day. For commerce with other peoples was very rare, but on such an occasion it was necessary to stop presenting the Celto-Scythian name; and that name remained, which they retained who always had communication with all human beings.

Their idiom, utterly abhorring anything from Italy, leads to another argument of Gaulish and not Roman origin. Besides, the custom and religious practice of consecrating sacred groves without any temples, according to the rite of the druids of the Gauls, is opposed to the Romans having buildings of the gods and ministries of the sacred rites. But neither the ceremonies of cremating bodies nor the chaining of slaves in the fields (with many other institutions which the ancient Lithuanians practised) could have come from the Romans—to whom they came quite late, when that people was already in Sarmatia. For the cultivation of fields by slaves was a more recent custom among the Romans, and we read that King Numa, the family of the Cornelii and many other famous men of Rome were buried. This makes the argument that any other kind of funerary practice is not an import, but new. Finally, their manner and custom of fighting does not at all match the Roman discipline.

---

[1] This text is based on Buonaccorsi, *Vita et mores Sbignei cardinalis*, ed. Finkel, 27–30.

XV. Sed, ut pluribus signis opinionem suam tuentur, qui Gallicam potius quam Romanam originem probant, ita non desunt argumenta illis, qui a Bosporanis p. 29 profectos aiunt, cum totius agendae vitae ratione, qua Bosprani degunt, prisci etiam Litifani inter se agitarent. Eadem utrisque populis licentia fuit ducendi uxores promiscue consanguineas et alienas; eadem dandi per viros non accipiendi dotes consuetudo; eadem in exhibendis recipiendisque muneribus hilaritas, par hospitalitas, nec minus similis negligentia educandorum liberorum sine ullis deliciis sub eodem tugurio promiscue cum pecoribus. Lavacris, sudatoriis ceterisque rebus, quae ad munditiam curamque corporis pertinent, tam Litifanos a principio caruisse constat, quam nunc quoque carent Bosporani. Aedificandi materia tam his quam illis crassa et informis, habitudo aedificiorum maxime rotunda et in conum fastigata, extat scriplum, relicto desuper foramine accipiendo lumini et ad fumum emittendum sine ulla contignatione aut discreto receptaculo; ignis in medio tugurii, circa quem accubitus ac discubitus sine loci alicuius electione aut observantia, neque ullius rei domesticae ordo aut disciplina. Vestis praeterea fluitans; idemque viris ac feminis habitus. Sed et multa carne ac pullis a primordio vescebantur, et lac equinum praecipuam potionem habebant, quae omnia Bosporanam arguunt originem.

Accedit ad haec, quod ab initio nullum praecipuum numen habuere, sed Bosporanorum ritu, quidquid colere coepissent, pro deo ducebant; hinc est quod lucos, lapides, solitudines, lacus et diversa animalia coluisse comperimus, sed ante omnia serpentem, quem Gyvotem lingua sua dicunt, cuius religionem utique non temere ipsorum animos occupasse crediderim. Nam et Phoenices, antiquae theologiae peritissimi, cetera animalia crassae admodum ac paene terrestris substantiae, serpentem spiritalissimum maximeque igneae ac divinae naturae putaverunt, quod spiritu solo mira celeritate feratur, sine alarum pedumve adminiculo, tumque quod imbecillitatem ac senectutem exuat et perpetuo, velut ex se ipso renascens, nisi vis aliunde accesserit, vix a natura conficiatur. Persae quoque tanquam diis maximis immolabant serpentibus et Aegyptii simulacro mundi serpentem implicabant, significantes spiritum illum, quo mundum et cetera, quae in eo sunt, animari et moveri putaverunt. In Graecorum praeterea sacrificiis serpens in spiram revolutus adhibebatur. Et Pherecydes Scyrus de deo Ophione, quem serpentem dicere possimus, librum conscripsit. Ad extremum nec Romani a serpentum veneratione abstinuere, quippe Aesculapium in serpentis effigie p. 30 coluere. Itaque, etsi nunc promptum sit recensere, quomodo serpentum adoratio Litifanos attigerit, tamen ferendi sunt, si in eadem superstitione fuere, qua tot sapientissimas nationes conflictatas scimus. Sed, ut ad institutum revertar, de origine, deque ipsorum religione, cum tot probabilia argumenta et coniecturae in diversum rapiant, assensum cuique, quod verisimilius putaverit sentiendum, relinquimus.

Chapter 15

But, since the opinion is upheld by many signs which prove a Gaulish rather than a Roman origin, arguments are not lacking from those who say they set out from the Bosphorus. The ancient Lithuanians agitated among themselves to set out with all the means of pursuing the life they led in the Bosphorus. It was similarly permitted for each of these peoples to take wives in marriage promiscuously, both strangers and relatives. It was similarly the custom for those being given by men not to receive dowries, and similarly for there to be merrymaking in the giving and receiving of gifts—equally, in hospitality; nor was there lacking a similar negligence in bringing up children (without any delights) all mixed together beneath the roof with the domestic animals. Baths, saunas, and other things that pertain to the cleansing and care of the body, which the Lithuanians lacked from the beginning, the Bosphorans now also lack. Their building materials are as coarse and shapeless as one another's, and the character of their buildings is round and gathered together in a cone; a small stone protrudes, with an aperture left above to receive the light and to let out smoke, without any upper storey or separate receptacle.[2] The fire is in the middle of the hut, around which they lie down to sleep or recline to eat without any observance, or anyone choosing a place, and without any order or discipline in domestic matters. Besides, their clothes are flowing, and men and women are dressed the same. Much meat and chicken was eaten by them from the beginning, and they had horsemilk as their principal drink—all of which argues for a Bosphoran origin.

The fact that from the beginning they had no principal spirit, but whatever they began to worship they took for a god (according to the Bosphoran rite), agrees with this. That is, we find that they worshipped groves, stones, deserted places, lakes, and different animals—but before all others they worshipped snakes, which in their language they call Gyvatės (a religion I would not have believed they would dare to taint their souls with). For the Phoenicians, the most skilful in ancient theology, thought that snakes were the most spiritual, the fieriest, and the most divine in nature; and thought other animals to be of quite a coarse and earthly substance. This was because they were borne by spirit alone with marvellous speed, without any support of legs and feet—and then, it is made almost immortal by nature (unless force carries it off somewhere), since it sloughs off dotage and old age—as if reborn from itself. The Persians, too, made sacrifices to snakes, as if they were great gods, and the Egyptians connected a snake to an image of the world, signifying the spirit which they thought animated and moved the world and the other things within it. Besides, a snake coiled in a spiral was used in the sacrifices of the Greeks. And Pherecydes of Syros wrote a book about the god Ophion, who we can call a snake. Finally, the Romans did not refrain from the worship of snakes, and of course worshipped Aesculapius in the form of a snake. Therefore (although it should now be set forth), it ought to be told how the worship of snakes reached the Lithuanians, if they were in that same superstition which we know assailed so many of the wisest nations. But, so that we may return to our task, we leave the origin of the same religion, since so many likely arguments and conjectures may be carried off in different directions, to which one might think agreement ought to be similarly given.

---

2 "Separate receptacle" may here refer to the lack of a chimney in Lithuanian huts.

TRACTATUS DE DUABUS SARMATIIS ASIANA ET EUROPEANA ET DE CONTENTIS IN EIS

[Extracts]

[sig. e II[v] ... **Capitulum secundum de Lituania et Samogithia.**

Magnus ducatus Lithuaniae est regio latissima: in ea sunt plures duces Lithuaniae et Russiae: unus autem praeses et monarcha cui caeteri omnes subsunt magnus dux Lithuaniae vulgo nuncupatus. Aiunt autem vetustiores et antiquitatum relatores quod quidam Italici, propter [sig. [e Vr]] romanorum dissensiones deserentes Italiam ingressi sunt terras Lithuaniae: et nomen patriae italia: genti vero itali indiderunt: quae per pastores terra Litalia et gens litali / littera praeposita coepit nuncupari Ruteni autem et Poloni, eorum vicini, maiorem immutationem facientes: usque in hodiernam diem terram Lithuaniam gentes vero Lithuanos appellant. Hi primum condiderunt oppidum Vilno: elevationis poli quinquagintaseptem graduum: et ex nomine ducis Vilii quo cum illas regiones ingressi sunt, Vilno vocaverunt, fluminibus quoque circa ipsum fluentibus Vilia et Vilna ex eiusdem ducis nomine indiderunt nomina. Samagithiam autem de suo sermone sic nominarunt: quod lingua eorum terra inferior sonat. Aliqui autem ignari historiae: a lituo quod est cornu et tuba venatorum: eo quod regio illa plures venationes exerceat: Lithuaniam appellare voluerunt: quod ad effectum, non ad historiae originem spectat. Haec gens Lithuanorum annis superioribus adeo obscura contempta et vilis apud rutenos fuit: ut principes Kiouienses ab ea sola perizomata et subera ob egestatem et soli nativi sterilitatem in signum tantummodo subiectionis exigerent. Donec Vithenen dux Lithuanorum rebellionem primum contra rutenos inducens: et seipsum ducem inter populares constituens: astu principes russiae aggressus conflixit: sensimque adeo crevit viribus, ut iugo principibus russiae iniecto etiam in tributa eos redigeret sibi pendenda, quae per plures aetates rutenis ipse penderat. ...

Tandem a cruciferis et christianorum exercitibus saepenumero [sig. [e Vv]] Iagello pressus: deo miserante ad Polonos declinavit: fideque christiana cum fratribus suis quos octo in numero habuit: unda baptismatis ablutus et in regem Poloniae coronatus, Heduigim, filiam Ludovici Hungariae et Poloniae regis illustrissimam ac speciosissimam in consortem accepit: anno Christi millesimo tricentesimo octuagesimo sexto: die Jovis quartadecima mensis februarii: quae fuit sancti valentini.

TREATISE ON THE TWO ASIAN AND EUROPEAN SARMATIAS AND ON THOSE THINGS CONTAINED IN THEM (1517)

MACIEJ Z MIECHOWA[1]

Chapter two on Lithuania and Samogitia

The Grand Duchy of Lithuania is a very extensive realm. There are many dukes in it, of Lithuania and Rus'ia, but one foremost monarch, commonly called Grand Duke of Lithuania, to whom all the others are subject. But the oldest writers and relaters of antiquities say that certain Italians, on account of disagreements of the Romans, deserted Italy and entered the lands of Lithuania. And the Italians gave the name of their fatherland, Italy, to the people. But the land began to be called Litalia and the people Litali (by a letter "l" placed in front) by the Ruthenian and Polish shepherds, their neighbours, making a larger alteration. Even in the present day they called the land Lithuania, and the people Lithuanians.

These people first built the town of Vilnius, at a latitude of 57 degrees from the Pole; and they called it Vilnius from the name of Duke Vilius, with whom they entered these regions; and they gave the rivers flowing around it the names Viliya and Vilnia, from the same duke. But they name Samogitia thus in their speech because in their language it means a lowland. But others, ignorant of the history, have wanted to name Lithuania from a *lituo*, which is a horn and trumpet of hunters (because there are many hunts in that region). This regards the outcome, but not the origin, of the history.

In former years, this Lithuanian people was obscure, disregarded, and worthless among the Ruthenians, so that the princes of Kyiv exacted only bark and the coverings of trees from them, on account of their poverty and the sterility of the native soil, as a sign of subjugation, until Vytenis, Duke of Lithuania, led a first rebellion against the Ruthenians and established himself as duke among the people. He attacked and clashed with the princes of Rus' by cunning; and little by little his strength grew so great that they threw the yoke on the princes of Rus', and exacted from them in payment what they used to pay the Ruthenians for many years. ...

After a long time, when Jogaila had long been pressed by the crusaders and by many and numerous armies of Christians, God had mercy and bent down to the Poles; and with his brothers (of whom he had eight in number) he was baptized into the Christian faith with the water of baptism and crowned king of Poland. He received Jadwiga, daughter of Louis, king of Hungary and Poland, as a most illustrious and beautiful consort, in the year of Christ 1386, on Wednesday, February 14 (which was St. Valentine's Day).

---

1 This text is based on Maciej z Miechowa, *Tractatus de duabus Sarmatiis* (1518), sigs e IIJv–fv, f IIJv–(f vr).

Coepitque praefatus rex Vladislaus, secundum promissa, vigilare et instare ut gentem lithuanicam a tenebris erroris ac idolatria expurgaret: assumptis quoque secum Bodzanta archiepiscopo Gneznensi et pluribus viris ecclesiasticis atque religiosis. Item regina hedvigi: Semovito et Joanne Mazoviae: Conrado Olesnicensi ducibus: et complurimis baronibus: anno domini millesimo tricentesimo octuagesimo septimo in lithuaniam intravit et baptisma percipere lithuanos procuravit. Colebant autem ab origine lithuani numina: ignem: silvas aspides et serpentes: ignem qui per sacerdotem lingua eorum zincz nuncupatum subiectis lignis adolebatur. Silvas autem et lucos sacrosanctos et habitacula deorum putabant. Aspides vero atque serpentes in singulis domibus velut deos penates, nutriebantur et venerabantur. Rex itaque Vladislaus ignem sacrum putatum in civitate Vilnensi barbaris inspectantibus extingui: templum et aram in quibus fiebat hostiarum immolatio dirumpi: silvas vero succidi et confringi: serpentes quoque necari praecepit: barbaris flentibus deorum suorum falsorum exterminium. Contra regem autem nec mussitare audentibus: mirantibus quoque quod Poloni sacrorum violatores ignis silvarum et serpentium intacti illaesique a diis eorum secus quam ipsimet quotiens violabant fuerunt. Exterminatis itaque idolis gens lithuanorum per aliquot dies de articulis fidei et oratione dominica per sacerdotes Polonos: magis tamen per regem Vladislaum qui linguam gentis noverat edocebatur et sacra baptismatis unda renascebatur. Largiente pio rege Vladislao singulis ex popularium numero post susceptum baptisma: ex panno de Polonia adducto novas vestes qua provida liberalitate effecit: ut natio illa rudis et pannosa: lineis in eam diem contenta: fama huiusmodi liberalitatis vulgata: pro consequendis laneis catervatim ad suscipiendum baptisma ex omni regione accurrebat: et quoniam labor erat immensus unumquemque credentium baptisare singillatim mandante rege multitudo sequestrabatur in turmas et cuneos: et universis de qualibet turmarum benedicta aqua sufficienter conspersis: cuilibet turmae et universis, qui in ea constiterant nomen usitatum petrus secundae paulus: terciae ioannes: etc. Feminis per turmas divisis. Katherina Margaretha. etc. iuxta numerum turmarum imponebatur. [sig. fi] Militaribus tamen spiritualis impendebatur baptismus. Fundavit insuper rex Vladislaus in Vilna ecclesiam cathedralem sub titulo sancti Stanislai, patroni Polonorum: principalemque aram in loco ubi ignis qui falso perpetuus credebatur constituit: ut error gentilis fieret cunctis patentior. Constituit etiam in eadem ecclesia Vilnensi episcopum virum spectatae virtutis Andream Vazilo: natione Polonum: genere nobilem: de domo accipitrum: professione fratrem ordinis minorum: olim Elizabet, reginae hungariae confessorem et praedicatorem insignem episcopum Ceretensem.

And the aforesaid King Władysław, according to his promise, began to watch and see to it that the Lithuanian people was purged of the shadows of error and idolatry; and he therefore took with him Bodzanta, archbishop of Gniezno, and many ecclesiastical and religious men. And he entered Lithuania in the year of Our Lord 1387 with the same Queen Jadwiga, Dukes Siemowit and John of Masovia and Konrad of Oleśnica, and a great many lords, and arranged for the Lithuanians to gain baptism.

But from their origin, the Lithuanians worshipped spirits: fire, forests, snakes, and serpents. They worshipped a fire which was kept alive by timber piled on by a priest (called *žinis* ["knowledge"] in their language). But they thought that forests were sacrosanct, and the habitations of the gods. Snakes and serpents were nourished and worshipped in individual houses like household gods. Therefore King Władysław ordered the fire (thought to be sacred) in the city of Vilnius to be extinguished, with the barbarians looking on; he ordered the temple and altar on which the sacrifice of victims took place to be destroyed, the forests to be cut down and smashed, and the snakes killed.

The barbarians wept at the extermination of their false gods, but they did not dare mutter against the king. They also marvelled that the Polish violators of the sacred fires, forests, and snakes were untouched and unhurt by their gods, when they themselves had been whenever they violated them. Therefore, with the idols destroyed, the Lithuanian people were taught for several days about the articles of faith and the Lord's Prayer by Polish priests—but more by King Władysław, who knew the language of the people—and they were reborn by the holy water of baptism. King Władysław, showing generosity to each of the number of the people after they received baptism, caused them to be liberally provided with new tunics from clothes brought from Poland, so that the primitive and ragged nation (content in those days with linen) ran from every region in large numbers to receive baptism after the rumour of liberality of this kind spread abroad—on account of the woollen clothes.

And since it was an immense labour to individually baptize every one of the believers, by the king's order the multitude was divided into squadrons and battalions, and all in every squadron sufficiently sprinkled. Those who were standing in them were established with a common Christian name: Peter; the second, Paul; the third, John, etc. The women, divided by squadrons, were assigned Catharine, Margaret, etc., according to the number of the squadrons. However, spiritual baptism for the soldiers was imminent.

Furthermore, Władysław founded in Vilnius a cathedral church under the title of St. Stanislaus, the patron of the Poles, and established the principal altar in the place where the fire falsely believed to be perpetual had been, so that the error of the pagans might be more completely clear. And he also established as the first bishop in the same church of Vilnius a man of attested virtue, Andrzej Wasilko. He was of the Polish nation, of noble birth, of the house of Jastrzębiec, and by profession a brother of the Order of Friars Minor. He was once confessor to Queen Elizabeth of Hungary, a notable preacher, and bishop of Siret.

Eodem quoque Vladislao rege instante Samagithia fidem Christi et baptisma suscepit. Ad cognoscendum autem naturam provinciae et gentis illius animadverte quod regio Samagithia est septemtrionalis et gelida. Lithuaniae livoniae et Prussiae contermina: silvis: collibus et fluminibus circumsepta. In hos districtus distincta scilicet Iragola: Miedniki: Chrosse: Rosena: Viduki: Vielunia: Kelthini: Czethra: gentes regionis procerae et altae staturae agrestes et incultae pauco et castigato victu viventes: sitim aqua sedare solitae raro cerevisia aut medone. Auri argenti aeris ferri vini in illa tempestate expertes et ignarae: apud quos licitum erat uni viro plures habere uxores: et patre mortuo novercam fratreque glotem in uxorem accipere. Nullus illic stubarum nullus aedificiorum nobilium: sed tantummodo tugurii unius usus ventrem distensum et porrectum: extrema vero habens coartata: ex ligno et culmo structura largius ab imo sensim operis incremento aedificium in artius cogitur: in carinae seu galeae maxime similitudinem elaborata in cacumine fenestra una superne lumen reddens: subter quam focus et cibos parabiles coquens et frigus quo regio pro maiori anni parte constricta est repellens: in ea domo se: uxores: pignora: servos: ancillas: pecus: armentum: frumentum et omnem supellectilem condunt gens ad divinationes et auguria proclivis. Praecipuum numen Samagitticum erat ignis: quem sacro sanctum et perpetuum putabant: qui in montis altissimi iugo super fluvium Neviasza sito assidua lignorum appositione a sacrorum sacerdote alebatur. Accedens itaque Vladislaus rex turrim in qua consistebat incendit et ignem disiecit et extinxit. Succidit deinde per milites suos Polonicos silvas: quas non secus quam sanctas et deorum habitacula Samagittae iuxta illud poeticum. "Habitarunt dii quoque silvas": venerabantur: in eam caliginem mentis prolapsi: quod et silvae praefatae et aves: feraeque in illis consistentes sanctae forent: et quicquid in illas ingrederetur ut sanctum deberet censeri: violanti quoque nemus: feras vel alites: manus aut pedes demonum arte curvabantur. Maxima itaque barbaros tenebat admiratio: quod Polonorum milites nemus ritu eorum sanctum [sig. fv] excidentes nulla laesio qualem ipsi in se frequentius experti erant sequeretur. Habebant praeterea in silvis praefatis focos: in familias et domos distinctos: in quibus omnibus charorum et familiarium cadavera cum equis sellis et vestimentis potioribus incendebant: locabant etiam ad focos huiusmodi ex subere facta sedilia: in quibus escas ex pasta in casei modum praeparatas deponebant:

Also, at the urging of the same King Władysław, Samogitia received the faith of Christ and baptism. But in order to understand the nature of this province and people, consider that the Samogitian region is northerly and frozen. It borders Lithuania, Livonia, and Prussia, and is surrounded by forests, hills, and rivers. In these there are distinct districts, that is to say Ariogala, Raseiniai, Medininkai, Kražiai, Viduklė, Veliuona, Kaltinėnai, and Šėta. The peoples of the region are noble and tall in stature, rustic, and unsophisticated, living on a sparing and severe diet. They are accustomed to quench their thirst with water, and rarely with beer or mead. In their season, they are ignorant and lacking in experience of gold, silver, bronze, iron, or wine.

It was permitted among them for one man to have many wives, and, on the death of his father, to take his stepmother or his brother's wife as a wife. There are no rooms or noble buildings among them, but just a single hut is customary; it has a distended and stretched out middle, having a narrow top. The structure of the building is of wood and thatch, getting larger little by little from the ground, the work is then gathered together into a point. They are decorated very much like a ship or helmet; at the top there is one window, admitting the light from above. Beneath is the hearth and materials for preparing food, and keeping off the cold by which that region is held for the larger part of the year. In this house they keep themselves, their wives, their hostages, their slaves, their slave-girls, their sheep, their cattle, and all their apparatus. And they are unacquainted with other buildings, upper storeys, palaces, storehouses, rooms, or stables, but enclose themselves and their sheep, cattle, and other domestic animals in the same homes. The people are prone to divinations and auguries.

The foremost god of the Samogitians was fire, which they thought sacrosanct and perpetual, which was situated on the high ridge of a hill near the River Nevėžis, and was kept going by the constant laying on of timbers by a priest of the rites. Władysław, therefore, burning the tower in which it stood, dismantled and extinguished the fire. Then, by his Polish soldiers, he cut down the forests which the Samogitians worshipped as nothing less than holy, and as the habitations of their gods—following that poet, "The gods also have dwelt in the woods."

They fell into that darkness of mind because they thought the aforesaid forests and the birds and wild animals living in them were holy, and that whoever made an entry into them ought to consider them sacred. No-one among the Samogitians dared hew wood in the aforesaid forests or hunt birds or wild animals. The hands or feet of those who violated the groves were made to curve over by art of the demons. Therefore, by long habit, the birds and wild animals living in the aforesaid forests, resembling domestic animals, were neither terrified at nor avoided human sight. Very great wonder seized the barbarians that no injury befell the Polish soldiers cutting down the groves—which they had frequently tested—that were sacred to their rite.

Furthermore, they had fires in the aforesaid forests, for different families and households, on which they burnt the bodies of their family and loved ones with horses, chairs, and useful clothing. They even put at the fire little chairs of a kind, made of bark, on which they placed food prepared in the manner of cheese pastry cakes.

medonemque focis infundebant ea crudelitate[1] illusi: quod mortuorum suorum animae quorum illic combusta fuerant corpora nocte venirent escaque se exsatiarent. Insuper prima octobris die: maxima per samagittas in silvis praefatis celebritas agebatur et ex omni regione universus utriusque sexus conveniens illuc populus: cibos et potus quilibet iuxta suae conditionis qualificationem deferebat: quibus aliquot diebus epulati diis suis falsis praecipue deo lingua eorum appellato Perkuno: id est tonitru: ad focos quisque suos offerebat libamina. Rex itaque vladislaus primum eos pater noster: deinde simbolum docuit: quoniam nullus sacerdotum linguam samagitticam noverat: et undis baptismatis ablui iussit. Unus autem ex maioribus samagittarum pro omnibus respondit. "Ex quo," inquit, "serenissime rex, dii nostri veluti inertes et languidi a deo Polonorum deleti sunt: deos nostros et sacra eorum deserimus et deo tuo atque Polonorum fortiori adheremus." Sicque baptisati sunt. ...

Capitulum tertium de amplitudine et contentis Magni ducatus Lithuaniae.

... [sig. f [I]v] Habuit hoc linguagium quadripartitum tempore idolatriae pontificem maximum unum: quem Crive appellabant: morantem in civitate Romovae a roma dicta: quoniam hoc linguagium de italia iactat sese advenisse: et habent nonnulla vocabula italica in suo sermone. De isto Crive et civitate Romovae in legenda sancti Adelberti pontificis et martiris legitur. Et scias quod in Prussia iam pauci proferunt Prutenicum: subintravit siquidem lingua polonorum et almanorum: sic et in Lothua pauci villani profitentur hanc linguam [sig. [f Vr]] quia subintravit Almanicum. In Samagithia autem quae est longitudinis quinquaginta miliariorum et in lithuania quae in longum triginta miliaria continet: in villis lithuanicum loquuntur: et in magna parte Polonicum profitentur: nam et sermone Polonico sacerdotes eis praedicant in ecclesiis: insuper scito quod hoc linguagium quadripartitum totum est de obedientia et fide Romanae ecclesiae: in aliis autem provinciis circumiacentibus ut in novigrod: in pleskovia: in polocko: in Smolensko et in meridiem usque post Kiow Ruteni sunt omnes et rutenicum seu Slavonicum loquuntur ritumque graecorum observant: et obedientiam Constantinopolitano patriarchae praestant. Amplius sunt in ducatu Lithuaniae thartari circum Vilnam: et habent proprias villas: colunt agros more nostro laborant et vehunt merces: ad mandatumque Magni ducis lithuaniae omnes ad bellum assurgunt: loquuntur thartaricum et colunt Machometem quia saracenorum sectam profitentur. Insuper sunt Hebraei in lithuania praesertim in civitate Troki: hi laborant et mercantur thelonea et officia publica tenent de usurisque non vivunt.

I Probably an error for *credulitate*.

And they also poured mead on the fires—deceived, in their cruelty,[2] that the souls of their dead whose bodies were burnt there would come at night and satisfy themselves with the food and drink the mead poured on the fire (long since absorbed by the ashes). Since it was not souls, but ravens, crows, and other forest birds and animals who, by continual custom, took away the food left behind.

Furthermore, on the first day of October there was a great celebration by the Samogitians in the aforesaid forests, and this people gathered together from every region (everyone of both sexes), and they brought food and drink, according to the ability of their condition. Feasting for several days, they offered libations to their false gods at their fires—especially to the god called in their language Perkūnas (that is, thunder). Therefore King Władysław taught them first the Our Father, then the Creed, since no priest knew the Samogitian language; and he ordered them to be washed with the water of baptism. But one of the elders of Samogitia replied for all: "On account of the fact that our gods, whose cults and rites we received from our ancestors, were destroyed by you and your soldiers, most serene king, and were defeated by the God of the Poles as if they were inert and powerless, we desert our gods and their rites, and adhere to your God and that of the Poles as stronger." And thus they were baptized. ...

Chapter three on the size and contents of the Grand Duchy of Lithuania

... This quadripartite language[3] had a single high priest in the time of idolatry, who was called Krivė, living in the town of Romuva, so called after Rome. Since this language boasts that it arrived from Italy, it has many Italian words in its speech. This Krivė and the town of Romuva may be read about in the legend of St. Adalbert, bishop and martyr. And know that in Prussia few now speak Prussian; the Polish and German languages have entered there, just as in Latvia few villagers speak that language because German has entered there. But it is found in Samogitia, which is forty miles in breadth and in Lithuania, which is thirty miles in breadth. In the villages they speak Lithuanian, and to a great extent Polish is spoken, for their priests preach to them in Polish in the churches.

Furthermore, know that this quadripartite language is all of the obedience of the Roman church. But in the other provinces lying around (as in Novhorod, in Pskov, in Polotsk, in Smolensk, and in the south up to Kyiv) they are all Ruthenians and speak the Ruthenian or Slavonic language and observe the rite of the Greeks, and they owe obedience to the Patriarch of Constantinople. There are many Tatars in the Grand Duchy of Lithuania around Vilnius; they have their own villages. They cultivate the fields, work in our manner, and transport goods; all of them rise for war at the command of the Grand Duke of Lithuania. They speak Tatar and worship Mohammed, since they profess the sect of the Saracens. Furthermore, there are Jews in Lithuania, especially in the town of Trakai. These work and trade in goods; they hold the toll-booths and public offices and do not live from usury.

---

2 Długosz has *credulitate* (credulity) in the same passage.

3 Miechowa is here referring to his distinctive theory of the Baltic languages as a single "quadripartite" language, consisting of Yotvingian, Lithuanian/Samogitian, Prussian, and Latvian. For a full discussion of this theory see Dini, *Prelude to Baltic Linguistics*, 83–94.

DE BORUSSIAE ANTIQUITATIBUS LIBRI DUO

[Extracts]

[p. 12] Terram hanc Borussi undiquaque foecundam longe lateque incolentes, ipsam tamen minime excoluere, vel ob ignorationem rei rusticae, vel ne bonitate soli deprehensa, et ipsi finitimorum metui obnoxii fierent, indeque eliminarentur: vel quod victum e terrae nascentibus nondum novere, carnibus namque ferinis et quidem crudis pro cibo, lacteque pro potu vescebantur, quandoque etiam sanguine equino mixto, et eo usque ad ebrietatem. Domos non figebant, sed specubus et arborum subere, unde etiam Subaria dicta comperitur, ab imbribus et algoribus sese ac infantes protexere. Nulla eis sacra aliquamdiu fuere, tandem in eam deducti insaniam, ut serpentes, ferasque et arbores religiose colerent, ceu de his in subsequentibus dicemus. Non leges, non magistratus novere, tantum cuique licet, quantum audebat: nihil a feris vita illorum distabat. Erga tamen naufragos, aut maris tempestate iactatos, humaniores, et illius ipsis undiquaque auxilio fuere, in reliquis mira foeditas ac foeda paupertas. Nam eis, nec arma, nec ferrum [p. 13] fuerat, si quando ad praelia inter se concurrerent, sudibus praeustis et perticis utebantur. ...

[p. 19] Habuere enimvero hii populi, ut de moribus eorum aliquid transeunter dicam, regulos suos quorum legibus obtemperabant, agrosque coluere, et commercia novere. Vestium cultus apud eos fuit, ut mares lanea, foeminae linea tunica uterentur, circuloque ex aere vel orichalco colla circumdabant; Auribus etiam crotalia suspenderunt, rem frivolam, quod tamen neque hodie desitum. Domos in villarum modum extructas inhabitavere, vicosque, ac sine muro et vallo omnia, quod forte ab externis, ipsos commercii gratia adeuntibus didicere, alioquin alienum a Sarmatis. Sed ut ad Borussios repedamus, societatem cum Sudinis eos iniisse diximus ob Germanorum finitimorum metum. Nec a Sudinis aspernati sunt. Verum eorum potentia adiuti, et contra quosvis conterminos populos tutiores facti. Aliquandiu in sua foedita degerunt, de qua post hac. ...

TWO BOOKS ON THE ANTIQUITIES OF THE PRUSSIANS (1518)

JOHANNES STÜLER (ERASMUS STELLA)[1]

The Prussians, dwelling in the whole length and breadth of this land, do not however cultivate it; either from ignorance of agricultural matters; or, not prevented by the goodness of the soil, they become afraid of their neighbours in their guilt, and they are thus compelled to come outside. Because they do not yet know a diet generated from the earth, they feed on the flesh of wild animals and anything raw for food, and milk for drink, which they even mix with horse blood (and that to the point of drunkenness). They do not fix their houses in one place, but have them in caves or from the bark of trees, whence they are called "bark houses'; and thus they protect themselves and their children from showers and cold. For a considerable while, nothing was sacred to them; but at last they were so far seduced into insanity that they devoutly worshipped snakes, wild animals, and trees (of which we shall speak more in what follows). They know neither laws nor magistrates; and as much as is permitted to each one, that much he dares to do. Their life differs in no way from that of wild beasts. Shipwrecked people, or those tossed up out of the sea from a storm, are more civilized; and even though there is assistance for them all around, there is remarkable filthiness and filthy poverty among the rest. For them there were neither arms nor iron, and if ever they came together in conflict, they used charred stakes and poles. ...

This people, as I said in passing concerning their customs, used to have princelings whose laws they obeyed; and they used to cultivate fields and know commerce. The fashion of clothing among them used to be wool for men, while women wore linen tunics, and a collar of bronze or brass encircled their necks; and from their ears they suspended earrings—a frivolous thing, which is not even abandoned today. They inhabit houses constructed in the manner of halls,[2] and villages are alien to the Sarmatians; everything is both without any wall or protective ditch—except what may have been taught by foreigners, thanks to their coming there on account of trade. But to return to the Prussians; we have said that they have entered into fellowship with the Sudovians on account of their fear of the neighbouring Germans. And they are not despised by the Sudovians. Indeed, they assist them with power, and they are thereby made more secure against any neighbouring peoples (on how long they have endured in this alliance, more hereafter). ...

---

1 This text is based on Johannes Stüler (Erasmus Stella), *De Borussiae antiquitatibus* (1518), 12–13, 19, 27–29.

2 It seems likely that *villarum* has here the sense of large communal hall-like dwellings, rather than large country houses.

[p. 27] Utque pueri non adeo incerto patre nascerentur, coitum promiscuum prohibuit, et sub conubii specie instituit, ut quotquot et quacumque paterfamilias puellam suscipiendae prolis gratia iniret, sive ex servitiis peculiaribus, vel alienis foret, sive ex liberis, eam secum suo detineret tugurio, aleretque: Alieni tamen iuris puellam, non nisi precio, quasi aere emptam, a quocumque deduci pro prole procreanda inhibuit: Adulteria tamen non usque adeo prohibuit, sed abigendos moechos potestate castigavit. Quo autem populum hunc ferocem ad vitam produceret mansuetiorem, comessationes frequentes et publicas instituit, quibus feros hominum animos demulctos iri credidit, nec in eo hallucinatus est. Nam brevi ad eam devenere mollitiem, ut eos quocunque vellet perduceret, hinc hospitalitatem maxime colendam esse statuit, quia ipsa amicitiae firmissime glutinarentur. Potum ex aqua et melle concinnare docuit, qui latine Mulsum dici potest, quo in commessationibus et publicis et privatis uti concessit, cuius dulcore mirum in modum dum barbari delectati, facile ad enervationem pervenire. Ad religionem autem se vertens sacerdotes a Sudinis sociis populis accersivit, qui insana superstitione contaminati eos immunda quoque animalia, ut serpentes colubres, proinde ac deorum famulos [p. 28] nuntiosque religiose colere docuerunt, quos intra domos nutriebant, eisque ut diis penatibus litabant. Deos in sylvis ac lucis habitare dixerunt, illis victimis ibidem ut placarentur immolandum esse. Ab his solem pluviasque expetendas fore. Sacra eorum aditu advenarum pollui, nec aliter quam humana victima expiari constanter crediderunt. Feras omnes Alcem praecipue, has sylvas incolentes, ut deorum servos venerandos esse monuerunt, ideoque ab eis abstinendum. Solem et lunam deos omnium primos crediderunt. Tonitrua fulgetrasque ex consensu gentium adorabant, tempestates advertendas citandasque precationibus dixerunt.

In order that children should not be born with uncertainty about their paternity, [Widewuto[3]] forbade promiscuous intercourse, and instituted a kind of matrimony. Whenever and as often as the head of a family undertakes to receive a young woman on account of her descent, he shall maintain her; whether from exceptional services, or from outsiders (whether or not, on account of children, he detains her with him in a hut). However, he forbade a woman to be taken in marriage for the procreation of descendants otherwise than by law; and not without a price: she is bought as if with money. He did not, however, go so far as to prohibit adultery, but he castigated seducing adulterers with his power. So that he might lead this fierce people to a life less wild, he instituted frequent and public feasts, by which he believed the souls of those wild men might be soothed. And in this he was not deceived; for they become briefly gentle enough to receive whoever they want; and it is established among them that this hospitality is greatly to be cultivated, so that by this they are most firmly joined in friendship. He taught them to make drink from water and honey, which may be called *mulsum* in Latin, which he allowed them to use in their public and private feasts. The barbarians, delighted in a remarkable way by its sweetness, quickly become weak.

But turning himself to religion, he summoned priests from the Sudovians—an allied people who, contaminated by insane superstition, taught them thenceforth to worship unclean things and also animals such as snakes and serpents as the servants and messengers of the gods. They used to feed them in their homes, and made offerings to them and the household gods. They said that the gods live in woods and groves, and that victims had to be offered to them so that they might be placated. The sun and rains had to be sought from them. I shall not pollute what follows by adding their rites; but they believed steadfastly that the gods could not be expiated otherwise than with a human victim. They taught that all wild beasts dwelling in these forests should be venerated as servants of the gods, and especially the elk, and therefore they had to abstain from them. They believed that the sun and moon were the first gods of all. They used to worship thunder and lightnings (by the common consent of pagans), and uttered prayers to avert or raise up storms.

---

3 Stüler is elaborating the myth of Widewuto, a legendary sixth-century ruler of the Old Prussians (see Beresnevičius, "Prūsijos amfiktionijos steigtis"). Stüler describes Widewuto as *Biotterus*, an attempted Latinization of Old Prussian *buttataws* ("house father"), the title given to a Prussian leader (Amato, "Morfologia dei composti nominali," 198).

Hirco in sacrificiis usi sunt, ob foecundam animalis istius naturam. Nam ad coniunctionem sexuum maxime defertur, sine qua generatio est nulla in animantibus. Praecellentes arbores, ut robora, quercus, deos inhabitare dixerunt, ex quibus sciscitantibus responsa reddi audiebantur, ob id nec huiuscemodi arbores caedebant, sed religiose ut numinum domos colebant. In eo numero et Sambucum et plerasque alias habuere. Statuit et dies natalitios et funera pari modo celebranda, mutuis scilicet commessationibus et compotationibus, tum lusu et cantu, absque moerore cum summa hilaritate et gaudio, utque alterius vitae spem prae se ferrent, illo saltem ostenderunt, quod exutos spiritu, armatos, vestitosque ac magna supellectilis parte circumposita humarunt. Quo more usque nunc [p. 29] sepeliuntur: Addito etiam potu melleo, aut ex frumentis facto in testaceis vasis. In funebri epulo partem ob sonii potusque vita defuncti manibus libarunt, hodieque libant. His et caeteris populo illo instituto religioneque firmata, Viduutus hanc oram prudenter et quietissime rexit, nullis excursionibus in vicinos populos permissis, nec aliqua rursus ab eis perpessus incommoda.

They are accustomed to make use of a he-goat in their sacrifices, on account of the fertile nature of this animal. For it is often brought to the joining of the sexes, without which there is no generation in those giving life. They said that the gods lived in the most prominent trees, as if in the trunk of an oak, from which answers to questions were heard returned. On account of this they did not cut down trees for any cause whatsoever, but devoutly worshipped them as the dwellings of spirits. Among their number is the elder, and they have many others.

Their funerals and birthdays must be celebrated in like manner, that is to say with mutual feasting and drinking, then games and songs, without mourning and with the greatest merriment and joy. And they show that they carry with them another hope of life—so much so that when someone's spirit has gone out, they bury them with arms and clothes and a great part of their household goods placed around them. Even now they are still buried in this fashion, when a drink made from honey or fruit is added in clay vessels. During the funeral feast they pour out part of the drink in libation for the deceased's shades, on account of their speech about their life, and they make this libation today. Having confirmed the people in their religion by the institution of this and other rites, Widewuto wisely and peacefully ruled this shore, permitting no incursions into the lands of neighbouring peoples; and neither was such an inconvenience endured by them in return.

CATECHISMUSA PRASTY SZADEI

[Pastoral Preface]

[sig. A IIr] Pastoribus et ministris ecclesiarum in Lituania gratiam et pacem.

Quidem nimis arctis limitibus scripturae sacrae possessionem includunt, dum eam sola sacerdotum famillia terminant, plebe interim exterminate. Pollui sacra, prophanari mysteria clamitant, et quasi magnam publicis domesticisque seditionibus fenestram aperiri, si populum admittendum censeas. His igitur cautio est, nequis in Apostolorum, Prophetarumque sacrarium introducatur, lingua vernacula loquens. Sed haec iniuria est intolerabilis. A communibus sacris arceri populum, quibus tamen abesse sine animae vitaeque aeternae detrimento, possit nemo, quid quaeso potest iniquius: Quae nostra sacra communiora, quae magis necessaria populo, quam doctrina coelestis: Haec et enim sola ceu leophoros[1] certam aeternae salutis viam omnibus aeque praescribit atque demonstrat. Quia enim tam plebs, quam proceres, coelesti opus habent doctrina, quae quid Deus a nobis postulet, quid nos possimus praestare, doceat, ostendatque quae sint causae consequendae salutis sempiternae, etc. Ergo cumbae doctrina excludat neminem, haud recte intra [sig. A IIv] privata septa concluditur. Commune bonum, publicumque est aeterne salutis possessio. Hoc quis poterit negare? Deus noster vult omnes salvos fieri. Cur non eodem pacto scriptura, quae est de ista, quam dixi, possessione privilegium, vel syngrapha, publicum bonum et commune aestimaretur? Quamobrem populum admittite O Proceres, et ad ea quidem sacra, quae ipsius sunt propria, vel certe vobiscum communia. Non loquor de abstrusioribus controversiis religionum, de quibus promiscua multitudo ut nec iudicium praestare, ita tamen Catechesim perdiscere, eo debet, et potest. Opus est noster pro se, conscientiaque sua, ut fidei suae confessionem edere, ut in periculis, in afflictionibus, in mortis agone recte, vereque se consolari possit, atque erigere fiducia Christi salvatoris.

---

[1] Misprinted *leopboros* in the text.

SIMPLE WORDS OF CATECHISM (1547)
[PASTORAL PREFACE]

MARTYNAS MAŽVYDAS[1]

Grace and peace to the ministers of the churches in Lithuania!

The sacred Scriptures certainly include possession by the furthest northern lands. While the family of priests alone limited them, the people were in the meantime banished from them. They cry again and again that the rites will be polluted, that the mysteries will be profaned, and that a great window would be opened for public and domestic sedition if they allowed the people to be admitted [to the Scriptures]. For these men, it is a stipulation that no-one may be introduced into the holy place of the apostles and prophets speaking the vernacular tongue. But this harm is unbearable. No-one can keep the people away from Holy Communion, from which no-one can be absent without detriment to their soul and their eternal life; what, I ask, could be more unjust? What is more of a participation in the sacred for us, what is more necessary for the people, than heavenly doctrine? For this alone prescribes and shows equally to all the sure high road and way of eternal salvation.

Since God demands from us that the people, as much as the nobility, has a need for heavenly doctrine (which we are able to fulfill), he teaches and shows us what should be the consequent causes of eternal salvation, etc. Therefore the barque of doctrine excludes no-one, and is not rightly shut off by a private fence within. The common and public good is the possession of eternal life. Who can deny this? Our God wants all to be saved. Why is Scripture not considered, by this same agreement (as I have said), to be a privilege by possession or by contract, and a common and public good? Wherefore, o nobles, admit the people! And admit them to those rites which are proper for them, and certainly in common with you. I do not speak of the more abstruse controversies of religion; in order that these are not presented for judgment to the promiscuous multitude, the Catechism can and must be taught. This is our work for them, and for their conscience: to publish a confession of their faith, so that they may be rightly and truly consoled in dangers, afflictions, and in the agony of death, and to establish the faith of Christ the Saviour.

1 This text is based on Martinas Mažvydas, *Catechismusa prasty szadei* (1547), sigs A ɪJr–A ɪɪɪJr.

Itaque in primitiva ecclesia, nemo admittebatur ad communionem caenae dominicae, nemo ad suscipiendum infantem e Baptismo, nemo copulabatur matrimonio, qui non probe ex catechesi confessionem fidei potuisset exhibere. Ac officii erat vestri Pastores, hanc puerilem (quam catechesim dixerunt veteres) doctrinam, rudiori populo proponere: hanc reiterare atque inculcare subinde, ut saltem his religionis Christianae seminariis imperitorum pectora implerentur. Vobis noster grex iste pascendus, vobis curandus atque tuendus ab ipso principe Pastore Christo [sig. A II]r] commissus est: vos illi accepti expensique, et fidei, diligentiaeque vestrae reddens rationem: imo animas illorum de manibus postulabit vestris. Perpendite, quaeso quam res horrenda sit ignoratio Dei, cuiusmodi animarum pestis idolatria, quantus furor Diaboli grassantis atque excitantis subinde idolomanias novas et opiniones pravas. Tum, quod non sine magno dolore commemoro, quam prae caeteris nationibus nostra gens ignara, rudisque et expers omnis pietatis, ac religionis Christianae? quam paucos reperias de plebe, qui non dicam catecheseos integram doctrinam probe teneant, sed qui vel primam Dominicae praecationis syllabam queant recitare. Imo quod auditu horribilius est, multi etiamnum manifestam idolatriam et exercent et profitentur palam: alii arbores, alii flumina, alii serpentes, alii aliud colunt, honorem exhibentes divinum. Sunt qui Percuno vota faciant, quibusdam ob rem frumentariam, Laucosargus, et propter pecuariam Semepates colitur. Qui ad malas artes adiiciunt animum, Eithuaros et Caucos Deos profitentur suos. Cuiusmodi autem adversus haec mala, ira Dei exardescat, pauci considerant: cum tamen Divus Paulus pari crimine reos pronuntiet tam hos, qui dum non obstant, assentiantur, quam etiam illos, quos manifesta delicta redarguant.

Quamobrem in primis vos moneo, hortorque Pastores, [sig. A II]v] aliquando tamen ut sitis officii, functionisque vestrae memores: ac ut cogitetis, tot animarum causam curamque vos suscepisse: Vobisque pro singulis magnam in extremo iudicio dicendi coronam restare: nullam istis futuram esse translationem culpae, nullum inscitiae praetextum. Vobis populus fecit ocium,[1] ut ecclesiae procurarens negotium, quod qua fide, quaque diligentia gesseritis, in coelesti senatu vos referre oportebit. Id autem ut bona conscientia facere, et intrepide possitis, huc animum intendite vestrum, huc omnis cura propendat, ne catecheseos doctrina ignota sit populo.

---

[1] Sic. for *otium*.

Therefore, in the primitive church, no-one was admitted to the communion of the Lord's Supper, no-one's child was received for baptism, no-one was joined in matrimony, who was not properly able to expound the confession of faith from the catechism. And it was your office, Pastors, to propound this childlike doctrine (as the ancients called the catechism) to a very unsophisticated people, and to constantly reiterate and inculcate it, so that their breasts might be filled with the Christian religion like seminaries of experts. You must feed this flock; you must care for and guard it as your commission from Christ himself, the foremost pastor. You will give account to him of what you have received and expended, and of your faith and diligence; indeed, he will demand their souls from you. Weigh carefully what an abominable thing is ignorance of God; how idolatry is a plague of souls; how much the fury of the devil grows and stirs up new manias for idols and wicked opinions.

Then, as I cannot recollect without great pain, before other nations our people is ignorant, unsophisticated, and lacking in all piety and the Christian religion. How little you will find from this people; I will not say they hold their entire catechized doctrine rightly, but they are able to recite the first words of the Lord's Prayer. Indeed, it is horrible to hear that many even now both practise and openly profess manifest idolatry. Some worship trees, some rivers, some snakes, and others other things, offering them divine honour. There are those who make vows to Perkūnas, and Laukasargis is worshipped by some for matters pertaining to grain; and Žemėpatis on account of flocks. Those who join their souls to evil arts profess the Aitvarai and Kaukai to be their gods. But few consider that God's anger burns against this kind of evil; yet St. Paul declares those who do not stand against [idolatry] to be guilty of an equal crime with those who assent to it; and their manifest failings prove it to be true.

Wherefore, first of all, I admonish and exhort you, Pastors, forasmuch as you are mindful of your office and duties, that you should think upon how many causes and cures of souls you have received; and you will be left a great crown for each one in the pronouncement of the final judgment. For these things there will be no passing on of guilt, and no pretext for ignorance. The people has made leisure for you, as if administering business for the church; since by the faith and the diligence you bear you ought to recollect this in the heavenly assembly. But if you have done this as if in good conscience, and as fearlessly as you can, exert your soul to this end, and expend every care, lest the doctrine of the catechism should be unknown to the people.

Principio discant homines ex decalogo, quid Deus a nobis exigat, et econtra quid nos valeamus, hoc est discamus de nostris viribus desperare, atque nullum mortalium esse, qui possit obedientiam, quam lex requirit, praestare integram. Quemadmodum testatur Psalmus, Non iustificatur in conspectu tuo omnis vivens. Item illud, Maledictus, qui non manserit in omnibus, quae scripta sunt in lege, ut faciat ea. Deinde cum hoc pacto constet, legi divinae non satisfacientes damnari, necessario consequetur, omnes aut aeternae mortis reos fore, aut ipsis quaerendum esse auxilium, quod doctrina Evangelii promittit. Quippe ad aeterni Patris misericordiam confugiendum esse, fiducia solius Christi salvatoris nostri. Hic etenim omnes, quicunque in ipsum confidunt, redimit a maledicto [sig. A IIIJr] legis, ab ira Dei, a condemnatione aeternae mortis, idque gratis, absque ulla vel antecedentium, vel consequentium operum conditione, ac dignitate. Postremo hoc quoque docendum est, Deum ab his, qui se grautito[2] solius Christi beneficio redemptos confidunt, postulare fidei atque poenitentiae fructum. Non id tamen ideo, quia opera aliquid conferant ad iustificationem nostri: sed quia eucharistica sint, non quae vitae aeternae salutem (haec nobis solius Christi merito contingit gratis) sed quae mereantur mitigationem temporalium poenarum, et praemia quaedam alia, tam hic, quam in vita futura. Haec in summa docet catechesis, Cuius iam vobis reverendi Pastores ac ludi magistri rude exemplum, et breve, et quidem lingua Lituanica nostra damus, daturi, Deo volente, mox copiosius aliquod et melius, Si prius in hoc exiguo, promptitudinem et benevolentiam erga me vestram intellexero.

Valete

---

2 Sic. for *gravitato.*

First of all, let them teach men from the Ten Commandments, which the Lord established for us; and, by contrast, let us teach what we must; that is, to put no hope in our strength; and that no mortal is able to offer complete obedience, as the law requires. Just as the Psalm testifies, "for in thy sight shall no man living be justified."[2] And again, "Cursed is every one that continueth not in all things which are written in the book of the law to do them."[3] While this stipulation remains, then—that we are to be damned while not satisfying the divine law—it follows necessarily that all will either be deserving of eternal death, or that they must seek the aid which the doctrine of the Gospel promises. Obviously, we must flee to the mercy of the eternal Father, trusting solely in Christ our Saviour. For he redeems all—whoever trusts in him—from the accursed law, from the wrath of God, from condemnation to eternal death; and he does this freely, without any prior or subsequent condition and dignity of works.

Lastly, this also must be taught: that God requires those who have resolved to trust solely in the benefits of Christ to show forth the fruits of faith and penitence. This is not, however, because works confer anything for our justification; but because they are given in thanks; not because they merit the salvation of eternal life, but because they merit the remission of temporal punishment, and certain other rewards, both in this and in the life to come.[4] Above all, the catechism teaches this; it is now, Pastors and teachers, your crude and brief exemplar, and we give it in our Lithuanian language so that, God willing, it may soon be given better and at greater length; if I fail in this beforehand, I shall have understood your promptness and benevolence.

Farewell!

---

2 Psalm 143:2 (Psalm 142 in the Vulgate).

3 Galatians 3:10.

4 Mažvydas's interpretation of Lutheran doctrine is close to Catholic teaching in his emphasis on the rewards obtainable for good works, especially "in the life to come." This was a view later repudiated by most Protestants.

DE MORIBUS TARTARORUM, LITUANORUM ET MOSCHORUM

[Extracts]

[p. 14] Epitome fragminis secundi

Mosci et Tartari, longe sunt Lituanis inferiores viribus: sed superiores industria, frugalitate, temperantia, fortitudine, caeterisque virtutibus, quibus regna firma consistent. Afferunt Tartaris hae virtutes ista commoda ut gaudeant copia peculii nostri abacti, et statu temporum sic exigente, placentur annuis muneribus a S[acra] Maiestate vestra, amici scilicet foederati, cum quibus antea quoque semper fuerunt Lituanis foedera. Iidem in equitatu sunt assidui, absque curribus bella gerunt, equis peregrinis abundant, urbibus quas tutentur carent. Mosci quolibet vere ex Orda Tartarica Nohaiensi, permutatione vestium, et rerum aliarum vilium, multa millia equorum bello aptissimorum accipiunt. Turcae Thraces immittunt nobis magno pretio equos partus ultimi, senes, laboribus exhaustos, morbis occultis obnoxios: **[p. 15]** valentes vero, aut ipsa arma vendere Christianis, religio ipsis est ac scelus. at maiores nostri contenti erant domi suae natis cantheriis: parati semper ad bellum cum lanceis, clipeis, loricis et refertis farre culeis. Heroidae Lituanicae vel templum vel convivium accessurae, senis vel octenis eiusdem coloris pilentis, id est, rhedis pensilibus vehuntur: totidemque homines loris vinctos Scytha trahens, evadit impune. at Tartari equorum ditissimi, ne Principis quidem suae vehiculo iungi patiuntur equum. Turcae aliique Saraceni accessuri die quolibet quinquies in fanum ad orandum, excalceant se lavantque frigida, etiam pudenda membra. iidem atque Tartari, Moscovitae, Livones, Pruteni, consulentes parsimoniae iugiter retinent uniusmodi vestitus, quos nos et pretiosos et varios habemus.

ON THE CUSTOMS OF THE TATARS, LITHUANIANS, AND MUSCOVITES (ca. 1550)

MICHALO THE LITHUANIAN[1]

Epitome of the second fragment

The Muscovites and Tatars are greatly inferior in strength to the Lithuanians, but superior in industry, frugality, temperance, courage, and other virtues, with which they firmly establish their realms. These virtues bring the Tatars these rewards—that they rejoice in the abundance of our stolen goods; and as the state of the times requires, they are placated with annual gifts by Your Sacred Majesty,[2] as friends and allies, since previously they were always allies with the Lithuanians. The same people are diligent in horsemanship, and wage war without chariots. They abound with exotic horses where they lack cities which are guarded by them. The Muscovites, indeed, received many thousands of horses—extremely suitable for war—from the Noghay Tatar Horde,[3] by swapping clothes and other inconsequential things. The Turks sent us Thracian horses at great price; they were runts, old, exhausted by labours, and liable to hidden diseases—strengthening themselves, therefore, by selling their own arms to Christians, a religion that to them is wicked.

But our ancestors were content with their nags born at home; they were always ready for war, with lances, shields, breastplates, and leather sacks filled with corn. Lithuanian heroines who are about to arrive at a temple or a feast are conveyed in carriages with six or eight horses of the same colour—that is, in suspended wagons; and drawing along as many men bound with Scythian leather straps, it passes them without harm. But even though the Tatars are very rich in horses, they do not suffer horses to be yoked to a vehicle, even that of their prince. The Turks and other Saracens[4] who are about to enter a mosque to pray five times a day take off their shoes and wash themselves with cold water, even their private parts. And the same Tatars, Muscovites, Livonians, and Prussians, preferring thriftiness, always wear the same kind of dress, while we have various different and precious clothes.

---

1 This text is based on Michalo Lituanus, *De moribus Tartarorum, Lituanorum et Moschorum, fragmina x* in *De moribus Tartarorum, Lituanorum et Moschorum*, ed. Grasser (1615), 14–18, 23–25, 39–41.

2 Grand Duke Sigismund II Augustus (1520–72), to whom Michalo's book was originally dedicated.

3 The Noghay Horde were nomadic Tatars living between the lower Volga and the Turgay Valley (Barisitz, *Central Asia and the Silk Road*, 158–59).

4 Michalo here uses the term "Saracen" as a generic term for Muslims.

Tartari tunicas habent absque plicis et rugis longas, equitanti dimicantique commodas, leves et pileos albos acutos non ad fastum paratos, quorum eminentia atque nitore in agminibus, licet minime galeati esse soleant, apparent illustriores, et hostibus formidandi. quas technas Mosci quoque imitantur. hi vero ex ovili lana fiunt, et saepe abluti diu durant, uno emti grosso.

Etsi Mosci soli, Sobolis aliarumque ferarum genere abundent: tamen vulgo Sobolos pretiosos non ferunt. Sed missos in Lituaniam, molles mollibus, aurum pro eis auferunt: gestantque in lacini is galerorum suorum cilicinorum laminas aureas, et gemmas pretiosas. quibus nec humor, nec sol, nec tinea, ut Sobolis, nocet.

Finis Fragminis secundi. ...

Epitome fragminis tertii

... [p. 16] Aqua amara.

Tartari, Precopenses itidem aromata aversantur, vivuntque potu lactis et aquae putealis, quae in ambitu Tauricae campestri, raro invenitur non amara, clara autem rarius, nisi in visceribus terrae, profundissime quaesita. Progenitores nostri cibos potusque peregrinos vitabant. Sobrii et frugales, omnem suam gloriam in re militari, voluptatem in armis, equis, famulis numerosis, et qualibus Mars gaudet, duris strenuisque ponebant, et cum exteras gentes arcerent, sua a mari uno ad alterum prolatarent, vocabantur ab hostibus Chorobra Litwa, i[d est] ferox Lituania. Nullum est in oppidis Lituanicis opificium adeo frequens, ut coquendae ex siligine cerevisiae, et aquae ardentis. Sequuntur hae potiones in bellum euntes, et ad sacrificia Missalia confluentes. Quibus homines domi assueti, simulatque insolitum sibi aquae potum in militia attingunt, torminibus et dysenteria pereunt. Rustici omissa agricolatione, in cauponas conveniunt. Ubi dies et [p. 17] noctes pergraecantur, ursis etiam arte cicuratis, ut potantes sua delectent ad cantum utricularii saltatione. Unde fit ut facultatibus consumtis, fames sequatur homines, ad furta et latrocinia convertantur, adeo ut in unaquaque Lituanica regione, intra unum mensem, plures propter haec facinora capite plectantur, quam centum et ducentis annis per omnes Tartarorum et Moscorum ebrietatem vetantium provincias.

The Tatars have tunics without folds and long creases, suitable for riding and fighting, and soft pointed white caps, not worn out of pride. In an armed host, by their height and brightness they seem to be shining and threatening to their enemies—although they are not accustomed to wear armour at all. The Muscovites imitate these artifices too. These men dress in sheep's wool, and when they are frequently washed they last for a long time, having been coarse at the time they were bought.

Although the Muscovite soil is abundant with sables and other kinds of wild animals, they do not commonly consider the sables to be precious. But, sending them to Lithuania (the soft for the soft), they receive gold for them. And they wear gold pendants and precious gems on the edges of their goat-hair hats—which neither the weather, nor the sun, nor moths harm as they harm sable.

The end of the second fragment. ...

Epitome of the third fragment

...

Bitter waters

The Perekopian Tatars[5] are averse to the same tastes, and they live off a drink of milk and well water, which is rarely found not bitter in the area of the Crimean region, and even more rarely found clear unless it is sought most deeply in the bowels of the earth. Our ancestors avoided foreign food and drink. Sober and frugal, all their glory was in military affairs—richness in arms, horses, numerous slaves—and such things as Mars rejoices in they established with the hardest efforts. And since they drove off external peoples, they enlarged themselves from one sea to another. They were called by their enemies *chorobra Litva* (that is, fierce Lithuania). There is no craft more common in Lithuanian towns than brewing beer from wheat and boiling water. These drinks follow them when entering war, and gathering together at the sacrifices of the mass. Men become accustomed to them at home, and at the same time the unaccustomed drink of water affects them in the army, and they perish from torments and dysentery.

The country people, having forgotten to cultivate the fields, gather in taverns. Here they pass both day and night in the manner of the Greeks, with bears tamed by art, so that while they are drinking they might take pleasure in their dancing to the song of the bagpiper. It happens, therefore, that having consumed their resources, hunger pursues men, who are turned to thievery and robbery, so that in one particular Lithuanian region more people were punished with death for these crimes within one month than in one hundred or two hundred years in the provinces of the Tatars and Muscovites, who forbid drunkenness.

---

5 A reference to the Tatars of Crimea, after the Perekop Isthmus that links Crimea to the mainland.

Poena vinipotatorum.

Certe apud Tartaros, qui modo vinum gustaverit, is et octoginta fustuariis ictibus percutitur, et totidem nummis multatur. In Moscovia vero nusquam est taberna potatoria. Quod si apud aliquem patremfamilias vel gutta sicerae deprehendatur: huius tota domus diruitur, fortunae confiscantur, familia atque vicini eiusdem vicus vapulant: ipsemet vero in perpetuum carcerem detruditur. In viciniam ideo saevitur, quod sit eo infecta contagio, et nefandi conscia criminis.

Bibacitas Lituanorum.

Nostros vero, non quidem magistratus, sed ipsa intemperies perdit potatores, aut mutua arma inter potandum enata. Dies ab aquae ardentis potu inchoatur. Vinum adhuc in lectis clamitantes. bibitur deinde idem virus a viris, foeminis, iuvenibus in plateis, foris, secus vias, Quo infecti nihil post agere possunt, quam dormire, ac qui huic malo semel assuesit, in eo crescit potandi continenter cupiditas. Nec Iudaei nec Saraceni quenquam e suo populo patiuntur perire egestate, tanta inter illos charitas viget: nec quisquam Saracenus cibarii sui edere vilum frustum audet, nisi id prius comminutum et commistum fuerit, ut unicuique praesentium cibus cedat eadem quantitate.

Abstinentibus autem ebrietate Moscis, oppida illorum celebria sunt variis et assiduis artificibus, qui mittendo nobis crateres ligneos, et baculos ad fulciendum gradum infirmis, senibus ebriis, ephippia, frameaes, phaleras et diversa arma, auro nos spoliant. ...

p. 18

Moscus Lituanis multa adimit.

Nam se suosque ab hac tyrannide Iohannes avus huius Iohannis Basilii, qui hodie rerum gubernacula tenet, redacto populo ad sobrietatem cauponisque unique interdictis vindicavit. Quin subiectis sibi Rezani, Twer, Susdal, Volodow aliisque finitimis Comitatibus ditionem suam protulit. Idem etiam, Casimiro rege Poloniae et Duce Lituaniae in Prussia contra Cruciferos pro regni finibus pugnante, populoque nostro in luxum prolapso, ademit suoque adiunxit patrimonio Lituanicas provincias Novohrod, Pskow, Siewer, et alia, heroum sanctorum catalogo a suis adscriptus, liberator et auctor patriae. Nam et metropolim suam, arce lateritia, et regiam lapidibus arte Phidiaca sculptis, inauratis quibusdam eius sacellorum cacuminibus decoravit.

Punishments of wine-drinkers

Certainly, among the Tatars, he who only tastes wine is both beaten with eighty strikes of clubs, and sentenced to pay the same amount in coins. Indeed, in Muscovy there is nowhere a tavern for drinking: because if a drop of strong drink is detected at the home of the head of any household, his whole house is knocked down, his fortune is confiscated, and his family and neighbours in the village beat him; and he is cast into perpetual prison. In the neighbourhood it is therefore met with rage, if the contagion has infected anywhere, and those who are conscious of the abominable crime.

The bibacity of the Lithuanians

But not only the magistrates, but they themselves cast our people into intemperance—or mutual conflicts arise whilst drinking. The day begins with a drink of boiling water; they call out for wine while still in their beds. The poison is then drunk by men, by women, by youths in the streets, in the marketplaces, and along the roads. Thus infected, they are afterwards able to do nothing other than sleep; and the desire for drinking grows continually in those who become accustomed to this evil. Neither Jews nor Muslims suffer people of their race to perish from poverty, so greatly does charity flourish among them; nor does any Muslim dare to eat an inconsequential crumb of food, unless it has been previously broken up and mixed, and he allows food in the same quantity to one of those present.

But the towns of the Muscovites, who abstain from drunkenness, are famous for various and first-class crafts. They despoil us of our gold by sending us wooden cups, and walking sticks to support the steps of infirm and drunken old men, horse blankets, ornaments for horses, and diverse arms. ...

The Muscovites take much away from the Lithuanians

For [the Muscovites] vindicated themselves when the people had been returned to sobriety by that tyrant Ivan,[6] the grandfather of the Emperor Ivan who today holds the government,[7] and the innkeepers had been everywhere forbidden. Indeed, he advanced his wealth after subjecting to himself Ryazan, Tver, Suzdal, Vladimir, and other border regions. The same ruler even took away from the Lithuanian patrimony and annexed to his own territory the provinces of Novhorod, Pskov, Severia, and others when Casimir, king of Poland and duke of Lithuania,[8] was fighting the crusaders at the borders of his realm. He was inscribed into the catalogue of holy heroes by his people as the liberator and founder of the country. For he decorated his capital city with a citadel of many sides and a royal palace from stones sculpted by the Phidian art, and gilded the tops of certain holy places.

---

6 Grand Prince Ivan III of Moscow (1440–1505; reigned 1462–1505).

7 Tsar Ivan IV "the Terrible" (1530–1584; r. 1547–1584).

8 Casimir IV Jagiellon (1427–1492; r. 1440–1492).

Sic et genitus ab eo Basilius eadem usus sobrietate atque disciplina morum, anni mille-
simi quingentesimi decimiquarti ultima Iulii ademtam nobis perfidia Michaelis Hlinscii
arcem et provinciam Smolensco, addidit suo patrimonio. Unde Moscwam metropolim
suam auxit, condito in ea vico Nalewki, opera mercenariorum nostrorum militum indito
ei in opprobrium gentis nostrae ebriosae cognomine. Naley enim Infunde significat.
Similiter huius natus qui nunc regnat, etsi arcem unam ad nos amisit: tamen interea intra
regionis nostrae fines tres arces condidit, Sebesz, Velisz, Zawlocz. Nulla recedit Tartaris,
quorum olim servus fuit, ita suos habet sobrios: tueturque libertatem non panno molli,
nec auro splendido, sed ferro: tenetque gentes suas in armis, munit arces perpetuis pra-
esidiis, pacem precariam non curat, vim vi repellit, continentiam Tartaricam continentia
populi sui, sobrietatem sobrietate aequat, artem arte Vitoudum heroem nostrum imita-
tus elidit. ...

[p. 23] Epitome fragminis quinti

Moscovitae irati imprecantur alicui suorum, ut fiat Romanae siue Polonicae religionis.
Adeo eam exosam habent. Gymnasiis literariis, dolendum, caremus. Literas Moscoviticas
nihil antiquitatis complectentes, nullam ad virtutem efficaciam habentes ediscimus,
Cum idioma Ruthenum alienum sit a nobis Lituanis, hoc est, Italianis, Italico sanguine
oriundis.

Lituani ab Italis orti.

Quod ita esse liquet ex sermone nostro semilatino, et ex ritibus Romanorum vetustis,
qui non ita pridem desiere apud nos, videlicet excrematis humanis cadaveribus, augu-
riis, auspiciis, aliisque superstitionibus, adhuc in quibusdam locis durantibus maxime
cultu Aesculapii, qui sub eadem, qua olim Romam ab Epidauro commigraverat, serpentis specie colitur, et in veneratione habetur. Coluntur et sacri penates, manes,[1] lares,
lemures, montes, specus, lacus, luci. Sed nec admodum diu sacer ille perpetuusque qui
cremandis victimis Romanorum Hebreorumque more fovebatur, extinctus est per baptismatis undam ugnis, id est, ignis.

---

[1] Misprinted *mares* in Grasser's text.

Thus the emperor born of him,[9] accustomed to the same sobriety and discipline in manners, added the citadel and province of Smolensk to his patrimony after it was taken from us by the treachery of Michael Glinsky on the last day of July 1514.[10] From this he enlarged his capital of Moscow, having founded in it the village of Nalewka, begun by the work of our mercenary soldiers, named out of contempt for our drunken people.[11] For *nalivat'* means "pour out."

Similarly, those born of him who now reigns have even taken one citadel from us. However, in the meantime he has built three fortresses within the borders of our realm: Sebezh, Velizh, and Zavolzhye. He does not shrink from the Tatars at all, whose servant he once was; and he guards his freedom not by a soft garment, nor by splendid gold, but by iron. He retains his peoples in arms, he reinforces his fortresses with continual protection, and he does not care for a precarious peace. He repels force with force, his people containing Tatar continence, and Tatar sobriety with sobriety, and imitating our hero Vytautas he crushes their art by art. ...

Epitome of the fifth fragment

The Muscovites angrily denounce anyone of theirs who adopts the Roman or Polish religion, so great a hatred do they have of it. Regrettably, we are lacking in schools of literature. Embracing no Muscovite literature in former times, we learn nothing effective for developing virtue, since the Ruthenian manner of speech is alien to us Lithuanians— that is, Italians, born of Italian blood.

The Lithuanians originated from the Italians

That this is the case is proved from our semi-Latin speech, and from the old rites of the Romans, which were not abandoned so long ago among us—that is to say, the cremation of human corpses, auguries, omens, and other superstitions. The cult of Aesculapius still very greatly endures in certain places, who is worshipped under the form of the serpent who once migrated to Rome from Epidaurus, and is had in veneration. And the sacred household gods, shades of the dead, guardian spirits, ghosts, hills, caves, lakes, and groves are worshipped. But it is not long since that holy and perpetual *ugnis* (that is, fire) was extinguished by the water of baptism, which was favoured in the manner of the Romans and Hebrews for burning victims.

---

9 Grand Prince Vasili III of Moscow (1479–1533; r. 1505–1533).

10 The Lithuanian nobleman Michael Glinsky (d. 1534) rebelled against Grand Duke Sigismund I in 1507 and defected to Vasili III of Muscovy, helping the Grand Prince capture Smolensk from the Lithuanians on June 30, 1514.

11 *Nalewki* (*krupnikas* in Lithuanian) is a traditional honey-based spirit; Michalo is saying that the Muscovites jokingly nicknamed a neighbourhood of Moscow built by and inhabited by Lithuanian mercenaries after the spirit they drank.

Verba Lituanica.

Etenim et ignis, et unda, aer, sol, mensis, dies, noctis, ros, aurora, deus, vir, devir, i.e. levir, nepotis, neptis, tu, suus, ▓p. 24▓ meus, suus, levis, tenuis, vivus, iuvenis, vetustus, senis, oculus, auris, nasus, dentes, gentes, sta, sede, verte, inverte, perverte, aratum, occatum, satum, semen, lens, linum, canapum, avena, pecus, ovis, anguis, ansa, corbis, axis, rota, iugum, pondus, culeus, callis, cur, nunc, tractus, intractus, pertractus, extractus, merctus, immerctus, sutus, insutus, versus, inversus, perversus, primus, unus, duo, tres, quatuor, quinque, sex, septem, et pleraque alia, idem significant Lituano sermone quod et Latino. Devenerant vero in haec loca maiores nostri, milites et cives Romani, missi olim in colonias, ad arcendum a suis finibus gentes Scythicas. Seu ut certior fert opinio, sub C. Iulio Caesare appulsi, Oceani adversis procellis. Nempe cum is Caesar, ut scribit Luc[ius] Florus, victis Germanis et in Gallia caesis, Rhenum proxima parte Germaniae domita superans, ac deinde Oceano in Britanniam disiecta tempestatibus classe, parum prospere navigaret, delatae enim naves maiorum nostrorum ad litus, ubi nunc est arx Samagitiae Ploteli, creduntur egressi in terram. Quin et nostro tempore pervenerunt naves quaedam transmarinorum in illud idem litus. Ubi nostri progenitores laborum et periculorum maris pertaesi, et captivis tam viris quam foeminis onusti, coepere in tabernaculis ad focos, more militari, adhuc in Samagitia durante, vitam degere. Unde ulterius progressi, subegerunt vicinos populos Iaczuingos, deinde Roxolanos seu Ruthenos, quib[us] tum ut Moscis dominabantur Tartari Zaulhenses: et singulis Ruthenorum arcibus praesidebant ii, qui appellabantur Basskaki, e quibus exacti sunt a parentibus nostris Italis, qui postea Litali, deinde Lituani appellati sunt. Tum innata fortitudine, populis Ruthenicis, regionibus arcibusque e Tartarica atque Baskakorum servitute ereptis, ditionem suam a mari Samagitico, quod Balteum dicitur, ad pontum Euxinum ubi ostia Borysthenis, et ad fines Valachiae, alterius Romanorum coloniae, et terras Voliniae, Podoliae, Kijoviae, Sievvier, atque campestres regiones usque ad terminos Tauricae, ac Towani[2] traiectum Borysthenis, omnia occupando, et illinc aquilonem versus ad ultimam et proximam metropoli Moscoviae arcem Mozaisco, ipsa quidem exclusa, sed Wiazmam, Dorohobusz, Biela, Toropetz, Luki, Pskow, Novihorod, ▓p. 25▓ omnibusque citerioribus arcibus et provinciis inclusis protulerunt.

---

2 *Sic.* for *Tamani?*

Lithuanian words

The words for fire, water, air, month, day, night, dew, dawn, god, man, husband's brother, grandson, granddaughter, you, his/hers, my, light, thin, alive, young man, old, old man, eye, ear, nose, teeth, people, stand, sit, turn, turn over, pervert, ploughed, harrowed, sown, seed, lentil, linen, hemp, reed, flock, sheep, eel, goose, basket, axle, wheel, yoke, weight, leather sack, track, why, now, drawn, undrawn, dragged, drawn out, purchased, unpurchased, sewn, unsewn, turned, turned over, perverted, first, one, two, three, four, five, six, seven, and many others mean the same thing in the Lithuanian language as in Latin. For our ancestors arrived in this place, Roman soldiers and citizens, sent out at one time in colonies in order to ward off the Scythian peoples from their borders. Or a more certain opinion is spoken of: that they were put ashore by adverse storms of the Ocean under Julius Caesar.

For this Caesar (as Lucius Florus writes), having defeated the Germans and slaughtered in Gaul, dominating the Rhine in the nearest part of conquered Germany, did not sail at all successfully.[12] His fleet was broken up in Britain by storms on the ocean, and the ships of our ancestors were carried to the shore of Samogitia where the castle of Plateliai is now; and there they are believed to have come ashore. And even today, the ships of those crossing the sea come to that same shore. There our ancestors, tired of the labours and perils of the sea, and weighed down by both male and female captives, began to lead a life in tents at open fires, in a military fashion that still endures in Samogitia. Having advanced further from there, they subjugated the neighbouring peoples of the Yotvingians, and then the Roxolani or Ruthenians, who were then dominated as if by the Muscovites, or as the Tatars dominate the people of Zavolzhsky. And those who were called *baskaks* were driven out of certain Ruthenian strongholds,[13] from which they were driven out by our Italian forebears, who were afterwards called Litalians, and then Lithuanians.

Then, by inborn strength, having kept the Ruthenian peoples in check and taken them out of Tartary and the servitude of the *baskaks*, they advanced their dominion from the Samogitian Sea (which is called Baltic) to the Black Sea where the mouth of the Dnieper is, and to the borders of Wallachia (otherwise a Roman colony) and the lands of Volhynia, Podolia, Kyiv, Novhorod-Seversky, and the steppe regions as far as the edges of Crimea, and the Strait of Kerch of the Borysthenes,[14] occupying everything. And turning from here to the north, they advanced to the furthest fortress of Mtsensk, and nearest to the city of Moscow, which indeed was excluded, but including Vyazma, Dorogobuzh, Byela, Toropets, Velikiye Luki, Pskov, Novhorod, and all the other fortresses and provinces.

---

12 The reference is to Lucius Annaeus Florus, *Epitomae Historiae Romanae* bk. 1, chap. 14, §§ 9–17, a summary of the events of Caesar's Gallic War including the first invasion of Britain in 55 BCE, when much of Caesar's fleet was destroyed by storms on the return to Gaul. The story of the survivors finding their way to the Baltic is a much later invention and not found in Florus.

13 *Baskaki*: collectors of Tatar tribute.

14 I take *Towani traiectum* to be a misspelling of *Tamani traiectum* ("the Strait of Taman"), an alternative name for the Strait of Kerch that divides the Sea of Azov from the Black Sea.

Postmodum amplificata sic virtute militari ditione sua, diadema quoque cum nomine regio obtinuerant Principi suo Mindawgo, sacri baptismatis charactere insignito. Sed extincto illo rege, etiam nomen regium atque Christianum interierat, donec rursum vicina nobis et Christiana gens Polona, ad sacrum baptisma et regale fastigium anno Christi 1386 invitaret feliciter hic dominantem proavum Sacrae Maiestatis vestrae, divum Wladislavum, Lituanice Iagelonem nuncupatum, quo virtus duarum gentium confinium consociata fortior foret in reprimendo communi Christiani nominis hoste.

Iudaei.

Quam in regionem confluxit ex aliis provinciis omnium pessima gens Iudaica, iam per omnia Podoliae, Voliniae, et alia fertiliora oppida aucta; perfida, callida, calumniatrix, quae nostras merces, monetas, Syngrapha, Sigilla adulterat, in omnibus emporiis victum Christianis praeripit, nullam artem praeter imposturas et calumnias exercet: ex progenie Chaldaeorum natio pessima, ut tradunt sacrae literae, adultera, peccatrix, infidelis, nequam, perversa. ...

Epitome fragminis decimi

[p. 39] ... Arcana divina scrutari nefas prophanumque esse existimant, nostram temeritatem execrantes, quod quidam ex nobis de iudiciis et secretis divinis, quae magna abyssus vocantur, in suis commessationibus disputent, nomen Divinum frustra usurpent. Irrident Tartari nostros Ecclesiast[icas] seu prophetas, taxant templa [p. 40] supellectilis, sediliorum, ararum, simulacrorum, et Dei ad senectutem vergentis, et mulierum venustarum, lasciviam moventium plena. Quibus in sedilib[us] honoratiores molliter recumbant, cum res divina agitur, dormiant. Iidem obscurioris conditionis homines a consessu arceant, in templa multis cincti stipatoribus veniant, eosdem ante se, suam ostentantes superbiam stare sinant. At ne ipse quidem Tartarorum Tyrannus, ante quenquam apparitorem, stipatoremque in Synagoga stare, aut se prae vulgo illustriorem esse patitur. Non ullam sedem quaerit, quanto maior est, tanto se humiliorem praestat.

Nos aeris pulsu, illi certis laudis divinae verbis ab vociferationibus ad templa se invitant: nos quod in laudibus divinis aures delectemus nostras buccinis, organis, harmoniis, verba precationis obscurantibus, et organis interea nostris naturalibus silentibus, reprehendunt.

Sacerdotes.

Quos habent sacerdotes ii, nec avari sunt, nec ambitiosi, neque voluptatibus, aut acquirendis possessionibus dediti, multominus negotiis secularibus implicati: sed sunt frugi, mansueti, modesti, officii sui studiosi, religioni intenti, qui tantum praecinunt, et legem interpretantur.

After having thus multiplied their dominions by military strength, they also obtained a crown with the name of king for their prince Mindaugas, who was signed with the sacred character of baptism. But on the death of this king, even the name of king and Christian perished, until our neighbouring and Christian people, the Poles, once again happily invited Your Sacred Majesty's ruling great-grandfather, the divine Władysław (called Jogaila in Lithuanian) to holy baptism and the summit of royalty in the year of Christ 1386. This allied strength of the two adjacent peoples (with the shared name of Christian) would be stronger in repressing the enemy.

The Jews

Into this region flooded from all provinces that worst people of all, the Jews, now increased through all Podolia, Volhynia, and other more fertile towns. They are deceitful, clever, and calumnious; and they adulterate our merchandise, coinage, signatures, and seals. In every market they snatch their livelihood from the Christians, and practise no art besides impostures and false accusations. This worst nation is descended from the Chaldaeans, and as the holy Scriptures relate that they are adulterous, sinful, unfaithful, wicked, and perverse. ...

Epitome of the tenth fragment

... [The Tatars] consider it unlucky and sacrilegious for the hidden things of God to be enquired into, denouncing our temerity; for they dispute at their meals about our judgments and divine secrets, which are called the great abyss, and use the name of God in vain. The Tatars laugh at our churchmen or prophets; how they value their temples by their supply of seats, of altars, and of statues of both God (tending to old age) and beautiful women, full of wanton gestures. In these churches they rest softly in the most honoured seats, and sleep while divine service is performed. The same people keep men of more obscure condition away from the assembly, and they come to the temple surrounded by many attendants; they allow them to go before them, showing that their pride stands. But not even the tyrant of the Tatars himself stands in the mosque[15] before some clerk or follower, nor is he suffered to be more illustrious than a common man. He seeks no other seat, however great he is, so much does he show himself to be humbler.

    We invite people to our temples by the striking of the air;[16] they by the repeated calling of words of divine praise. They censure us because we delight our ears with trumpets, organs, harmonies, obscure words of prayer, and organs in the middle of natural silences.

Priests

They have priests who are neither greedy nor ambitious, nor given to luxury nor to the acquisition of possessions, tied up in multifarious secular dealings. But they are frugal, gentle, modest, diligent in their office, attentive to religion, and they predict many things and interpret the law.

---

15 Michalo here uses the term *synagoga* as a generic term for a place of non-Christian religious assembly.

16 I.e., by ringing bells.

Taxantur etiam sacerdotes nostri non solum ab Ethnicis sed a vicinis nostris Ruthenis, quod vinum, quae est res luxuriosa, bibant, carnes manducent, neque habentes in se procreandi sibi simile appetentiam, uxores ducant. Cum nemo continens esse, nisi id ipsi Deus dederit, queat. Ab his abstinent caelibes monachi Graecorum. Porro habuisse antiquitus sacerdotes suas uxores, id ex multis Sacrae Scripturae locis liquet. Levit[icus] 21.3. Esd[ras] 9. Dan[iel] 14. Ezech[iel] 4.4. Baruch. 6. Luc[a] 1.10, 18. ad Titum 1.

Quod si nunc etiam nostri facerent, abstinendo ante triduum, cum vasa domini portanda essent: viverent sanctius quam in fucato coelibatu delicati epulones. Quos uri semper libidine aut concubinas alere, id est, ut Sophonias dicit, sanctum polluere necesse est. Et tamen nos in istos mercenarios officium laudandi Dei, nobis scil[icet] grave, reiicimus: cum ii irritant potius suis pravis moribus, quam placent Deum. Vices a nobis sibi delegatas, in vicarios negligentes reiiciunt: ipsi interea ociosi et voluptatibus ▓▓p. 41▓▓ intenti, ut fuci mel apum, sic isti labores populi comedunt, epulantur, seque vestiunt splendide. Ad munia Ecclesiastica, multa simul, nondum adulta aetate, nec sua natura perspecta, temere aspirant. Negotiis secularibus et profanis se immergunt.

Quaestus sacerdotum.

Et licet olim sacerdotibus nefas erat habere partem possessionum cum populo Dei, praeter Decimas: tamen nostri non contenti decimis, victimis, pro peccatis, primitiis, variis quaestibus, quos a divitibus, egentibus, nascentibus, nubentibus, aegrotantibus, morientibus, mortuis percipiunt: adhaec praeter opima praedia, multarum simul Ecclesiarum regimina, iactura publica, contra ius et rationem appetunt. Cum interim alibi potius quam in his Ecclesiis, ad quas ut dicit Dominus, non per ostium sed tanquam fures et latrones ingressi sunt, non vocati vivant, eas laicis, negotiatoribus, laenonibus locent, vendant. Multae sunt, quae nunquam viderunt suos pastores seu plebanos.

Si quis a Regni finibus ferme per omnem Lituaniam et Samagitiam atque Russiam, in Ecclesiis proventuum adeo bonorum, ut una multos alere queat, suos quaerat pastores, nulla invenietur in qua pastor assidue habitet, aut eam crebro invisat. Ideo vacillat ovium fides, friget Dei amor, cessant divinae laudes. Contra tales vero multis locis detonant divina oracula. Sed nolo me sacerdotibus, quibus nos et subiicere et ostendere debemus, post tot genera hominum a me lacessitorum reddere infensum. Satis sit haec recensuisse. Quibus in meliorem statum redactis, vivemus beatius, cum laude vestrae Regiae, sed in primis Divinae maiestatis.

Finis fragminum Michalonis Lituani.

Our priests are judged not only by the ethnic [Lithuanians] but also by our neighbours the Ruthenians, because they drink wine (which is a luxury) and eat meat; nor do they take wives, although they have in themselves the same desire to procreate. Yet no-one is able to be continent unless God himself should grant it. The celibate monks of the Greeks abstain from these things. In former times the ancient priests had their wives, and this is proven from many places in Scripture: Leviticus 21:3; Ezra 9; Daniel 14; Ezekiel 4:4; Baruch 6; Luke 1:10 and 18; Titus 1.

Even though our priests now abstain for three days before the cup of the Lord must be borne, they would live in greater holiness than wanton feasters in painted celibacy. They are continually consumed with lust, or maintain concubines—that is, as Sophonias says, it is necessary to pollute the sacred. However, we drive those mercenary men back to the office of praising God, which is of course serious for us—since these men rather offend God with their depraved morals, than please him. They cast off the offices delegated to them by us onto negligent vicars. Meanwhile, being lazy and eager for luxury, as honey is the glue of bees, these men thus consume the labours of the people, feasting and dressing themselves splendidly. They rashly aspire to ecclesiastical offices—many at the same time, not yet of adult age, nor perceiving their nature. They immerse themselves in secular and profane dealings.

The gains of the priests

It was once considered wicked for the priests to have any part of the possessions of the people of God, besides tithes. Ours, however, not content with tithes, profit from their victims for sins, and various profits: from the rich, from the poor, from those newly born, from those getting married, from the sick, from the dying, and from the dead. Besides these rich prizes, they desire at the same time the governance of many churches (at public expense) against justice and reason. As if not called, they live anywhere rather than in their churches (to which, as the Lord says, they entered not by the door but like thieves and robbers), and they sell and farm them out to laymen, to men of business, and to pimps. There are many of the common people who never see their pastors.

If someone were to seek the pastors, from the borders of the kingdom throughout almost all Lithuania, Samogitia and [Ruthenian] Rus', in churches supplied with so many goods (so that one can maintain many), he would not find a single one in which a conscientious pastor lives, however often he visits. Therefore the faith of the flock wavers, the love of God grows cold, and the praise of God ceases. Indeed, against these things the divine oracles thunder in many places.[17] But I do not want the priests, to whom we must both submit ourselves and show the same—attacked by me after every other kind of people—to return the hostility. It is enough to have examined this. Returned to this better state, we would live more happily, with the praise of Your Majesty, but first of all that of the divine majesty.

The end of the fragments of Michalo the Lithuanian.

---

17 Probably a reference to the prophets of the Old Testament.

8

SARMATIAE EUROPEAE DESCRIPTIO

[Extracts]

[fol. 44v] **Deductio et origo celeberrimae gentis Lituanorum, probabilis. Hactenus a nemine Historicorum Latinorum explanata.**

Ptolomeus ille universi orbis Geographus curiosissimus, hiis in regionibus quae hodie a Lituanis coluntur, et quae eorum ditioni utpote Russia, Podolia, Volhinia, Podlassia, Samogitiaque subsunt, hos populos colonias, suas, (quorum hodie ne vestigium quidem apparet) antiquitus habuere recenset, Galindos, Bodinos, Geninos, Sudinos, Cariones, Amaxobios, Stabanos, Sturnos, Nascios, Asubios, Wibiones, Ombrones, inter Lublinam et Brestiam, Sargatiosque. Quos omnes ex Cimbris, Gotisque, et Sarmatis ortum sumpsisse idem Ptolomeus asserit. Sarmatorum autem deductio cum latius a nobis descripta pateat, Cimbrorum nomen, et successiones mihi explanandae videntur. Cimbros itaque a Gomero nepote Nohae ex maximo natu filio Iapheto ortos esse, nomenque ab eo per tot secula paululum immutatum trahere consentiens omnium historicorum opinio est. Haec posteritas Iapheti, cum maiorem orbis terrarum partem, in Europa, Asiaque minori occupauerit, quod ipsi cum Etymon nominis dilationem significantis, tum fausta Nohae parentis imprecatio portendebant, pars eorum a Gomero orti, ad Bosphorum Cimerum Maeothidis paludibus proximum, (qui de illis Cimmerius est appellatus) ultra fontes Tanais fluvii, ubi in Ducatu Rhesanensi Moschouiae Principi subiecto oritur, sedes suas habuerunt. Postea successu temporis, quod haud difficile illis fuit, per regiones propinquas, Russiam, Lituaniam, et Borussiam nunc Prussiam appellatam, et Cimbricam Chersonensum ubi Sweci, Dani, Golandi[1] progressi, toto eo littore se passim diffundentes late dominati sunt, et castrato paululum nomine, litteraque interiecta Cimbri nuncupati. Quando vero et qua occasione haec migratio contigerit: quoniam nulla gentis ab eo tempore monumenta extant, ex quibus id constare possit, ignotum est. Caeterum fuerunt semper Cimbri gens bellicosa, strenua, manu prompta, id enim res ab ipsis fortissime audacissimeque gestae testantur. Hiis namque coloniis Septentrionalibus relictis in numero trecentorum millium, per Germanorum regiones in Heluetiam, Galliamque imprimis penetrarunt. Deinde Hispanias populabundi vastaverunt. Inde annum circiter centesimum decimum, ante natum Christum in Italiam excurrerunt, quam vastabundi passim depredarunt, Romanorumque Consulem Papirium Carbonem, cum universo exercitu fuderunt. Postea ab eisdem M. Iunius Silvanus, et ipse Consul contracta infoeliciter pugna, superatur. Aurelius deinde Scaurus Consulis legatus amissis copiis Romanis, in manus eorum vivus perveniens, a Bolo Rege Cimbrorum occiditur. Id Tacito affirmante actum est, anno sexcentesimo quadragesimo post urbem conditam. Tandem Romani maioribus copiis collectis in aditu Alpium contra Cimbros exercitum opponunt,

---

I Perhaps *sic.* for *Gotlandi.*

A DESCRIPTION OF SARMATIAN EUROPE (1581)

ALESSANDRO GUAGNINI[1]

The settlement and probable origin of the most celebrated Lithuanian people, so far not explained by any Latin historians

Ptolemy the Geographer, who was most curious about the entire world, recounts that there were in antiquity colonies of peoples in those regions now inhabited by the Lithuanians (and which are known under their rule as [Ruthenian] Rus', Podolia, Volhynia, Podlachia, and Samogitia). No trace at all today remains of the Galindi, Bodini, Genini, Sudini,[2] Cariones, Amaxobi, Strabani, Sturni, Nasci, Asubi, Wibiones, Ombrones, and Sargati between Lublin and Brest. The same Ptolemy asserts that all these took their origin from the Cimbri, Goths, and Sarmatians. But since the origin of the Sarmatians, described by us, lies more widely open, it seems that in what follows I ought to explain the name of the Cimbri.

It is the opinion of all historians, therefore, that the Cimbri descend from Gomer, the grandson of Noah and son of his eldest son Japheth, agreeing that the name was changed little by little over so many centuries. This posterity of Japheth would occupy the greater part of the world in Europe and Asia Minor, because the origin of the name signifies "expansion." Then the happy pronouncement of father Noah portended that the line born of Gomer should have its seat beyond the sources of the River Tanais, near the marshes of the Cimmerian Bosphorus of Maeotis (which is called from this Cimmerius), where it rises in the Duchy of Ryazan (subject to the Prince of Muscovy). Afterwards, by the passage of time they advanced through the neighbouring regions (which was not difficult for them): Russia, Lithuania, and Borussia (now called Prussia), and Cimbrian Chersonesus where the Swedes, Danes, and Gotlanders had advanced. Spreading out widely here and there along that shore they dominated it, and having cut their name a little short, and by the insertion of a letter, they were called the Cimbri.

When and for what reason this migration came about is unknown, since no monuments of that people survive from that time, by which we might understand this. Of all the others, the Cimbri were always warlike and vigorous, prompt to violence—something which their very brave and daring deeds testify. Having left thirty thousand colonists in northern regions, they first penetrated into the regions of the Germans in Switzerland and Gaul. Then this devastating people laid waste to Spain. From here, in around the year 110 BCE they ran into Italy. Devastating it, they plundered here and there, and routed the Roman Consul Papirius Carbo with his whole army. Marcus Junius Silvanus,

---

1 Text taken from Guagnini, *Sarmatiae Europeae descriptio* (1581), fols 44v–45v, 52v–53r, 60v–61r.

2 The Sudini were in fact identified with the Sudovians by other authors.

fusi tamen et ad internitionem prostrati, ubi C. Manlius in pugna intersectus occubuit. Octuaginta vero millia Romanorum militum caesa. Q. Servilius Coepio Imperator exercitus, ex conflictu funesto vix cum denis elapsus, Romam tante cladis nuncius perveniens, bonis omnibus publicatis, ex decreto Senatus, quod temeritate sua exercitum perdiderit, iugulatur. Aiunt Romanos uno in praelio maiori clade et detrimento unquam affectos esse, quamobrem suspensis metu animis, de exitu imperii sui magnopere soliciti, praesentique rerum suarum periculo vehementer conturbati, cum hostes exitium, ubi minitantes propediem adventare nunciarentur. Caium Marium ex Libia ubi Iurgutam devicerat, Ducem bellicosissimum, et fortunatum vocaverunt, duobusque annis ab illa clade Romanorum elapsis. Marius, Cimbrorum et Tewtonum, ad aquas Sextias cruento praelio ducenta millia fudit, tantaque fertur caesorum multitudo, ut Massilienses congestis defunctorum ossibus, vineas eisdem obsepserint, sanguineque humano [fol. 45r] agri quasi stercore multo pinguescentes uberrimi, feracissimique redditi sint. Itaque Cimbri attenuati numero et viribus, sed animo minime fracti, in unum conglobati, Q. Catuli Proconsulis exercitum in fugum verterunt, ad fluviumque Atesin castrametati sunt. Quo Marius summa celeritate advolans, coniunctis copiis suis, cum exercitu Catuli, inito praelio 29. die Iulii centum quadraginta millia Cimbrorum occidit. Qua clade ad extrema redacti Italia egressi, patrias oras utpote Daniam, Prussiam, Suetiam, Livoniam, Lituaniamque petierunt, ex quibus illi qui Lituaniam occupaverant Gepidae nuncupati fuere. Hac vero in Regione ubi Samogitia, Aeneas Silvius Massagetas, gentem Plinio, celebrem consedisse testatur. Lituanorum vero gentem, qui antiquitus Gepidi vocabantur ex Gotis oriundam. Erasmus Stella pulchris rationibus affirmat cum Duce Litalalano, sive Litwone Vedenuti Prussiae Regis filio, anno Domini 573. in has regiones vicinas patris imperio quas olim Alani incolebant, venisse. Lituaniaeque nomen a sui denominatione eiusdem indidisse. Samogitiam vero a fratre eiusdem Lituonis Saimone principe appellatam, idem Erasmus Stella in Prussia historia testatur, quae tunc temporis longe in Prussiam, et Livoniam usque extendebatur. Similiter Lotialos, sive Lotwonos, qui nunc Livones post Germanorum ingressum Latinis dicuntur, ab eodem Litwone cum Litwania pariter nomen traxisse. Hae autem gentes, utpote Pruteni, Polowci, Samogitae, Gepidae, Lituani, Livones, Curlandi, Iatwingi sive Iaziges et Iaczwingi appellati, et unum idioma, ita eosdem mores, consuetudines, legesque et bellorum expeditiones in Christianos concordi Marte, semper habebant, nisi singulae singulis principibus finibusque certis dirimebantur.

himself Consul, was defeated by the same people after joining an unlucky battle. Then the Suffect Consul Aurelius Scaurus, having lost the Roman forces, fell into their hands alive and was killed by the Cimbrian king, Boiorix. Tacitus says that this happened in the six-hundred and fortieth year after the founding of the city [113 BCE]. Eventually, the Romans sent their army against the Cimbri, having gathered more troops for an Alpine attack; but they were routed and put to the slaughter when Gaius Manlius, having been cut in two in the battle, lay dead.

With eighty thousand Roman soldiers dead, the commander of the army Servilius Caepo was strangled by decree of the Senate, with all his goods being confiscated, because he had lost the army by his temerity. He slipped away from the deadly battle with a tenth of the army, and came to Rome as the messenger of such a catastrophe. They say that the Romans were weakened as one in the battle by a major disaster and catastrophe. This was because their spirits were frozen in fear, being very greatly concerned by the departure of their commander, and intensely disturbed by the present danger of their affairs when they were warned that the enemy would arrive before long, threatening death. Two years after this disaster for the Romans, they summoned Gaius Marius from Libya, where he had subdued Jugurtha, a most warlike and fortunate leader. Marius routed two hundred thousand of the Cimbri and Teutones in a bloody battle at Aquae Sextiae. And so great was the number of the slaughtered that the Massilians gathered up the bones of the dead and enclosed their vineyards; and the fields were rendered very fertile and fruitful by human blood like dung, being much strengthened.

The Cimbri, therefore, diminished in numbers and in strength (but not broken in spirit) gathered into one and put the army of the Proconsul Quintus Catulus to flight and pitched camp by the River Adige. Marius flew there with the utmost speed, and having joined his forces with the army of Catulus, he killed one hundred and forty thousand Cimbri in a battle begun on July 29. With this catastrophe, leaving Italy at long last, they made for the shores of their fatherland—namely Denmark, Prussia, Sweden, Livonia, and Lithuania, from which those who occupied Lithuania were called Gepidae.

In this region, where Samogitia is, Aeneas Silvius testifies (by Pliny) that the famous people of the Massagetae were settled, and that the famous Lithuanian people, who were anciently called Gepidi, originated from the Goths. Erasmus Stella affirms, by attractive reasoning, that they came into these regions (which the Alans once inhabited) with their leader Litalalanus, or Lituon the son of the Prussian king Widewuto (neighbouring his father's realm) in the year of Our Lord 573. And that they assumed the name of Lithuania from the name of the same man. Erasmus Stella, in his history of Prussia, testifies that Samogitia is so called from Lituon's brother, the prince Saimon, which has now been extended by length of time to Prussia and Livonia. In the same way, he says that the Lotiali (or Latvians), who are now called Livonians in Latin after the arrival of the Germans took their name from the same Lituon, just as much as Lithuania.

But these peoples—namely, the Prussians, Polovtsians, Samogitians, Gepidae, Lithuanians, Livonians, Couronians, and Yotvingians (otherwise called the Jatvians)—always had the same speech, the same manners, customs, laws, and expeditions against Christians in a martial alliance, unless they were separated one from another by princes with established borders.

Iaczwingi autem fuerunt populi crudelissimi, in finibus Lituaniae iuxta Masoviam, ubi hodie Podlassia colonias suas habebant, qui in bello non referebant pedem, quin vincerent, aut vincerentur: ideo bellis assiduis interierunt, reliqui eorum in Lituanos Russos, et Masovitas ob vicinitatem abierunt. Opinantur alii Lituanos, a Lituo quod cornu venatorium significat, dictos esse, quorum opinio, ut anilis et stulta iure ab omnibus irridetur. Mathias autem Miechoviensis, et Dlugosus Polonicae historiae indagatores, ac annales Rutenorum testantur. Italos Duce Palemone, vel ob tyrannidem Neronis, vel promeritum exilium, aut ab Attila Hunnorum Reges crudelissimas Patriae vastationes fugientes, has regiones, longa navigatione superata, ex sinu maris Baltici, quod Prussiam, Samogitiam, Livoniamque alluit, per Nemnam fluvium Crononem Ptolomeo dictum, classe ingressos fuisse, qua et ipsa gens Lituanica strenue asserit. Quamplures enim dictiones Latinae, et Italicae idiomati eorum intermixtae habentur. Aiuntque hunc Palemonem (quem ipsum nomen Latinum, Italumque esse prodit) cum certa comitiva ex nobilibus propinquitate iunctis collecta, quorum praecipuos, Ursinos, Columnas, Iulianos, Caesarianos, Gastaldos recensent, Lituaniae nobilibus familiis et Stemmatibus principia dedisse, vulgum vero Lituanorum utpote colonos, et agrestes ex Gotis natos asserunt, in hancque sententiam plurimi Polonicae et Germanicae, ac Russorum historiae scriptores astipulantur, quorum iudicio et autoritati, nos quoque acquiesccentes cum eiusdem sentire volumus.

Hic itaque Polemon ob innatam industriam, a gente barbara Princeps salutatus, eam coram nomine Patriae suae Italiae (praeposito articulo Italis in faeminini generis nominibus efferendis consueto) *La Italia* appellasse creditur, quae postea longo temporis successu Italicis moribus, idiomateque in barbariem populi commutatis, Lituania dicta est. Quidam etiam eosdem Italos a littore maris Baltici, quod Prussiam, Livoniam, ac Lituaniae, Samogitiae extrema alluit, eo quod ibi prius consederint, Lituaniam connominasse putant. Succedente postea Palemoni quodam ex eadem gente Principe, Itali recens Latinorum nomen non modo deposuerunt: sed ignatam quoque et peregrinam eorum incolarum linguarum, apud quos principatum arripuerant addiscentes, in suam cooptarunt, vivendique normam et modum cum eiusdem barbaribus susceperunt. Caeterum haec gens Lituana longo tempore a sui imperii primordiis, obscura fuit, Rutenorumque iugo subiecta, ut Princeps Kiouiensis Russiae quondam [fol. 45v] Monarcha, ab eis periomata, suberaque ob aegestatem et soli sterilitatem, in signum tantummodo subiectionis exigeret: Donec Mendolphus sive Mendog, et Witenen, Gediminusque Duces Illustres Haeroica Magnanimitate illa innata, dudumque segnitia rei militaris oppressa excitata, rebellionem contra Rutenos, ab antecessoribus suis inceptam[1] continuentes, unus post alium in Lituaniae imperio succedentes, Russiae Principibus partim strenuo marte, partim astu frequentius aggressis, et quasi debellatis, sensim adeo viribus creuerunt, ut iugo Rutenis omnibus iniecto, etiam ad tributa sibi pendenda eos compellerent, quae pluribus ab annis Rutenis ipsi pendebant, ac pro periomatibus et subere aurum, argentumque exigunt. ...

I The original text has *inseptam*.

But the Yotvingians were a most cruel people at the borders of Lithuania next to Masovia (where Podlachia has its colonies today); those whom they defeat, or who are defeated by them in war do not bring back a foot. Therefore they were ruined by eager wars—the remainder of them against the Lithuanians and Russians, and the Masovians left the vicinity on account of them.

Others opine that the Lithuanians are so called from *lituo*, which means a hunter's horn; an opinion that is derided by all as a stupid old wives' tale. But Maciej z Miechowa and Długosz, the investigators of Polish history, and the Ruthenian annals bear witness that Italians led by Palaemon came to these regions—either on account of the Neronian tyranny, or deserving exile, or fleeing the most cruel devastations of their fatherland by Attila the Hun. Having overcome a long sea journey, they entered the River Nemunas (called Cronones by Ptolemy) with a fleet out of the Baltic Sea, which laps at Prussia, Samogitia, and Livonia—and the Lithuanian people themselves strenuously claim this. Thus there are so many Latin words and Italian idioms mixed in among them.

And they say that this Palaemon (whose name itself comes from a Latin and Italian name), when he had gathered together a certain retinue from nobles joined together by closeness of blood, gave the rule to the noble families and dynasties of Lithuania (among the foremost they listed the Ursini, the Columnae, the Juliani, the Caesariani, and the Gastaldi). But they assert that the common people of the Lithuanians—namely, those who live on the land, and the rustics—were born of the Goths. And many of the Polish, German, and Russian writers of history join in this opinion—with whose judgment and authority we also wish to agree, acquiescing with the same. Therefore this Palaemon, by innate industry, was hailed as prince by this barbarian people; and it is believed that he called it *la Italia* after the name of his Italian fatherland (after the Italian custom of putting an article before words of the feminine kind). Afterwards, after a long time had elapsed from Italian customs, and with their speech truncated among a barbarian people, "Lithuania" was said. They also think that those same Italians named Lithuania from the shore (*litus*) of the Baltic Sea, which laps at Livonia and the edges of Lithuania and Samogitia, because they first settled there. When someone else from the same people succeeded Palaemon as prince, the Italians did not, however, set aside their recent name of Latins; but learning as they snatched the rule from them, they adopted in their own language the native and foreign languages of the inhabitants; and they adopted a norm and way of living with the same barbarians.

For a long time after the beginnings of its rule this Lithuanian people was obscure among all others, and subject to the yoke of the Ruthenians, so that the Prince of Kyivan Rus' (at one time their monarch) took bark and the outer coverings of trees as a sign of subjugation, on account of the poverty and barrenness of the soil; until the illustrious dukes Mindaugas, Vytenis, and Gediminas, by their inborn heroic greatness of soul, continued the rebellion against the Ruthenians begun by their predecessors, having awoken a long oppressed weakness in military matters. Succeeding one after another to the rule of Lithuania, and attacking the princes of Rus' ever more frequently (partly by martial exertions and partly by cunning) until they were almost defeated, little by little their strength grew so great that they threw the yoke on all the Ruthenians. They even compelled the Ruthenians to pay them the tribute which they used to pay the Ruthenians for many years, and for bark and the outer coverings of trees they exacted gold and silver. ...

[fol. 52v] De prisca religione Lituanorum.

Ad Iagielonis Wladislai Regis Poloniae ex Ducibus Lituaniae tempora, de quo in Polonorum Regum descriptione copiosius diximus, tota gens Lituanica, et Samagitica priscae multorum Deorum, seu potius Daemonum superstitioni dedita erat. Imprimisque ignem, (quem sua lingua Znicz, ut rem sacram appellabant) cultu divino prosequebantur, eumque in celebrioribus locis, atque oppidis perpetuum observabant, et sacerdotes cum ministris ad hoc munus obeundum adhibebant, quod si in curia ministrorum ignis extingueretur capite plectebantur. Huiusque modi ignis Vilnae Metropoli Lituaniae in arcis medio (ubi nunc Basilica divo Stanislao dicata, erecta est) perpetuo asservabatur. Fulmen quoque quod Perunum Slavonica lingua appellabant, pro Deo colebant. Lucos praeterea et eximias procerasque arbores, in silvis singuli sacrosanctas habebant, easque cultu latriae venerabantur, ita ut violare eas ferro iniuriave aliqua nephas esset, quod si Lituanus eiusdem fidei perpetraret, ut videlicet aliquam arborem, vel ignem quolibet modo dehonestaret, statim vel Daemonum violentia interibant, vel membro aliquo arrepti privabantur. Solem forte nubibus obscuratum credebant sibi succenseri, ideo sese illi quo placaretur, devovebant. Viperas item atque serpentes Deos esse credebant, eisque cultum praecipuum exhibebant, et singuli patresfamilias, cives, coloni, et nobiles singulos, serpentes domi asservare solebant, quos pro Paenatibus, et laribus familiaribus adorabant, lacque et gallos gallinaceos, eis immolabant, eratque inauspicatum et exitiabile toti familiae, quempiam ex eis violasse dehonorasseve, aut domi non fovisse, tales enim, vel bonis omnibus privabantur, vel crudeliter lacerati interibant. Erat autem apud eos quottannis solemne sacrificium, sub initium mensis Octobris post collectas fruges, ad quod frequentes, cum uxoribus et liberis servisque, conveniebant: ac toto triduo opipare epulabantur, de hiis quae Diis ad offerendum mactarant. Quod et nunc in Samagitia, Lituania et quibusdam locis Russiae, ab agrestibus observatur, prout inferius suo loco dicetur. Ex bellis revertentes manubias et unum aliquem de captivis praecipuum, et insignem virum victimae loco igni consecrabant.

On the ancient religion of the Lithuanians

Up to the time of Władysław Jagiełło, king of Poland, from the line of the dukes of Lithuania (of whom we have said a great deal in our description of the kings of Poland), from ancient times the whole Lithuanian and Samogitian people had been given to a superstition of many gods (or rather demons). And first of all they worshipped fire (which in their language they call *žinis* ["knowledge"], as if a holy thing), and observed a perpetual fire in the best-known places, and in towns;[3] and they employed priests with assistants to attend to this task—because if the fire went out in the care of the ministers, they were punished with death. And a fire of this kind was observed perpetually in the middle of the citadel of Vilnius, the capital of Lithuania (where the basilica dedicated to St. Stanislaus now stands).

They also worshipped thunder as a god, which was called Perún in the Slavonic language. Furthermore, they had sacred groves and outstanding and noble trees in certain woods. They venerated them with a cult of worship, so that to violate them with iron or any injury was wicked. If any Lithuanian of this faith perpetrated it—that is, dishonoured such a tree in any way, or with fire, they either died at once by the violence of the demons, or were deprived of some member which was torn from them. They believed they would be set alight if the sun happened to be obscured by clouds, and therefore they vowed themselves to those whom they were placating.

And they believed that serpents and snakes were gods, and offered them the foremost worship. Each head of a family, citizen, inhabitant, and noble was accustomed to host snakes in their home, which they worshipped as gods of the household and family. And they made sacrifice to them of milk, chickens, and poultry products. And it was unlucky and deadly to the whole family if any one of them violated, dishonoured, or did not favour the snakes in their home; such were either deprived of all their goods, or died cruelly maimed.

But there was among them every year a solemn sacrifice, before the start of October, after the harvest, to which they frequently came together with their wives and children. And for three whole days they used to feast sumptuously on those things which they had offered the gods in sacrifice. And this is now observed by the rustics in Samogitia, Lithuania and certain places in Rus', as will be said below. Returning from war, they consecrated the booty and one of the foremost captives in the place of fire, making the important man a victim.

---

3 Guagnini has here garbled Długosz's earlier account; Długosz, *Historiae Polonicae* (1711–1712), 1:109 says that the oracle priest who tends the sacred fire was called *Zincz*, and not the fire itself. Guagnini's error probably arose from the ambiguity in the construction of Miechowa's sentence describing the sacred fire, where *zincz* could be either the name of the fire or of the priest: *ignem qui per sacerdotem lingua eorum zincz nuncupatum subiectis lignis adolebatur* (Miechowa, *Tractatus de duabus Sarmatiis* (1518), sig. (e vv)).

Corpora mortuorum cum pretiosissima suppellectili, qua vivi maxime utebantur, cum equis, armis, et duobus venatoriis canibus, falconeque cremabant, servum etiam fideliorem vivum cum domino mortuo, praecipue vero magno viro, cremare solebant, amicosque servi, et consanguineos, pro hac re maxime donabant. Ad busta propinquorum lacte melle mulsato, et cervisia parentabant, choreasque ibidem ducere solebant, tubas inflantes, et timpanas percutientes. Hic mos adhuc hodie in partibus Samagitiae confinibus Curlandiae ab agrestibus quibusdam observatur. Quos omnes errores et vanas superstitiones Iagielo postquam cum Hedwigi haerede Regni Poloniae, unica ut supra in serie Regnum[2] Poloniae patet, matrimonium contraxit, abstulit, sedavit, et Christianum nomen Lituanis Baptismi lavacro ablutis, indidit. Rebus enim in Polonia recte constitutis, volens ne Lituania patria sua ulterius Daemonum cultui vacaret, Comitia generalia Vilnae Lituaniae Metropoli, anno Domini 1387 ad initium quadragenarii ieiunii indixit, ad quas ingenti procerum et equitum Polonorum caterva stipatus, una cum [fol. 53r] Regina in Lituaniam se contulit, Archiepiscopum Gnesnensem, et multos sacerdotes, ac pios homines, secum duxit. Semovitus quoque et Ioannes Masoviae, Conradusque Olesniciae, Duces, eum commitati sunt. Convenerunt quoque Vilnam, Skergelo Trocensisum, Vitoldus Grodnensium, Volodimirus Kioviensium, et Koributus Novogrodensium Duces, fratres Principis, et infinita equitum plebisque multitudo. Ibi de religione Christiana populariter suscipienda, ac de exterminando cultu falsorum Deorum, et omni superstitione diligenter actum, ipso Rege, maximam ei rei operam navante, non solum hortando, et praemiis alliciendo, sed etiam docendo, cum Polonici sacerdotes linguae gentilis ignari essent. Porro gens barbara maiorum suorum, religiones aegre relinquebat, sed cum mandato Regis ignis sacer extinctus, templum araque eius unde oracula a sacerdote edebantur, eversum esset Vilnae, ubi nunc divi Stanislai templum, necatique serpentes, et succisi luci, arboresque, sacrae, absque cuiusquam laesione, Lituani admirantes stupidique dicebant, quomodo Dii nostri istis perversis Polonis Christianis, hanc iniuriam dissimulant, seque laedi scelestis manibus sinunt, quod si hoc aliquis nostrum perpetraret, confestim ira Deorum interiret. Sed cum Poloni praeter opinionem barbarorum, Idola everterent, tum vero Lituani vanitate sua agnita, alacriores, ad Principum suorum religionem facti sunt, plurimam ex his multitudinem Rex advectis ex Polonia pannis laneis albis, ad Baptismum perduxit. Porro cum immensi laboris esset, singulos sacro fonte tingere, nobilioribus tantum hic honor tributus est: reliquum vero vulgus turmatim distributum, aqua sacra a sacerdotibus aspergebatur, unumque nomen singulis turmis, tam virorum quam mulierum, in nomine Patris et Filii et Spiritus Sancti, inditum erat, atque una die triginta millia barbarorum baptisati sunt, exceptis nobilioribus, et illis qui ante sacro fonte, in Polonia lavati erant, atque ab eo tempore Lituani in fide Christi permanent. ...

---

2 *Sic.* for *Regum?*

They were accustomed to cremating the bodies of the dead with the most precious equipment, which they made great use of when alive; with horses, arms, and two hunting dogs and a falcon—and they even burnt a most faithful servant alive with the master, especially with a great man, and the friends and relatives of the servant gave great gifts towards this matter. At the pyre they fed the shades of their relatives with milk mixed with honey and with beer, and were accustomed to dance there, blowing trumpets and striking drums. This custom is still observed by certain rustics in parts of Samogitia and the edges of Courland.

Jogaila, after he had contracted a marriage with Jadwiga, heiress of the kingdom of Poland (as appears uniquely and above in the order of the kings of Poland), took away and suppressed all these errors and vain superstitions, and bestowed the Christian name on the Lithuanians, having been washed by baptism.

For when things had been rightly established in Poland, wishing that Lithuania his fatherland should in future be free from the cult of demons, at the beginning of the Lenten fast in the year of Our Lord 1387 he proclaimed public assemblies at the capital of Vilnius, to which a huge packed crowd of nobles and Polish knights brought themselves. They brought with them the archbishop of Gniezno and many priests and pious men. Dukes Siemowit and John of Masovia and Konrad of Oleśnica were also sent with them. Skirgaila, duke of Trakai, Vytautas, duke of Grodno, Vladimir, duke of Kyiv, and Kaributas, duke of Novhorod, the prince's brothers, also came, and an infinite multitude of knights and ordinary people. Here, with great zeal, the same king not only exhorted but also taught, enticing with rewards, about the people receiving the Christian faith, and about exterminating the worship of false gods, and every superstition diligently performed (since the Polish priests were ignorant of the people's language).

Thereafter the barbarian people reluctantly abandoned the religions of their ancestors. But when the sacred fire was extinguished by the king's order, and the temple and altar from which they received an oracle from the priest were destroyed; when the temple was overturned at Vilnius, where the church of St. Stanislaus now is; when the snakes were killed, and the groves and sacred trees were cut down without any injury, the stunned and wondering Lithuanians said, "How do our gods ignore this injury by these perverse Polish Christians? And how do they allow themselves to be hurt by disgraceful hands? For if one of us had perpetrated this, at once the wrath of the gods would have killed him." But when the Poles, contrary to the opinion of the barbarians, overturned the idols, the Lithuanians recognized their emptiness and were turned more quickly to the religion of their princes. The king, having brought robes of white linen from Poland, brought very many of this great multitude to baptism.

Furthermore, since it would have been an immense labour to dip each one at the sacred font, this honour was accorded to the most noble. The remaining common people, having been divided into squadrons, were sprinkled with holy water by priests, and a single name was given to each squadron, of men or of women, in the name of the Father, and of the Son, and of the Holy Spirit. And on one day thirty thousand barbarians were baptized, apart from the higher nobles, and those who had previously been washed at the sacred font in Poland; and from that time the Lithuanians remain in the Christian faith. ...

[fol. 60v] Ducatus Samogitiae

Samogitia Regio satis ampla proxima Lithuaniae, a Septentrione Livoniae contermina est, marique Baltaeo sive Germanico ab occidente, nonnihil in Septentrionem reflectendo adiacet: Prussiam quoque in vicinia habet. Nullo castro munito insignis est, civitates tamen in ea cum pagis tam Regiae, quam nobilium complures sunt. Huic Regioni praefectus sive Capitaneus supremus, a Rege Poloniae magno Duce Lituaniae praeponitur, aeque temere is nisi gravissimas ob causas officio movetur, sed quoad vivit perpetuo manet. Episcopum habet Romanae obedientiae. Agrestis turba in humilibus casis, iisque oblongioribus vitam ducit, in quibus ignis in medio accensus ardet, ad ignem vero paterfamilias cum domesticis, servisque sedit, iumentaque, et totam suppelectilem domesticam cernit. Solent enim sub eodem quo ipsi habitant tecto, sine ullo interstitio peccora habere. Maiores eorumdem cornibus animalium urorum videlicet pro poculis utuntur. Audaces sunt et strenui homines et ad bellum prompti, loricis aliisque plurimis armis praecipue autem cuspide venatorum utuntur, equos adeo parvos habent, ut vix credibile sit ad tantos labores eos posse sufficere, quibus foris in bello, domique, in colendis agris utuntur. Terram non ferro sed ligno proscindunt, quod eo magis mirandum, cum terra eorum tenax et non arenosa sit. Araturi ligna complura quibus vomeris loco utuntur secum portare solent, scilicet ut uno fracto, aliud atque aliud ne quid in mora sit in promptu habeant. Quidam ex provinciae praefectis quo provinciales graviore labore levaret, multos ferreos vomeres fabricare fecerat, cum autem eo, sequentibusque, aliquot annis segetes quadam caeli intemperie expectationi agricolarum non responderent, vulgus agrorum suorum sterilitatem ferreo vomeri pertinaciter adscribebat nec aliud quicque in causa esse putabat. Praefectus eorum vulgi seditionem timens amoto ferro suo, eos more agros colere permisit.

Provincia haec naemoribus, silvisque abundat, in quibus horrendae quandoque visiones fieri dicuntur. Mel nusquam melius nobiliusve, quodque, minus caerae habeat, albumque sit quam in Samogitia reperitur. Silvaeque illic summas divitias ferunt, stipitibus enim cavatis mela passim promuntur. Sunt etiam nunc illic inter agrestes, idolatrae complures, qui serpentes quosdam quatuor brevibus sacerdotum instar pedibus, nigro obesoque corpore Givoiitos patria lingua dictos, tanquam penates domi suae nutriunt, eosque domo lustrata certis diebus ad appositum cibum prorepentes, cum tota familia quoad saturati, in locum suum revertantur, timore quodam circumstantes venerantur. Quod si adversi illis quid acciderit, serpentem deum domesticum male acceptum ac saturatum esse credunt.

The Duchy of Samogitia

The large Samogitian region is sufficiently close to Lithuania, bordering Livonia to the north, and the Baltic or German Sea to the west, and turning back on itself, it neighbours a great deal to the south; it also has Prussia as a neighbour. It is not endowed with any important castle. However, there are many towns in her, with lands of both the king and of the nobles. A prefect or supreme captain is appointed for this region by the king of Poland as Grand Duke of Lithuania, and normally this man is not removed from office except for the gravest reasons, but remains for as long as he lives. It has a bishop of the Roman obedience. The crowd of rustics lead their life in humble oblong huts, in which a fire burns that is lit in the middle. The head of the family sits at the fire with his household and servants and animals, and perceives the whole domestic apparatus. For they are accustomed to live under the same roof, without having any dividing wall from the sheep. Their ancestors used to use bison horns for drinking cups.

They are daring and vigorous men, and quick to wage war, and they use breastplates and many other arms, but above all the hunters' spear. They have horses so small that it is hardly believable they can be adequate for such labours, which they use in foreign wars, at home, and for cultivating the fields. They do not break the earth with iron, but with wood—which is the more to be wondered at, since their earth is obstinate and not sandy. The ploughmen use entirely wood, and are accustomed to carry the ploughshares with them from place to place—so that if one breaks, they have another ready without delay. Certain of the prefects of the province had caused many iron ploughshares to be made, by which he might lift the people of the province from such heavy labour. But when that year, and for several years following, the crops of the farmers did not respond to the intemperateness of the heavens, the common people stubbornly ascribed the barrenness of their fields to the iron ploughshare and would not think anything else the cause. Their prefect, fearing an uprising of the common people, removed their iron, and allowed them their custom of cultivating the fields.

This province abounds in woods and forests, in which horrendous visions are said to occur. No honey is better, more noble or more white, and has less wax, than is found in Samogitia. The forests here bear great riches, and they sometimes draw the honey out with sharpened stakes. And there are also many idolatries there among the rustics, who (on the instructions of their priests) nourish certain snakes like household gods that are four feet long, black, and with a fat body, and called Gyvatės in the language of the country. Having purified the house for several days, the snakes are worshipped when creeping towards food put out for them. Having been fed by the whole family, they return to their place, with those around standing in fear. But if something bad happens to them, they believe that the domestic serpent god was badly received and fed.

Accidit hoc nuper in Lithwania sex a Vilna miliaribus in pago quodam iuxta civitatem Troki, quod quidam Christianus ab eiusmodi serpentis cultore, aliquot alvearia apum emit, quem cum ad verum Christi cultum multo labore adduxisset, utque serpentem quem colebat occidere persuasisset, aliquanto post, cum ad visendas apes suas eo reversus fuisset, hominem facie deformatum, ore aures tenus, miserabilem in modum diducto offendit, tanti mali causam interrogatus, respondit sequod serpenti deo suo domestico manus nepharias iniecisset ad piaculum expiandum hac calamitate puniri, multoque, graviora si ad priores ritus suos non rediret cum pati oportere. Est etiam quatuor a Vilna miliaribus Lauariiki villa Regia, in qua a multis adhuc serpentes coluntur. Haec quamvis non in Samogitia sed in Lithwania gesta sunt, pro exemplo tamen adduxi.

Agrestis turba in Samogitia Sacrificium quoddam, solennesque epulas gentilium more sub [fol. 61r] finem Mensis Octobris collectis frugibus, quotannis celebrant hoc modo. Ad locum convivio, aepulisque sacris delectum, omnes cum uxoribus, liberis, et servis conveniunt, mensam feno supersternunt, desuper panes apponunt, et ex utraque panis parte duo cervisiae vasa statuunt. Postea adducunt vitulum, porcum et porcam, gallum et gallinam, et caetera domestica iumenta, ex ordine mares et femellas. Haec mactant gentili more ad sacrificandum hoc modo, in primis augur sive incantator quispiam, verba quaedam proferens animal verberare baculo orditur, deinde omnes qui adsunt iumentum per caput pedesque, baculis verbarant, postea tergum, ventrem, et caetera membra concutiunt dicentes, Haec tibi o Ziemiennik deus, (sic enim illum daemonem agrestis turba appellat) offerimus gratiasque tibi agimus, quod nos hoc anno incolumes, et omnibus abundantes, conservare dignatus es, nunc vero te rogamus, ut nos quoque hoc anno praesenti favere, tueri ab igne, ferro, peste, et inimicis quibuslibet, defendere digneris. Postea carnes, iumentorum ad sacrificium mactatorum comedunt, et ab uno quoque ferculo anteque comedant, portiunculam amputant; et in terram omnesque angulos domus proiiciunt dicentes: haec tibi o Ziemiennik nostra holocausta suscipe et comede benignus. Omnesque tunc temporis lautissime solenniter et opipare aepulantur. Hic vero ritus gentilis et in Lituania, Russiaque ab agrestibus, quibusdam in locis observatur.

In a certain locality next to the town of Trakai, six miles from Vilnius, it happened recently that a certain Christian bought a number of beehives from a serpent worshipper, whom he brought to the true faith of Christ with much labour, so that he persuaded him to kill the snake he worshipped. A little while afterwards, when returning to visit his bees, he offended the man with a deformed face (with a mouth as wide as his ears), who was reduced to a miserable state. Having asked him the cause of such a great evil, he replied that he raised wicked violent hands against his domestic serpent god, and was punished in order to expiate the sin; and that he ought to have suffered more and more seriously if he had not returned to his former rites. Four miles from Vilnius is the royal village of Lavoriškės, in which many snakes are still worshipped. Although these things happened not in Samogitia but in Lithuania, I have adduced them as an example.

Every year, the rustic crowd in Samogitia celebrate in this way a certain solemn sacrifice, and solemn feasts in pagan fashion before the end of the month of October when the harvest has been gathered. In the place of the feast, having delighted in sacred banquets, they spread on top of the tables and put bread on them, and from each part of the bread they set two vessels of beer. Afterwards they lead in a calf, a boar and a sow, a cockerel and a hen, and other domestic animals, the males and females each in order. They slaughter these in the pagan fashion in order to sacrifice them in this way: first of all, some augur or enchanter, offering a few words, begins to beat the animal with a staff; afterwards they slice into the back, stomach and other members, saying:

> We offer this to you, o Žemininkas, god! (for thus the rustic crowd calls the demon) and give you thanks, because you have deigned to keep us safe this year, and abundant in all things; now we ask you to favour us also in this present year; and deign to defend us from being killed by fire, violence, plague, and any enemies.

Afterwards they eat the flesh of the animals slaughtered in sacrifice, and before they also eat from a single dish, they cut off a small portion, and throwing it onto the floor and into all of the corners of the house, they say, "Accept this our sacrifice, o Žemininkas, and eat kindly." And then everyone at this time sumptuously, solemnly, and liberally feasts. This pagan rite is observed in both Lithuania and Rus' by the rustics in several places.

LIBELLUS DE SACRIFICIIS ET IDOLATRIA VETERUM BORUSSORUM, LIVONUM, ALIARUMQUE VICINARUM GENTIUM

[p. 177] **Libellus De Sacrificiis Et Idolatria Veterum Borussorum, Livonum, aliarumque vicinarum gentium, Ad Clarissimum Virum Doctorem Georgium Sabinum, Illustrissimi Principis Prussiae etc. Consiliarum, scriptus per Ioannem Maeletium.**

Ista sacerdotis speciem pictura vetusti
Cornigero capro sacrificantis, habet.
Cornua praendebat laeva, dextraque patellam,
Lumine privatus, vel pede claudus erat.
Spicea cingebant pendentes serta capillos:
Non trahat hic surdos in sua vota Deos?

[p. 178] **Ad lectorem.**

Prisca Borussorum fuerat gens inclyta bello
Sed coluit multos impietate Deos.
Quos inter, veluti monstrat brevis iste libellus,
Maxima consuevit sacra litare Capro.
Finis et auspicium quorum completa fuerunt
Pocula, quid faceret plebs temulenta boni?
Hanc extirparunt diuturnis funditus armis
Fratres, qui sancta de cruce nomen habent.
Instaurant nova sacra adytis, placitura Tonanti
Fermento nimium sed scatuere Papae.
Quo pulso rediit verbi lux aedita coelo,
Pro qua grata Deo pectora ferre decet.

[p. 179] Clarissimo Doctissimoque Viro D. Doctori Davidi Voit S. Theologiae in Academia Regiomontana Professori primario etc. Hieronymus Maeletius Illustrissimi Principis Prussiae etc. interpres Polonicus. S[alutem] P[lurimam] D[icit].

LITTLE BOOK ON THE SACRIFICES AND IDOLATRY OF THE OLD PRUSSIANS, LIVONIANS, AND OTHER NEIGHBOURING PEOPLES (1553/1561)

JAN MALECKI and HIERONIM MALECKI[1]

A little book on the sacrifices and idolatry of the Old Prussians, Livonians and other neighbouring peoples, to the most famous man, Dr. George Sabinus, counsellor to the most illustrious Prince of Prussia; written by Jan Malecki

This picture has the image of an ancient priest
sacrificing a horned goat;
with his left hand he grasped the horns, and with his right a dish;
he was deprived of sight, or was lame in his foot;
wreaths of corn adorn his hanging hair;
does this one not summon up deaf gods in his offerings?

To the reader

The ancient people of the Prussians were renowned in war,
but they worshipped many gods in impiety;
and among them, as this little book shows,
the greatest rite is accustomed to be the sacrifice of a goat.
When an end was made, the auspices were complete,
And the cups were full, what good does this drunken people do?
The brothers who have the name of the Holy Cross
eradicated this to the root with long-lasting arms;
they install new rites in the sanctuaries, no longer to please the Thunderer
in their ferment but to pour them forth for the pope.
Having been driven off by the word, light returns from heaven,
for which hearts ought to return thanks to God.

To the most famous and most learned man, Dr. David Voit, foremost professor of sacred theology in the University of Königsberg, etc. Hieronim Malecki, Polish interpreter to the most illustrious prince of Prussia, etc., sends many greetings.

Among the remaining benefits which the eternal God, out of his immense mercy, has heaped up for Prussia and its neighbouring regions, this is the highest and foremost

---

1 This text, which includes Jan Malecki's 1561 verses and letter to David Voit prefacing the work of his father Hieronim Malecki (but not his parallel German version), is based on Hieronim Malecki, *Libellus de sacrificiis et idolatria*, ed. Schmidt-Lötzen, 177–96. This text was based on Hieronim Malecki's letter to George Sabinus, originally published as *De sacrificiis et idolatria veterorum Borussorum, Livonum, et aliarum vicinarum gentium*, ed. Horner (1551).

Inter reliqua beneficia quibus aeternus Deus ex immensa misericordia sua Borussiam et finitimas regiones cumulavit, hoc summum ac praecipuum est, quod etiam ibi lumen verae cognitionis Dei exortum sit. Nam ante haec tempora non tantum tristissimis tenebris impiorum cultuum, quos veteres Borussi, Livones et Sudini suis numinibus exhibuerunt: Verum etiam horrendis Pontificiorum furoribus immersa fuit, quibus homines in tantam confusionem opinionum prolapsi sunt, ut existimarent Deum his qualibuscunque sacrificiis et cultibus audacia rationis humanae introductis propitium et placatum fore. Cum ipsi tamen interea nihil neque de Essentia neque de voluntate Dei tenerent. Non dubium est igitur hoc magnum Prussiae decus et ornamentum esse, quod Deus etiam in ea sibi colligit Ecclesiam a qua in aeternum agnoscatur et glorificetur, et multos ad societatem Ecclesiae vocat, nosque [p. 180] aeternae vitae participes facit. Unde et immensa bonitas et Φιλανθρωπία dei elucet ac conspicitur, quia summa eius et immutabilis voluntas est, ut verbum suum in toto orbe terrarum spargatur, et omnes homines audiant atque agnoscant Filium Mediatorem, quem ipse nobis sua voce divina coelitus emissa commendavit, clamans: Hunc audite.

Quemadmodum autem omnibus temporibus aliquos pios et fideles gubernatores in propaganda verbo suo excitavit. Ita etiam Deus in repurgandis his regionibus ab Idolorum cultibus selegit Illustrissimum Principem Albertum Seniorem primum Borussiae ducem etc. Hic etenim illustratus luce Evangelii accensa a Deo in Germania virtute et efficatia Spiritus Sancti per Reverendum D. Doctorem Lutherum omnes cum Pontificiorum corruptelas atque furores, tum veterum Borussorum idolatrias profligavit et extirpavit, ac verum Dei cultum restituit, concedens in suo Ducatu halcyonia, in quibus laetissima vox Evangelii miseris conscienciis et papistarum traditionibus illaqueatis, annunciaretur. Quin etiam ut nihil deesset, erexit hanc laudabilem Academiam, et docentium et discentium coetus non sine magnis sumptibus in eam convocavit, ut omnibus nodis verbum Dei in Prussia maxime innotesceret et iuvetur in doctrina coelesti educaretur et probe institueretur.

Gratis igitur animis hoc ingens beneficium Dei agnoscamus et Deo vicissim nostram gratitudinem exhibeamus, et ardentibus votis eum precemur, ut nos in vera agnitione sui conservet, nec iterum in tantas tenebras et furores nos coniici patiatur. Agnoscamus etiam magnam gratiam Principi nostro clementissimo referendam esse, qui voluntati Dei obtemperans, veterum Borussorum cultus e medio sustulit atque delevit, et Pontificiorum furores heroicos animo repressit atque funditus extirpavit: huius etiam ministerio intercedente virtute et ope Spiritus Sancti, tota ferme Sarmatia repudiatis Pontificiorum dogmatibus ad veram Dei agnitionem perducta est, quam ut Deus penitus ad societatem ecclesiae vocet atque pertrahat ipsum toto pectore precor atque oro.

of them, that even here the light of true knowledge of God has come forth. For before these times it was in the saddest shadows of impious cults, which the Old Prussians, Livonians, and Sudovians exhibited for their deities. Then it was submerged in the horrible furies of the popes, from which men fell into such confusion of opinions that they considered that God might be placated and propitiated by whatever sacrifices and rites were brought in by the audacity of human invention. Then, however, they meanwhile understood nothing either of the being nor of the will of God. There is no doubt, therefore, that it is the great honour and adornment of Prussia that God gathered his church even in her, by which he is acknowledged and glorified forever. He calls many to the society of the church, and makes us participants in eternal life. From this, the immense goodness and love for humankind shines forth and is seen, since his supreme and immutable will is that his word should be dispersed throughout the whole world, and that all men should hear and acknowledge his Son, the mediator, whom he himself commends to us in his divine voice sent from heaven, crying: "Listen to him."

But to this end, in all ages he has raised up pious and faithful governors to propagate his word. Thus God, in cleansing these regions from cults of idols, chose the most illustrious prince Albert the Old, the first duke of Prussia, etc.[2] This man, illuminated by the light of the Gospel, and set alight by God in Germany by the virtue and efficacy of the Holy Spirit, by the reverend Dr. Martin Luther, overthrew and eradicated all the corruptions and furies of the popes, and then the idolatrous practices of the Old Prussians, and restored the true worship of God. He granted in his duchy a peaceful place in which the most joyful voice of the Gospel might be announced to those trapped in miserable consciences and popish traditions. Therefore, so that nothing would be lacking, he founded this praiseworthy academy,[3] and called together a gathering of learners and the learned (not without great beneficence), so that in Prussia the word of God might be greatly renowned in every corner, and so that Prussia might be assisted, brought up and rightly etablished in heavenly doctrine.

Therefore, let us acknowledge with grateful souls this huge benefit of God, and let us show our gratitude once again to God; let us supplicate him with ardent vows, so that he may preserve us in the true confession, and that we may not be suffered to be cast again into such shadows and tumults. Let us also acknowledge that great thanks should be rendered to our most merciful prince who, submitting to the will of God, removed and eradicated the cult from the midst of the Old Prussians, and with a heroic spirit repressed the furies of the popes and cut them down to the ground. By his efforts, assisted by virtue and the work of the Holy Spirit, almost the whole of Sarmatia was brought to confession of the true God, having repudiated the dogmas of the popes—so that I pray and beseech God to call and draw him fully to the society of the church.[4]

---

2 Albert, duke of Prussia (1490–1568), the last Grand Master of the Teutonic Knights who converted to Lutheranism and became the first secular ruler of German Prussia.

3 The University of Königsberg (the Albertina), founded by Duke Albert of Prussia in 1544.

4 Malecki here implies that Duke Albert himself, in spite of spreading the Lutheran faith, was not himself an orthodox Lutheran. This is probably an allusion to Duke Albert's support for the theologians Andreas Osiander (1498–1552) and Johann Funck (1518–1566), who advocated a theology of justification that differed from Luther's.

Valde autem prodest videre ritus ceremoniarum et sacrificiorum quibus veteres Borussi, Livones et Sudini usi sunt. Ex illis enim agnoscimus in quantis tenebris homines non illuminati luce Evangelii versentur, quibus sane et nos adhuc obrueremur, nisi a Deo inde erepti fuissemus. Proinde ex cognitione horum sacrificiorum intellegimus etiam, quod Deo gratias maximas, ut dixi, pro tantis suis beneficiis nobis exhibitis agere debeamus, quod nos ex tam tetris idolatricorum cultuum confusionibus liberavit et Evangelii sui luce illustraverit.

[p. 182] Quapropter parens meus pastor et Archipresbyter ecclesiae Liccensis (qui fuit apud quosdam eiusmodi homines idolatricos et eorum rituum ac sacrificiorum spectator fuit, ante annos ab hinc decem) libellum de veterum Borussorum sacrificiis conscripsit, quem ad Clarissimum Virum Doctorem Georgium Sabinum misit, cuius authoritate in publicum exire dignus visus est. Quem ego in nonnullis locis nunc emendavi et auxi, et propter rationes paulo ante recitatas quae mihi quidem videntur esse probabiles typis vicissim excudi curavi. Ideo autem ornatissime Vir, eum sub tui nominis auspiciis edidi, quod intelligam te veterum historiarum lectione plurimum delectari, deinde ut studiosis adulescentibus tanto gratior et commendatior esset: et ipsi tua authoritate adducti agnoscerent bonitatem Dei, qui illos ex tam horrendis tenebris [p. 183] subducit et liberavit, quibus maiores nostri fuerunt oppressi, et mentes suas ad gratiarum actionem pro restituta hac Evangelii luce exuscitarent, et post emendationem vitae suae ad conservandum praeclarum hoc depositum flecterentur, ne ex hac luce prolapsi in deteriores tenebras immergerentur. Denique ut publicum animi mei erga te benevolentiae testimonium aederem, quod alia ratione quam hac praestare non potui. Quare omnibus modis te peto Vir ornatissime et omni observantia mihi colendissime, ut hunc conatum et voluntatem meam boni consulas, et munusculum hoc quantum vis exiguum aequo et prompto animo suscipias. Me tibi vicissim totum defero et dedico. His faeliciter in Christo vale, meque tibi commendatum habe. Regiomonti die 8 Iulii Anno 1563.

[p. 184] **De Sacrificiis et Idolatria veterum Borussorum Livonum aliarumque vicinarum gentium. Ad clarissimum virum Doctorem Georgium Sabinum Illustris[imo] Ducis Prussiae Consiliarum. Ioannes Maeletius.**

Cum elegiam illam tuam, quam ad Petrum Bembum cardinalem scripsisti mihi legendam, exhibuisset Hieronymus filius meus, qui tuis scriptis plurimum delectari solet, in qua de sacrificio capri et anguium cultu, quae nonnullae Sarmaticae gentes faciunt, commemoras: continere me non potui, quin ea quae de vano cultu earum gentium comperi, ad te scriberem, tibi utique non ingratum fore sperans, si earum [p. 185] gentium ad quas fato quodam vocatus es, et in quarum vicinia vitam agis, mores et idolatriam plenius cognosceres.

But it is of great benefit to see the rites of the ceremonies and sacrifices which the Old Prussians, Livonians, and Sudovians were accustomed to use. For from them we understand how much darkness people dwell in who are not illuminated by the light of the Gospel—by which we would surely have been covered, unless we had been snatched from it by God. So, then, from understanding these sacrifices we may also understand that we ought to give the greatest thanks to God, as I have said, for such great benefits shown to us, which freed us from the confusions of such foul cults of idolatry and illuminated us with the light of his Gospel.

Since my father, a pastor and the archpriest of the church of Lyck (who lived among certain idolatrous men of this kind and was a spectator of their rites and sacrifices) wrote a little book about the sacrifices of the Old Prussians, which he sent to the most celebrated man George Sabinus, it seemed worthy for it to be issued in public by his authority. I have improved and added to it in many places, and on account of the reasons related a little earlier, which seem to me to be necessary, I have taken care that it should be printed again. But therefore, most honorable man, he under whose auspices I have edited it in your name, because I understand that you delight greatly in reading old histories, it is so much more welcome and commendable to studious young people. And they themselves, having been brought under your authority, may acknowledge the goodness of God, who led them out and freed them from such horrible shadows by which our ancestors were oppressed; and let them rouse up their minds to give thanks for this restored light of the Gospel; and after amending their lives to safeguard this famous deposit, let them be persuaded—lest falling from this light they should be submerged in worse shadows.

Therefore, so that I might set up a public testament to your benevolence to my soul— for I can set this forth for no other reason than this—I therefore beseech you in every way, most honorable man, and most cherished in all my sight, that you would judge this will and effort of mine to be good, and that you would receive this meagre little gift as much as you wish, with a calm and eager spirit. Once again, I dedicate and submit myself completely to you. Farewell happily in Christ, and have my commendation to you! At Königsberg, July 8, 1563.

On the sacrifices and idolatry of the Old Prussians, Livonians, and other neighbouring peoples. To the most famous man Dr. George Sabinus, one of the counsellors of the Duke of Prussia. Jan Malecki.

Since I wrote that elegy of yours, which you wrote to Cardinal Pietro Bembo so that I might read it, my son Hieronim had it published, who is accustomed to be greatly delighted by your writings, in which you recall the sacrifice of the goat or snake (which many of the Sarmatians perform), I have not been able to contain myself. Therefore, I wrote to you what I have learnt about the vain worship of these people, hoping you would not be ungrateful to understand more fully the customs and idolatry of those peoples to whom you were once called by fate, and in whose vicinity you lead your life. For many superstitious rites and idolatrous cults are still secretly preserved in these regions, which perhaps were unknown to you upon your arrival. Therefore it seemed right for me to share with you what I have learnt about them; and, so that I may no

Multi enim superstitiosi ritus, idolatricique cultis passim in his regionibus adhuc occulte servantur, qui tibi advenae nondum forte cogniti sunt. Itaque visum est communicare tecum, quicquid de illis compertum habeo: Ac ne longiore utar prooemio, referam primo sacrificia, quibus olim Borussae, Samogitae, Lituani, Ruteni et Livones, coluerunt daemonia pro diis, atque etiam nunc multis in locis colunt occulte: deinde superstitiosos quosdam ritus, quibus nuptiae, funera et parentalia, apud easdem gentes celebrantur.

Die Georgii sacrificium facere solent Pergrubio, qui florum, plantarum, omniumque germinum Deus creditur. Huic Pergrubio sacrificant hoc modo. Sacrificulus, quem Vurschayten appellant, tenet dextra obbam cerevisiae plenam, invocatoque daemonii nomine, decantat illius laudes:

> Tu (inquit) abigis hyemen, tu reducis amoenitatem veris: per te agri et horti virent, per te nemora et sylve frondent.

Hac cantilena finita, dentibus apprehendens obbam, ebibit cerevisiam nulla adhibita manu: [p. 186] ipsamque obbam ita mordicus epotam, retro supra caput iacit. Quae cum e terra sublata iterumque impleta est, omnes quotquot adsunt ex ea bibunt ordine, atque in laudem Pergrubii hymnum canunt. Postea epulantur tota die, et choreas ducunt.

Similiter quando iam segetes sunt maturae, rustici in agris ad sacrificium congregantur, quod lingua Rutenica Zazinek vocatur, id est, initium messis. Hoc sacro peracto, unus e multitudine electus, messem auspicatur, manipulo demesso quem domum adfert. Postridie omnes, primo illius domestici, deinde caeteri qui volunt, messem faciunt.

Facta autem messe, sollenne sacrificium pro gratiarum actione conficiunt, quod Rutenica lingua Ozinek, id est, consummatio messis dicitur, in hoc sacrificio, Sudini Borussiae populi, apud quos succinum colligitur, capro litant, sicut in elegia tua ad Bembum scribis. Litandi vero ritus est talis. Congregato populi coetu in horreo, adducitur caper, quem Vurschaytes illorum sacrificulus mactaturus, imponit victimae utramque manum, invocatque ordine daemones, quos ipsi Deos esse credunt: videlicet, [p. 187] Occopirnum, deum coeli et terrae:

> Antrimpum, deum maris:
> Gardoaeten, deum nautarum, qualis olim apud Romanos fuit Portunnus:
> Potrympum, deum fluviorum ac fontium:
> Piluitum, deum divitiarum, quem latini Plutum vocant:
> Pergrubium, deum veris:
> Pargnum, deum tonitruum ac tempestatum:
> Pocclum, deum inferni et tenebrarum:
> Poccollum, deum aëriorum spirituum:
> Putscaetum, deum qui sacros lucos tuetur:

further prolong the prologue, I will first mention the sacrifices by which at one time the Prussians, Samogitians, Lithuanians, Ruthenians, and Livonians used to worship demons as gods—and even secretly worship today in many places; then certain superstitious rites with which weddings, funerals and the commemoration of ancestors[5] are celebrated among these same peoples.

On St. George's Day they are accustomed to sacrifice to Pergrubris, who is believed to be the god of flowers, plants, and all growing things. To this Pergrubris they sacrifice in this way. The priestling,[6] whom they call *Viršaitis*,[7] holds in his right hand a beaker full of beer, and having invoked the name of the demon, he chants these praises of him: "You drive off the winter," he says, "you bring back the comfort of spring; by you the fields and gardens flourish, by you the groves and woods come into leaf."

Having finished this little chant, gripping the beaker with his teeth, he drinks the beer, with no use of hands allowed, and having gnawed it, he throws the same emptied beaker back over his head. When it has been picked up from the ground and filled again, everyone present drinks from it in order, and sings a hymn in praise of Pergrubris. Afterwards they feast for the whole day, and take part in dances.

Similarly, when the crops are ready, the country people gather in the fields for the sacrifice which in the Ruthenian language is called *Zazinek*—that is, the beginning of harvest. When this rite has been performed, one chosen from the multitude divines the harvest from a cut handful which he takes home. The next day everyone—first those of that household, and then others who want to—gathers the harvest.

When the harvest has been gathered in they perform a solemn sacrifice as an act of thanksgiving, which in the Ruthenian language is called *Ozinek* (that is, the end of harvest). In this sacrifice the Sudovians (a people of Prussia), among whom sap is collected, perform divination from the sacrifice of a goat (as you write in your elegy to Bembo). The rite of sacrifice is thus: with the congress of people gathered in a granary, the goat is led in whom the *Viršaitis*, their priestling, is about to slaughter. He places each hand on the victim, and invokes in order the demons whom they believe to be gods, that is to say:

Antrimpas, the god of the sea:
Gardaitis, the god of sailors, such as Portunus
     once was among the Romans:
Patrimpas, the god of rivers and springs
Pilvytis, the god of riches, whom the Latins call Pluto;
Pergrubris, the god of spring;
Perkūnas, the god of thunders and storms;
Poklius, the god of hell and shadows;
Pokulas, the god of the spirits of the air;

5 Malecki here seems to use the pagan Roman term *parentalia* (the festival of honouring the ancestors) in a generic sense to refer to any rite of commemorating ancestors.

6 The word *sacrificulus* literally means "little priest."

7 For a thorough discussion of the origin and meaning of this title, which has many variations in the Baltic languages, see Kregždys, "On the Origin of the Mythonyms."

Auscautum, deum incolumitatis et aegritudinis:
Marcoppolum, deum magnatum et nobilium:
Barstuccas, quos Germani Erdmenlein hoc est, subterraneos vocant.

His daemonibus invocatis quotquot adsunt in horreo, omnes simul extollunt caprum, sublimemque tenant donec canatur hymnus: quo finito, rursus demittunt ac sistunt caprum in terram, Tum sacrificulus admonet populum, ut solenne hoc sacrificium a maioribus pie institutum, summa cum veneratione faciant, eiusque memoriam religiose ad posteros conservent. Hac conciuncula ad populum habita, ipse mactat victimam, [p. 188] sanguinemque patina exceptum dispergit. Carnem vero tradit mulieribus eodem in horreo coquendam. Hae interea dum caro coquitur, parant e farina siliginea placentas quas non imponunt in furnum, sed viri focum circumstantes, hinc illinc per ignem iaciunt absque cessatione, tamdiu quoad illae indurescant, et coquantur. His peractis, epulantur atque helluantur tota die ac nocte usque ad vomitum. Ebrii deinde summo mane extra villam progrediuntur, ubi reliquias epularum, quae remanserunt, certo in loco terra operiunt ne vel a volatilibus vel a feris diripiantur, Postea dimisso coetu suam quisque domum repetit.

Caeterum, ex omnibus Sarmatiae gentibus nominatis, multi adhuc singulari veneration colunt Putscaetum, qui sacris arboribus et lucis praeest. Is sub arbore Sambuco domicilium habere creditur. Huic passim homines supersticiosi litant pane, cerevisia, aliisque cibus sub arbore Sambuco positis, precantes a Putscaeto, ut placatum efficiat Marcoppolum deum magnatum et nobilium, ne graviore servitute a dominis ipsi premantur: utque sibi mittantur Barstuccae, qui (ut supra dictum est) subterranei vocantur. His enim daemonibus in domo versantibus se fieri credunt fortunatiores: eisque collocant vesperi in horreo super mensam, mappa stratam, panes, caseos butyrum, et cerevisiam: nec dubitant de fortunarum accessione, si mane reperiant cibos illic absumptos. Et si quando intactus cibus in mensa remanet, [p. 189] tunc magna anguntur cura, nihil non adversi metuentes.

Eaesdem gentes colunt spiritus quosdam visibiles, qui lingua Rutenica Coltky, Graeca Cobili, Germanica Coboldi, vocantur. His spiritus credunt habitare, in occultis aedium locis vel in congerie lignorum: nutriuntque eos laute omni ciborum genere, eo quod afferre soleant nutritoribus suis frumentum ex alienis horreis furto ablatum.

Cum vero hi spiritus alicubi habitare ac nutriri cupiunt, hoc modo suam erga patrem familias voluntatem declarant. In domo congerunt noctu segmenta lignorum, et mulctris lacte plenis imponunt varia animalium stercora. Quod ubi paterfamilias animadverterit, nec dissipaverit segmenta, nec stercora e mulctris eiecerit, sed de inquinato lacte cum omni familia sua comederit, tunc illi apparere et permanere dicuntur.

> Puškaitis,[8] the god who guards the sacred groves;
> Aušautas the god of health and illness;
> Markopolas, the god of magnates and nobles;
> The Barstukai, whom the Germans call *Erdmenlein*
> (that is to say, dwellers under the earth).

Having invoked these, as many as are present in the granary lift up the goat at the same time, and hold it aloft while a hymn is sung. When this is finished they put it down again on the ground. Then the priestling admonishes the people that they should perform the solemn sacrifice devoutly instituted by their ancestors with the utmost veneration, and preserve the memory religiously for posterity. After this brief harangue, he himself slaughters the victim, and having caught the blood in a dish scatters it. He gives the flesh to the women to be cooked in that same granary. In the meantime, while the flesh is cooked, they prepare pancakes of wheat. They do not put these in an oven, but the men, standing around fires, throw them here and there through the fire without stopping, until they harden and are cooked. Having done these things, they feast and overindulge all day and all night, to the point of vomiting. Then, on the last morning, they process outside the village. Here, in a certain place, they bury the remains of the feast in the ground lest it be taken away by birds or by wild animals. Afterwards, having been dismissed from the gathering, each returns to his house.

Of the other named peoples of Sarmatia, many still worship Puškaitis with singular veneration, who is in charge of sacred trees and groves. He is believed to have his dwelling beneath the elder. Everywhere people offer him sacrifice, putting bread, beer, and other foods beneath the elder tree, praying to Puškaitis to placate Markopolas, the god of magnates and nobles, lest they should be oppressed by heavy servitude to their masters; so that the Barstukai are sent from him, who (as was said above) are called earth-dwellers. With these demons living in their houses, they believe they become more fortunate. For these they put out bread, cheese, butter, and beer in the evening on a table draped with a cloth. And they do not doubt the arrival of good fortune if, in the morning, they discover the food consumed. But if any food remains untouched on the table, they are greatly troubled with anxiety, perceiving nothing as not unlucky.

The same peoples worship certain visible spirits who are called *kobaldy* in the Ruthenian language, *kobaloi* in Greek, and *Kobolde* in German. They believe these spirits live in hidden places of buildings, or in the crossing of beams. And they feed them sumptuously with all kinds of food, so much so that they are accustomed to bring grain to their nourishers, stolen by theft from other granaries.

When these spirits wish to live and be fed elsewhere, they declare their will to the head of the family in this way; they gather pieces of beams in the house at night, and put the dung of various animals in pails full of milk. When the head of the family notices this, he will neither break up the pieces, nor empty the dung from the milk pails, but will drink the contaminated milk with all his family; then [the Barstukai] are said to appear and remain.

---

8 The Lithuanian version of this theonym was reconstructed by Greimas, *Of Gods and Men*, 22–23.

Praeterea Lituani et Samogitae in domibus sub fornace, vel in angulo vaporarii ubi [p. 190] mensa stat, serpentes fovent, quos numinis instar colentes, certo anni tempore precibus sacrificuli evocant ad mensam. He vero exeuntes, per mundum linteolum conscendunt, et super mensam assident: Ubi postquam singula fercula delibarunt, rursus discedunt, seque abdunt in cavernis. Serpentibus digressis, homines laeti fercula illa praegustata comedunt, ac sperant illo anno omnia prospere sibi eventura. Quod si ad preces sacrificuli non exierint serpentes, aut fercula super mensam posita non delibaverint, tum credunt se anno illo subitures magnam calamitatem.

Adhaec eaedem gentes habent inter se sortilegos, qui lingua Rutenica Burty vocantur, qui Potrympum invocantes, caeram in aquam fundunt, atque ex signis sive imaginibus inter fundendum figuratis, pronunciant ac vaticinantur de quibuscunque rebus interrogati fuerint.

Novi ipse mulierculam, quae eum diu reditum absentis filii frustra expectasset: Erat enim filius ex Borussia in Daniam profectus: consulit sortilegum a que edocta est, illum naufragio periisse. Caera enim in [p. 191] aquam fusa, expressit formam fractae navis, et effigiem resupini hominis, iuxta navim fluitantis.

Apud Samogitas est mons ad fluvium Neuuassam situs, in cuius vertice olim perpetuus ignis a sacerdote conservabatur in honore ipsius Pargni qui tonitruum et tempestatum potens a supersticiosa gente adhuc creditur.

Hactenus de sacrificiis: nunc de ritibus nuptiarum, funerum, et parentalium, narrabo non minus ridicula quam supersticiosa.

Apud Sudinos, Curonenses, Samogitas, et Lituanos nubiles puellae multis in locis gestant tintinabulum, quod funiculo alligatum e cingulo dependet usque ad genum: nec ducuntur sed rapiuntur in matrimonium veteri Lacedemoniorum more a Lycurgo instituto. Rapiuntur autem non an ipso sponso, sed a duobus sponsi cognatis. Ac postquam raptae sunt, tunc primum requisito parentum consensu, matrimonium contrahitur.

Cum nuptiae iam celebrantur, sponsa ducitur ter circa focum. Deinde in sellam ibi [p. 192] collocatur. Sedenti super sellam pedes lavantur. Ea vero aqua, qua sponsae lavantur pedes, conspergitur lectus nuptialis ac tota suppellex domestica. Consperguntur item hospites, qui ad nuptias invitati sunt. Postea sponsae os oblinitur melle, et oculi teguntur velamine, velatis oculis ipsa ducitur ad omnes aedium fores, quas iubetur contingere ac pulsare dextro pede. Ad singulas fores circumspergitur tritico, siligine, avena, hordeo, pisis fabis et papavere.

Furthermore, the Lithuanians and Samogitians keep snakes warm underneath the stove, or in the chimney[9] corner where the table stands. At a certain time of year the priestlings, worshipping them as the image of a deity, call them by prayers to the table. Coming by a clean linen cloth they crawl up, and remain on the table. Having tried several dishes, they depart again, and likewise hide themselves in caves. When the snakes have gone, the people joyfully eat the pre-tasted dishes, and hope that everything will turn out prosperously that year. But if the snakes do not come out at the prayers of the priestlings, or they do not taste the dishes that have been put out, they believe a great calamity will befall them that year.

And those same people have sorcerers still among them who are called *burti[ninkai]* in the Ruthenian[10] language. These people, invoking Potrimpus, pour wax into water, and expound and divine from the images made during the pouring on whatever matters they are asked about.

I myself knew a little woman who had long awaited the return of her absent son who had set out from Prussia to Denmark. She consulted a sorcerer about him, from whom she learnt that he had perished in a shipwreck. For the wax, poured into the water, took the form of a broken ship, with the effigy of a man lying on his back floating next to the ship.

Among the Samogitians there is a hill situated by the River Nevėžis, on whose summit at one time a perpetual fire was kept burning by a priest in honour of the same Perkūnas, who is still believed by this superstitious people to be powerful in thunder and tempests.[11]

So much for sacrifices. Now I will tell about nuptial and funerary rites, which are no less ridiculous than they are superstitious.

Among the Sudovians, Couronians, Samogitians, and Lithuanians young women of marriageable age wear a bell in many places. Tied to a cord, it hangs from her girdle to her knees. And they are not taken in marriage but carried off, after the ancient Spartan fashion instituted by Lycurgus. But they are not carried off by the groom himself, but by two of his relatives. And after they are carried off, then the parents' consent is first sought, and a marriage is contracted.

When marriages are celebrated the bride is led three times around the hearth; then she is set in a seat there. As she sits on it her feet are washed. And the nuptial bed and all the household goods are sprinkled with the water with which her feet are washed. Similarly, the guests invited to the wedding are sprinkled. Afterwards the bride's mouth is smeared with honey and her eyes covered with a veil. Thus veiled, she is led to all the doors of the building and ordered to touch and kick them with her right foot. At each door corn, wheat, reeds, barley, peas, beans, and poppy seeds are sprinkled.

---

9 *Vaporarium* usually means "steam pipe," but the context here (the interior of a humble Samogitian hut) makes "chimney" more likely.

10 *Burtininkai* is a Lithuanian, not a Ruthenian/Belarusian word.

11 Długosz mentions this hill near the River Nevėžis (perhaps Burveliai or Burve) but says that the fire itself was worshipped as a god, rather than being lit in honour of any deity.

Qui enim sequitur sponsam, gestat saccum plenum omni genere frugum: cumque illam circumspergit, ait, nihil horum defuturum sponsae, si religionem pie coluerit, remque domesticam curaverit ea diligentia, qua debet. His actis aufertur sponsae velamen ab oculis, et convivium celebrantur. Vesperi cum sponsa ad lectum deducenda est, inter saltandum ei abscinduntur crines: quibus abscissis mulieres imponunt ei sertum niveo linteolo adornatum, quod uxoribus gestare licet donec filium filium pepererint. Tam diu enim uxores pro virginibus se gerunt. Ad extremum introducitur in cubiculum, ubi pulsata et verberata coniicitur in lectum sponsoque traditur. Tum pro bellariis afferuntur testiculi caprini, vel ursini, quibus ipso nuptiarum die commanducatis coniuges creduntur fieri foecundi. Hac de causa, nullum quoque animal castratum illic ad nuptias mactatur.

In funeribus hic servatur [p. 193] ritus a rusticanis. Defunctorum cadavera vestibus et calceis induuntur et erecta locantur super sellam, cui assidentes illorum propinqui, perpotant ac helluantur. Epota cerevisia fit lamentatio funebris, que in lingua Rutenica sic sonat:

> *Hà lele, lele, y proez ty mene umárl? y za ty nie miel szto yesty, albo pity? y procz ty umârl? Há lele, lele, y za ty nie miel krasnoye mlodzice? y procz ty umarl?*

Id est,

> Hei, hei mihi: Quare mortuus es? Num tibi deerat esca aut potus? Quare ergo mortuus es? Hei, hei mihi: An non habuisti formosam coniugem? Quare ergo mortuus es? etc.

Hoc modo lamentantes enumerant ordine omnia externa illius bona, cuius mortem deplorant: nempe, liberos, oves, boves, equos anseres, gallinas etc. Ad quae singula respondentes, occinunt hanc Naeniam, cur ergo mortuus es, qui haec habebas?

Post lamentationem dantur cadaveri munuscula, nempe mulieri fila cum acu: viro linteolum, idque eius collo implicatur. Cum ad sepulturam effertur cadaver, plerique in equis funus prosequuntur, et currum obequitant quo cadaver vehitur: eductisque gladiis verberant auras, vociferantes

> *Geygethe begaythe peckelle,*

id est,

> aufugite vos daemones in infernum.

For one who follows the bride carries a sack full of all kinds of grain, and as she[12] thus sprinkles them, she says there will be nothing wanting for the bride if she cultivates religion and carries out all her domestic duties as she should.

When these things have been done the bride's veil is lifted from her eyes and a feast is celebrated. In the evening, when the bride must be led to the bed, her hair is let down amid dancing; when it has been cut, the women place on her a scarf made of folded, decorated white linen, which wives are permitted to wear until they bear a son. Until then they bear themselves as if virgins. At last she is led into the bedroom, and after being pushed and pummelled she is thrown into bed and given to her husband. Then the testicles of a goat or bear are brought as sweetmeats; these, they believe, if eaten on the day of marriage, make the spouses fertile. For the same reason no castrated animal is slaughtered at the feast.

By contrast, at funerals this serves as a rite for the country people: for the bodies of the dead are dressed in clothes and shoes, and placed upright in chairs, and their relatives drink and make merry with them, sitting down. When the beer has been drunk, there is a funeral lamentation, which in the Ruthenian language sounds like this:

> *Hà lele, lele, y proez ty mene umárl? y za ty nie miel szto yesty, albo pity? y procz ty umârl? Há lele, lele, y za ty nie miel krasnoye mlodzice? y procz ty umarl?*

That is,

> Alas, alas, why are you dead to me? Did you not have food to eat or drink to drink? Why, therefore, are you dead? Alas, alas for me; did you not have a handsome wife? Why, therefore, are you dead? Etc.

Lamenting in this way, they enumerate in order all of the external goods of the one whose death they bemoan: children, sheep, cattle, horses, geese, chickens, etc. And each replying to this, they chant this dirge: "Why are you dead, who had all of this?'

After the lamentation little gifts are given to the body: to a woman, a needle and thread; to a man, a strip of linen with which his neck is wrapped. When the body is being borne to the tomb, many horses follow the funeral procession and ride up to the cart on which the body is carried. With drawn swords they beat the air, shouting:

> *Geygethe begaythe peckelle!*

That is:

> Flee, you demons, to hell!

---

12 The Latin does not make clear the gender of the person entrusted with sprinkling produce around the bride, but it is likely that a woman conducted this pre-nuptial rite so closely associated with the household sphere.

[p. 194] Qui funus mortuo faciunt, nummos proiiciunt in sepulchrum, tanquam viatico mortuum prosequentes. Collocant quoque panem, et lagenam cerevisiae plenam ad caput cadaveris in sepulchrum illati, ne anima vel siciat vel esuriat. Uxor mane et vesperi, oriente et occidente Sole super extincti coniugis sepulchrum sedens vel iacens lamentatur diebus triginta. Consignati vero ineunt convivia die tertio, sexto, nono, et quadrigesimo a funere. Ad quae convivia animam defuncti invitant precantes ante ianuam. In his conviviis quibus mortuo parentant, tacite assident mensae tanquam muti nec utuntur cultris. Ad mensam vero ministrant duae mulieres, quae hospitibus cibum apponunt, nullo etiam cultello utentes. Singuli de unoquoque ferculo aliquid sub mensam iaciunt, quo animam pasci credunt, eique potum effundunt. Si quod [p. 195] forte deciderit de mensa in terram id non tollunt sed desertis (ut ipsi loquuntur) animis relinquunt manducandum, quae nullos habent vel cognatos vel amicos viventes, a quibus excipiantur convivio. Peracto prandio sacrificulus surgit de mensa, ac scopis domum purgat: animasque mortuorum cum pulvere eiicit, tanquam pulices: atque his precatur verbis, ut e domo recedant,

Jely, pily, duszyce: nu wen, nu wen:

hoc est,

edistis ac bibistis animae dilectae, ite foras, ite foras.

Post haec incipiunt convivae inter se colloqui et certare poculis. Mulieres viris praebibunt, et viri vicissim mulieribus, seque mutuo osculantur.

De hac oblatione ciborum super tumulos defunctorum, meminit etiam Augustinus Sermone 15 de Sanctis, cuius verba haec sunt: Miror cur apud quosdam infideles hodie tam perniciosus error increverit, ut super tumulos defunctorum cibus et vina conferant, quasi egressae de corporibus animae, carnales cibos requirant. Epulas enim et refectiones caro tantum requirit: Spiritus autem et anima iis non indigent. Parare [p. 196] aliquis suis charis dicit, quod ipse devorat, quod praestat ventri imputat pietati etc. Hactenus Augustinus.

Haec, quae de supersticiosis ritibus, et ceremoniis illarum gentium narravi. partim ipse vidi, partim ab hominibus fide dignis audivi. Tu vero Sabine praestantissimae, qui variarum rerum cognitione delectari solitus es, pro ea qua excellis humanitate, meum hoc qualecunque scriptum ab homine tui amantissimo profectum, boni consulas oro.

Finis.

When they perform the funeral rites for the dead, they throw coins into the tomb, as if going with the dead person as provision for the journey. And they also put bread and a bottle full of beer in the tomb, laid at the head of the body—lest their soul should either be hungry or thirsty. The wife, sitting or lying on the tomb of her dead husband from sunrise to sunset, laments for thirty days. The relatives celebrate feasts on the third, sixth, ninth, and fortieth days after the funeral. To these feasts they invite the soul of the deceased, praying before the doorway. In these feasts in which they honour the dead, they sit down in silence at the table like mutes, and do not use knives. Two women serve at the table, who put the food before the guests, using no knife at all. Each one of them abandons a dish under the table, from which they believe the soul feeds, and they pour out drink for it. If anything should happen to fall to the floor from the table they do not pick it up; but they say that they leave it to be eaten by the lonely souls (as they say) who have neither relatives nor friends alive, for whom it is taken from the feast. When the meal is finished, the priestling rises from the table and, sweeping the house with brooms, ejects the souls of the dead with the dust like fleas: and utters these words, as if they leave the house:

> *Jely, pily, duszyce: nu wen, nu wen!*

That is,

> You have eaten, you have drunk, beloved souls; go outside! Go outside!

Afterwards the dinner guests begin to talk among themselves and compete in drinking.[13] The women outdrink the men, and the men are kissed again and again by the women, and by one another. Even Augustine, in his Sermon 15 on the saints, recalls this offering of food on the tombs of the dead:

> I marvel how among certain unbelievers such a pernicious error has grown, that they bestow food and wine on the tombs of the dead. As if, once souls have left the body, they require fleshly food. For the soul and spirit do not need feasts and refreshment, even though flesh requires it. Someone says he prepares edible roots for them, which he himself devours. That which supplies the stomach, he imputes to piety.[14]

Thus far Augustine.

I have narrated these things about the superstitious rites and ceremonies of those peoples. Some of this I have seen; some I have heard from men worthy of belief. I pray, most outstanding Sabinus, you who are accustomed to delight in understanding varied matters—on account of which you excel in humanity—that you would consult this writing of mine well, sent forth by a man who so dearly loves you.

The end.

---

13 Literally "compete with cups."

14 The quotation is, in fact, from Augustine's Sermon 190 (Augustine, *Sermones*, in *Opera omnia* 5, part 2, ed. Migne, Patrologia Latina 39, col. 2101).

DE DIIS SAMAGITARUM CAETERORUMQUE SARMATARUM, ET FALSORUM CHRISTIANORUM

p. 42 Amplitudo regni Polonici.

Samagitia mare attingit Balticum: cuius figura triangularis est. Longitudo septuaginta milliarum Germanicarum hanc separant fluvii: a Prussia Nemel, ab Curlandia regione Livonica, Helingegau. quae provincie, aliaeque usque ad Borysthenum, in Pontum Euxinum illabentem, regis Polonie imperium agnoscunt. In ea regionis silvosae parte, quae ad Regiomontanum, Academia, anno Christi 1544. 17. Augusti instituta, plurimum claret. Sunt antiqui Borussi: lingua, moribus ab iis diversi Germanis, qui hodie permisti Polonis, Prussiam incolunt.

Origo Samagitarum.

Tradunt veteres, maiores Samagitarum, (Zamagitis enim se ipsi vocant) Italos fuisse. Neronem Imperatorem de bellica expeditione cogitantem, illos etiam exsules Romanos, qui in Giaros sterili quadam insula habitabant, evocare in militiam voluisse. Verum hos metu crudelitatis imperatoriae conscensis eorum a quibus bis terue evocabantur navibus, ipsismet autem caesis, **p. 43** ad Pontum Euxinum appulisse.

Mare Varetzgoie.

Dehinc per saltus, ubi olim Romana venatio fuit, quique hodie magna ex parte excisi iam, Russiae, Podoliae, Lithuaniaeque cognomina habent, usque ad mare Balticum, quod Russi, a Varetzgois quibusdam populis Livonicis, quibus tum parebant, mare Varetzgoie appellant, penetrasse. rei huius ut idolatriam, gentisque calliditatem, Romanae similem: ita sermonem ex Latino quodammodo, barbaroque conflatum, indicium esse.

ON THE GODS OF THE SAMOGITIANS, OF THE OTHER SARMATIANS, AND OF THE FALSE CHRISTIANS (1582)

JAN ŁASICKI[1]

The size of the Polish kingdom

Samogitia borders on the Baltic Sea; its shape is triangular. Rivers separate it, a length of seventy German miles: the Nemunas separates it from Prussia; the Šventoji from the Courland region of Livonia. These provinces, and others up to the River Dnieper (which flows into the Black Sea), acknowledge the rule of the king of Poland. It is well known to many that the University of Königsberg was inaugurated on August 17, 1544 in a forested part of the region. Here are the Old Prussians—distinct in language and customs from the Germans, who today live mixed with the Poles.

The origin of the Samogitians

The old authors report that the ancestors of the Samogitians (who call themselves *Žemaičiai*) were Italians. The Emperor Nero, contemplating a warlike expedition, wanted to call into military service those Roman exiles who were living on a certain barren island of Gyaros.[2] Embarking on account of fear of the emperor's cruelty, they were summoned with two or three ships; but when the same had been broken up [by a storm], they came ashore on the Black Sea.

The Varangian Sea

From there, by a leap they penetrated [the interior], when one day there was a Roman hunt; they are today to a great degree cut off from one another and now have the names of Rus'ians, Podolians, and Lithuanians, right up to the Baltic Sea. This the Rus'ians call the Varangian Sea[3] from the Varangians whom the Livonian people were then obeying. In this matter—idolatry, and the cleverness of the people—the people are similar to the Romans. An indication of this is a speech derived in some way from Latin and conflated with a barbarous language.

---

1 Text based on Łasicki, *De diis Samagitarum* (1615), 42–58.

2 The island of Gyaros, in the northern Cyclades in the Aegean Sea, was used as a place of exile in the early Roman Empire.

3 Ališauskas (Łasicki, *Pasakojimas apie Žemaičių Dievus*, ed. Ališauskas, 101) translates *mare Varetzgoie* into Lithuanian as *Variagų jūra*, "the Varangian Sea."

Ploteli arx Samagitica.

Michalo fragmine quinto de moribus Tartarorum, et suorum Lituanorum, paulo haec aliter refert. Ait enim, classis Iulii Caesaris ex Gallia in Britanniam navigantis partem, coortis tempestatibus, ad littus Samagiticum, ubi nunc est arx Ploteli, pervenisse, saepeque etiam hodie in illud ipsum littus, naves navigantium, vi ventorum eiici solere. Ubi Lituanorum progenitores, periculorum maris pertaesi, et praedis onusti, in tabernaculis ad focos, more militari, et adhuc in eadem Samagitia recepto, habitarint. unde ulterius progressi, Iaczvingos atque Roxolanos subegerint. Haud absurda coniectura.

Zamagitiae terra inferior.

Nam et Zamagitia, propter mare vicinum, et Lituaniam superiorem, terrae inferioris appellationem habet: et Lituanorum cum Samagitis idem propemodum sermo est, idem habitus, iidem mores, eadem ferme religio. Quae regio cum aquilonalis sit, tam parvae sunt in ea media aestate noctis tenebrae, ut radii solis occumbentis excipiant orientem, tumque plurimum agricolae segetes demetant suas.

Solis ingens aestus.

Nempe quod duabus ante meridiem horis, totidemque post, solis aestum ferre in agris messores nequeant. Et licet vix ante, quam tribus post Pentecosten hebdomadis, agros conserant: tamen id ardor coelestis efficit, ut eodem quo et apud nos tempore, messis fiat: aestas haud diu duret. similis in Moscovia fervor, (mirandam divinam providentiam) sex hebdomadis, frugibus maturitatem adfert.

Dies sex mensium.

Secus fit in Irrlandia ultra Sueciam, sub ipso polo. Ibi enim sex mensium dies est, totidem est nox. Cuius tenebras focus perennis dispellit. Qui locus est a Stokholm metropolis et regia Sueciae, trecentis milliaribus Germanicis. Id Iohannes tertius, Rex Suecorum, qui nunc rerum potitur, cuique sua ditio bene nota est, cuidam medico, is autem mihi narravit. Sita est Stockholm in ipso littore, trans mare Balticum, e regione Samagitiae.

Plateliai, the castle of Samogitia

Elsewhere, Michalo the Lithuanian, in his fifth fragment on the customs of the Tatars and Lithuanians refers a little to this.[4] For he says that part of Julius Caesar's navy, sailing from Gaul to Britain, broken apart by storms, came to the shore of Samogitia where the castle of Plateliai is now. And even today, the ships of those sailing them are accustomed to be cast ashore by the force of the winds. There the ancestors of the Lithuanians, tired of the perils of the sea, and weighed down by plunder, and having been received in the same Samogitia, lived in tents at open fires in military fashion. Having advanced further from there, they subjugated the Yotvingians and Roxolani. The conjecture is not absurd.

Samogitia: a lowland

For both Samogitia and Lithuania Superior,[5] on account of the neighbouring sea, have the name of lowlands. And the speech of the Lithuanians is almost the same as that of the Samogitians; the same dress, the same customs, and almost the same religion. In this region, since it is northerly, the darkness of night is so little in the middle of summer that the rays of the setting sun follow its rising, and then many farmers reap their fields.

The immense heat of the sun

Indeed, in the two hours before noon, and for the same time after, the reapers cannot bear the heat of the sun in the fields. And they may scarcely sow the fields more than three weeks after Pentecost. However, this burning of the heavens ensures that, in the same way and at the same time as among us, the harvest arrives; the summer does not last long. Similarly, in Muscovy (marvellous divine providence!) the intense heat brings the crops to maturity in six weeks.

The day of six months

It happens otherwise in Finland,[6] beyond Sweden, beneath the pole itself. For here a day is six months long, and a night the same. Perpetual fires dispel the darkness. This region is three hundred German miles from the city of Stockholm. John III, the king of Sweden who now reigns, to whose sovereignty it is subject, told this to a certain physician who told the same to me. Stockholm is situated on the seashore, across the Baltic Sea from the region of Samogitia.

---

4 The reference is to Lituanus, *De moribus Tartarorum*, ed. Grasser (1615), 24.

5 Aukštaitija, i.e., "highland" Lithuania.

6 Ališauskas (Łasicki, *Pasakojimas apie Žemaičių Dievus*, ed. Ališauskas, 103) reads *Irrlandia* as an error for Finland (since Finland is in the geographical position described by Łasicki) rather than as a misspelling of *Islandia* (Iceland).

[p. 44] Solum Samagiticum fertile quidem est, sed cultores eius pigri, nec aliis quam ligneis, superstitione quadam, in arando utuntur vomeribus. Idcirco inopia panis laborant, eius loco rapis tostis, quae minori labore proveniunt, et instar humani capitis nascuntur, vesci soliti. His vero absumtis, ad panem comedendum se convertunt. Mellis albi, lactis, butyri, pecoris divites, pinguibus pascuis felices. Nec eis pisces desunt.

Cervisia.

Potus, hydromel et cervisia est. Haec in vasis, ex corticibus factis, positis intus saxis fervidis, ex aqua, frumento, lupulo, una nocte cocta, protinus faeces accipit, posteroque die bibitur. percommoda alvi purgandae ratio. Praecipui cornibus urorum ornatis (boves sunt silvestres, valde feroces) pro poculis utuntur: strenuos compotatores, cantharo hydromelis, indusio, mantili, manicis, sudariolo, seu re quavis alia operis domestici libenter donant. Quibus cervisia non est, ii aquam bibunt, proceri, agiles, animosi, robusti, ad arma promti.

Samagitae annosi.

Vivunt autem vulgo centum annos. Sunt enim frugales, et modicis exercitiis dediti.

Wladislai Iagiellonis Polonorum Regis opera, Anno humanae salutis 1413. (Lituani autem 1387.) Christiana religione initiati sunt. Quibus episcopum Miednicii praefecit. Duodecim paroecos dedit. Dandis pecuniis, pannis caeruleis, pileisque rubris, iuxta montem Schatria, ad baptismum amplectendum illexit. Ubi monacho regio, de mundo Adamoque a Deo creatis concionante; unus illorum hisce verbis Regem compellavit: "Mentitur," inquit, "o Rex, hic homo, non admodum senex, multi enim nostrum centesimum annum superaverunt: tamen haec minime recordantur. eadem illis pueris quae senibus coeli conversio, eadem temporum vicissitudo, idem cursus et fulgor siderum fuit." Cui Rex, officio et ipse concionatoris fungens, "Verum ais," inquit: "nec falsum sacerdos, qui non sua aetate, sed multis ante saeculis mundum divino mandatu ex nihilo extitisse dixit."

The Samogitian soil is fertile, but its cultivators are lazy; nor will they use anything other than wood for their ploughs, on account of some superstition. Therefore in poverty they work for bread, and they are accustomed to eat roasted turnips, which are grown with little labour, and are grown in the likeness of a human head.[7] Having eaten these, they turn to eating bread. They are rich in clear honey, milk, butter, and herds, and fortunate in fertile pastures. Nor do they lack fish.

Beer

Their drink is mead and beer. This is brewed for one night in vessels made from bark and placed within hot stones, from water, grain, and hops; then at once it takes the dregs, and is drunk the next day. It is very convenient for the purpose of purging the bowels. In particular, they use the decorated horns of the wild ox as cups (their cattle are forest-dwelling, and very ferocious). They gladly give strenuous drinkers a cup of mead, clothes, a cloak, a handkerchief, or any other domestic item whatsoever. Wherever there is no beer they drink water, and are prompt to arms.

The long-lived Samogitians

But they commonly live a hundred years, for they are frugal, and given to moderate exercises.

By the labour of Władysław Jagiełło, king of Poland, they were initiated into the Christian religion in the year of human salvation 1413 (but the Lithuanians in 1387). He erected an episcopal see for them at Medininkai. He gave twelve parish priests. Giving them money, blue shirts, and red caps, he enticed them next to the hill of Šatrija in order to receive baptism. Then, to a royal monk, who was addressing the crowd about the world and Adam, created by God, one of them addressed these words to the king: "He speaks falsely," he said, "O king, this man—not yet an old man; many of us have outlived our hundredth year, yet we do not remember this. The alteration of the heavens is the same to boys as it is to old men; the vicissitude of the times are the same, and the same are the course and brightness of the stars." The king said to him, exercising his office and addressing the crowd himself, "You speak truly, and it is not false that the priest speaks not on account of his own age, but by the divine mandate from many ages before the world came into being out of nothing."

---

7 This phrase may be a humorous Classical allusion to the birth of Greek gods from the head of Zeus; alternatively, Łasicki is implying that the superstitious Samogitians prefer to eat turnips because they resemble a human head.

Res pecuaria.

Rei pecuariae adeo sunt studiosi, ut unus agricola sexaginta, alius duplo plus, paullo minus alius cornuti pecoris, praeter oves et capras alat. Equi illorum parvuli: ob nimium opinor frigus: sed tamen robusti. quorum uno, Anno Domini 1554. duobus florenis Vilnae in Lituania emto, et trahae iuncto, p. 45 vectus sum cursu celeri usque Cracoviam, 120. milliarum Germanicarum. Foeminae pecori curando, viri agris colendis dant operam.

Linum.

Iidem deni aut viceni, plures vel pauciores, in uno tugurio linum, lanam, cannabim pectunt, nent, texunt, vestes conficiunt. Quicquid horum superest, id Rigam vel Regiomontum, hinc in Hollandiam, pretio tolerabili mittunt. lino enim maxime et cannabi, agros suos complent. Dispersi per silvas, campos degunt. rara oppida, nec pagos nimium multos, arces autem munitas nullas habent. quorum fenestrae meridiem versus spectant. Studio Sigismundi Augusti Regis, anno 1572. 7. Iulii mortui, in coetus et societates convocati.

Mapalia.

Mapalia, quae turres appellant, sursum angusta, atque qua fumus et foetor exeat, aperta ex tignis, asseribus, stramine, corticibus faciunt. In his homines cum omni peculio, in pavimento tabulato stante, habitant. ita paterfamilias omnia sua in conspectu habet, et feram noxiam, et frigus a pecore arcet, ad ostium cubat, deastro foci custodia commissa, ne vel ignis damnum domicilio det, vel prunae nocte extinguantur. Ubi crebro accidit, ut vel sus vel canis ex olla in foco stant, carnes auferat: aut rostrum, aqua fervente, laedat. Qui in pagis degunt, ii caulas separatas an aestuariis habent. Tam hi quam illi plumis concisis, culcitras farciunt. Quae non possunt non pungere, et vigilantem reddere cubantem. Paterfamilias, mactatis autumno avibus domestici, iisque pecudibus ac bobus, quos se brumae tempore non posse alere animadvertit, genio cum suis indulget: quaeque supersunt, ea doliis inclusa, maritimis vendit.

Matters pertaining to cattle

They are very careful in matters pertaining to cattle, and one farmer rears sixty, another twice as many (these cattle are a little less horned than others), besides sheep and goats. Their horses are very small; on account, I think, of the excessive cold—but hardy nonetheless. I bought one of them, in the Year of Our Lord 1554, for two florins in Vilnius in Lithuania, and harnessing it to a sleigh I was carried with a swift course to Kraków, one hundred and twenty German miles. The women give their labour to looking after cattle, the men to cultivating the fields.

Linen

In one cottage, in groups of ten or twenty (more or less), they card, spin, and weave linen, wool, and hemp, and make clothes. Whatever of theirs is left over they send to Riga or Königsberg (and from there to Holland) for a tolerable price. Their fields are very full of cotton and hemp. Dispersed throughout the forest, they spend their time in the fields. Towns are rare, nor are there many villages, but they have no fortified castles. Their windows look towards the south. By the zeal of King Sigismund Augustus, who died on July 7, 1572, they were called together in union and fellowship.

Huts

Their huts, which they call towers, rise up narrowly, and so that smoke and bad smells can leave they make them with open beams, rafters, straw, and outer coverings. In these the people live with all their wealth, standing on a pavement floor. There the head of the family has all within his sight, and wards off the harmful wild beast and the cold from the cattle. He sleeps at the doorway, committing the guardianship of the hearth to an idol,[8] lest the fire destroy the house, or the coals are extinguished at night. When darkness falls, like a hog or a pig he stands apart from them at the hearth, he takes away the meat; or like a beaked bird[9] strikes in rushing water. Those who bide their time in villages have apertures separate from the air vents; each as much as the other stuffs cushions with chopped up feathers. They are not able not to prick them, and return watchful to bed.[10] The head of the family, having slaughtered[11] domestic birds in the autumn, turns his attention to those sheep and cattle he is unable to feed during the wintertime, and indulges his appetite with his family. Whatever remains, enclosed in jars, he sells to sailors.

---

8 The Neo-Latin word *deaster* was invented by Sebastian Castellio (1515–1563) for a carved wooden pole venerated as an idol (Polish *bożyszcze*). See Frick, *Polish Sacred Philology in the Reformation and the Counter-Reformation*, 104. Ališauskas (Łasicki, *Pasakojimas apie Žemaičių Dievus*, ed. Ališauskas, 107) translates *deaster* into Lithuanian as *dievaičius*.

9 Literally "like a beak."

10 Łasicki seems to be suggesting that the Samogitians make pillows compulsively, and find themselves unable to stop.

11 *Macto* also has the meaning of "sacrifice," but it seems unlikely that Łasicki intends this meaning here.

Ferae.

Foras egressus, alcem, aprum, cervum, avem, sciurum, bombarda, venabulo, ballista, arcu conficit. Sunt enim iaculatores et sagitarii praestantes. In quorum curribus nihil omnino ferri invenias. Omnia lignea, rotae ex radicibus arborum inflexis, quas procul audias venientes, axibus, quod eas non illinant, stridentibus.

Virgines.

Virgo non ante nubit, quam triginta annos, aut minimum 24. expleat: et ipsa manibus suis, aliquot corbes vestium, omnibus cum sponso venientibus dispertiendarum paret. Tum enim dat singulis, vel indusium, vel mappam, vel mantile, vel texta e lana tibialia, vel chirothecas. Haec in agrum non prodit, ni prius p. 46 parentibus inserviat, et in omnibus morem gerat. Idem facit filius. Ac praemissi qui eam in matrimonium petant, primum omnium, num progenitoribus sit morigera, reique familiaris studiosa, considerant. Et viri et foeminae, sunt amantissimi honesti. Rarissima apud eos homicidia, furta, stupra, incestus.

Pudicitia.

Puella stricto persequitur cultro se ad impudicitiam solicitantem. quae duobus, ante et retro pendentibus de zona tintinnabulis, nocte autem semper cum face incedit. quibus rebus monentur parentes, ubi sit, quiddue agat filia. Pater filio uxorem quaerens, nec formam nec dotem spectat, satis esse ducens dotatam, si sit morata. Quae succi plena atque adulta, magna cum laetitia, in domum soceri inducitur.

Praefecti.

Praefectos, quos Civonias vocant, non adeunt, quin ipsis aliqua munuscula adferant. Summus toti regioni, dum vivit, praeest Lituanicus Senator. Hodie est vir eximius Iohannes Kisska Palatino Vitepscensi natus: inter eos qui minoris dignitatis sunt, fuit Iacobus Lascovius, Polonus nobilis, tractus Calissiensis, ex quo haec percepi: qui in hisce hominibus pie erudiendis, et in certa loca cogendis, Sigismundi Augusti iussu, plurimum operae impendit. Cui Deum Unum praedicanti, respondebant idolatrae: "Quid tu nobis Unicum Deum, quasi omnibus nostris potentiorum inculcas? Plus uno multi possunt, plura plures agunt." Idem agros illorum ad 40. iugerum millia dimensus est. Horum tria uni rustico assignata, praeter alia minutiora commoda, quinque florenos fructus annui Regi adferunt.

Wild animals

Going outside, he kills elk, wild boar, deer, birds, and squirrels with bombard, hunting spear, slingshot, and bow. For they are outstanding spear-throwers and archers. In their vehicles you will find nothing at all made of metal. Everything is made of wood, the wheels made from the roots of trees bent into shape, which you will hear coming from a long way off, with creaking axles that they do not grease.

Virgins

A virgin does not marry before the age of thirty— or, at the least, twenty-four may be sufficient. And she herself produces with her own hands several baskets of clothes, parcelled up into everything for coming to live with the husband. Even then she gives everyone a shirt, or a napkin, or a cloak, or stocking woven from wool, or gloves. She does not work in the field, nor does she serve her former parents, and in everything she conducts herself according to custom. A son does the same. And the first thing of all he considers (in those things which one seeking her in marriage contemplates) is whether she is compliant towards her parents, and eager in family matters. Both men and women are honest and very loving. Murder, theft, rape, and incest are most rare among them.

Modesty

A girl pursues a man soliciting her to immodesty with a drawn knife. She always ventures out at night with two little bells hanging from her girdle, front and back, and with a torch. By these things parents are advised where their daughter is, and for how long. A father seeking a wife for his son looks neither at her form nor at her dowry, taking it as a sufficient dowry if she is endowed with manners. Filled with ripe juice, and with great joy, she is led into the home of her father-in-law.

The officials

They do not visit the officials called *tivunai* without taking them some little gift or other. The highest man in the whole region, while he lives, is a Lithuanian senator. Today that is the exemplary man Jan Kisska, born in the Palatinate of Vitebsk. Among those who are of minor dignity are Jakub Łaszkowski, a noble Pole, drawn from Kalisz, from whom I received this. He expended much labour in piously instructing these people by order of Sigismund Augustus, and gathering them in certain places. To the one preaching the one God, the idolaters replied, "Who are you, one God, that you instruct us as if more powerful than all of ours? Many can do more than one, and more can do more." Their fields are forty thousand jugera in size. Three of them are assigned together to one rustic, besides other suitable smaller plots, and they bring five florins' worth of produce to the king each year.

Silvae.

Iussi autem a Lascovio arbores excindere, invitissimi id, nec prius, quam ipsemet inchoaret, fecerunt. deos enim nemora incolere persuasum habent. Sequitur persuasionem effectus. nam in silvis eorum horrenda quaedam visa ac spectra, tam auribus quam oculis spectantium sese offerunt. Tum unus inter alios percontari, num etiam decorticare arbores liceret. annuente praefecto, aliquot magno nisu haec repetens decorticavit: "Vos me meis anseribus, gallisque gallinaceis spoliastis; proinde et ego nudas vos faciam." Credebat enim demens deos rei suae familiari perniciosos, intra arbores et cortices latere.

Dii.

Quoniam tantus pene est numerus, quantus aliorum apud Hesiodum. Nam praeter eum, qui illis est Deus Auxtheias Vissagistis, Deus omnipotens atque summus, [p.47] permultos Zemopacios, id est, terrestres ii venerantur, qui nondum verum Deum Christianorum cognoverunt. Percunos Deus tonitrus illis est. quem coelo tonante agricola capite detecto, et succidiam humeris per fundum portans, hisce verbis alloquitur: *Percune deuaite niemuski und mana, diewu melsu tawi palti miessu.* "Cohibe te," inquit "Percune, neve in meum agrum calamitatem immittas. Ego vero tibi hanc succidiam dabo." Verum postquam nimbus praeterit, carnes ipse absumit. Percuna tete, mater est fulminis atque tonitrui: quae solem fessum ac pulverulentum, balneo excipit: deinde lotum et nitidum, postera die emittit. Audros deo, maris caeterarumque aquarum cura incumbit. Algis, angelus est summorum deorum. Ausca, dea est radiorum solis vel occumbentis, vel supra horizontem ascendentis. Bezlea dea vespertina, Breksta tenebrarum. Ligiczus, is Deus esse putatur, qui concordiae inter homines, et auctor est et conservator. Datanus donator est bonorum, seu largitor. Kirnis caerasos arcis alicuius secundum lacum sitae curat. in quos, placandi eius causa, gallos mactatos iniiciunt, caereosque accensos in eis figunt. nimirum sicut ille avarus Euclio apud Plaut[um] in Aul[ularia] ture ac corona laris gratiam aucupabatur:

> Nunc tusculum emi, et hasce coronas floreas,
> Haec imponentur in foco nostro lari:
> Ut fortunatas faciat natae nuptias.

Kremata porcorum ac suum est Deus cui similiter focos excitant, et cervisiam super eas fundunt. Pizio iuventus, sponsam adductura sponso, sacrum facit.

The forests

They were commanded by Łaszkowski to cut down trees; and they did this most unwillingly, and not before he entered upon the work himself. For they are persuaded that gods dwell in the forests. The effect of this conviction follows; for in their woods certain horrible things are seen, and spectres present themselves as much to the ears as to the eyes of those watching. Then one inquired among the others whether it was permitted to strip the bark from trees. When the official gave his assent, he stripped its bark with a great effort, repeating this: "You have despoiled me of my geese, cockerels, and hens; therefore I will make you naked." For the madman believed that gods harmful to his family dwelt within the trees and their bark.

The gods

For [the gods] are nearly as many as the number of others in Hesiod. For aside from the one who is to them the all-powerful and supreme god, the god Aukštėjas Visgalįsis,[12] a great many *žemėpačiai* (that is, terrestrial spirits) are venerated by those who do not yet know the true God of the Christians. Perkūnas is for these people the god of thunder. When the sky is thundering a farmer carries a shoulder of meat through the farm, with uncovered head, and he says these words: *Percune deuaite niemuski und mana, diewu melsu tawi palti miessu* ("Hold back, o Perkūnas, and do not send calamity into my field. Truly, I give you this joint of meat"). And after the clouds pass over, he himself consumes the meat. Perkūno Teta[13] is the mother of lightning and thunder, who bathes the tired and dusty sun; then, washed and shining, the next day she sends her forth. On the god Audros rests the care of the sea and other waters. Algis is a messenger of the supreme gods. Auska is the goddess of the rays of the sun, or of the sun setting or ascending above the horizon. Bežlėja is the goddess of the evening, Brėkšta of the darkness. Ligičius is considered by these people to be the author and preserver of concord among people. Duotojas is the giver of good things, or bountiful giver. Kirnis guards cherry trees next to the fortress by the lake, into which, in order to appease him, they cast slaughtered cockerels, and they place lit candles among them. Without doubt, like that miser Euclio according to Plautus in the *Aulularia*, they eagerly seek the thanks of the household god with incense and a crown:

> Now I have bought a little frankincense, and these wreaths of flowers,
> These are placed on the hearth for our household god:
> So that he may make fortunate our daughter's marriage.[14]

Kremata is the god of pigs and swine, for whom they simultaneously light fires and pour beer over them. A young man sacrifices to Pizius, so that he may take a wife in marriage.

---

12 A divine title rather than a name; literally "the highest almighty."

13 "Aunt of Perkūnas."

14 Plautus, *Aulularia*, lines 385–87.

Puellae quoque quendam Gondu adorant et invocant. Modeina et Ragaina silvestres sunt dii: uti Kierpiczus huiusque adiutor Siliniczus, musci in silvis nascentis: cuius in aedificiis magnus apud illos est usus. huic etiam muscum lecturi sacrificant. Tawals Deus, auctor facultatum. Orthus lacus est piscosus, quem colunt, quemadmodum et Ezernim lacuum Deum.

Sunt etiam quaedam veteres Nobilium familiae, quae peculiares colunt deos. Ut Mikutiana Simonaitem, Micheloviciana Sidzium, Schemetiana et Kiesgaliana Ventis Rekicziovum, aliae alios. Kurwaiczin Eraiczin agnellorum est deus: est et Gardunithis custos eorundem recens editorum. Prigirstitis hic est, ⸢p. 48⸣ qui murmurantes exaudire putatur. Iubent igitur ut quis summisso murmure, hoc vel illud loquatur, ne clamantem Prigirstitis audiat. Derfintos pacem conciliat. Ut et Bentis is creditur, qui efficit, ut duo vel plures simul, iter aliquo instituant. Lawkpatimo ituri aratum vel satum supplicant. Priparscis est, qui augere nefrendes existimatur. Ratainicza equorum habetur deus, ut Walgina aliorum pecorum. Kriksthos cruces in tumulis sepultorum custodit.

Divinationes.

Sunt et omnium auguriorum, divinationumque observantes. Habentque Apidome mutati domicilii deum. nato cuiusvis generis, vel coeco vel debili pullo, actutum sedes mutantur. Quin ipse quoque rex Wladislaus, gente Lituanus, has a matre superstitiones didicerat, ut eum diem infaustum sibi futurum crederet, quo primum calceum sinistrum fortuito accepisset. Adhoc movebat se interdum in gyrum stans pede uno, foras e cubili proditurus. quorum similia multa observantur ab Samagitis. Ita olim Germani, Plutarcho in Caio Caesare teste, non ante praelium cum hoste committebant, quam nova luna fulsisset. Et nostrum quidam infeliciter se venaturos sibi persuadent, si domo egressis mulier occurrat, seu quis certum numerum capiendorum leporum, vulpium, luporum nominet. Krukis suum est deus. Qui religiose colitur ab Budraicis, hoc est, fabris ferrariis. Lasdona avellanarum, Babilos apum dii sunt. Hunc Rossi Zosim cognominant. Sunt etiam deae, Zemina terrestris, Austheia apum. Utraeque incrementa facere creduntur: ac cum examinantur apes, quo plures in alveos aliunde adducant, et fucos ab eis arceant, rogantur.

Girls also worship and invoke a certain Gandas. Medeina and Ragaina are forest goddesses, as is Kerpičius and his helper Silinčius, the god of moss that grows in the forest, which is in great use among them in buildings. To this god they sacrifice when they go to collect moss. The god Tavalas is the originator of skills. Orthus is the god of lakes rich in fish, whom they worship as the god of the lakes of Ežerinis.

There are even certain old families of the nobility who worship particular gods, as the Mikučiai worship Simonaitis, the Michelovičiai worship Sidzius, and the Šemetos and Kęsgailos worship Ventis Rekičionis. Others worship others. Karvaitis Ėraitis is the god of lambs, and Gardunytis is their guardian when they have been recently born. Prigirstytis is he who they think hears murmurers; they therefore command that anyone who speaks should do so in a subdued murmur, lest Prigirstytis should hear the one shouting. Derintojas conciliates peace, and Bentis is believed by these people to be the one who causes two or more to go on a journey anywhere at the same time. Those about to go out to plough or sow supplicate Laukpatis. Priparšis is the one who is considered to increase toothlessness.[15] Ratainyčia is held to be the god of horses, and Valgina of other cattle. Krikštas guards the crosses on the tumuli of the buried.[16]

Divinations

And they are observers of all auguries and divination. And they have Apidomė, the god of a changed abode. When he has been born in whichever way, either from a blind or a feeble chick, their dwelling is immediately changed.[17] Indeed, King Władysław [Jagiełło] also, a Lithuanian by nation, learnt these superstitions from his mother, so that he believed it would be an unlucky day whenever by chance he put on his left shoe first. For he would turn himself around in a circle, standing on one foot, in order to go outside his bedroom. Many similar things are observed by the Samogitians. Thus Plutarch testifies in his life of Julius Caesar that at one time the Germans would not commit to battle with the enemy before the new moon had shone.[18] And certain of our people[19] persuade themselves it is unlucky to hunt if he runs into a woman on leaving the house, or if he foretells the taking of certain numbers of hares, foxes or wolves.

Krukis is their god. He is venerated religiously by the Budraičiai—that is, the blacksmiths. Lazdona is the god of hazelnuts and Babilas the god of bees; this one the Rus'ians call Zosim. There are also goddesses: Žemyna of the earth, Austėja of bees, and each is believed to bring about growth. And they are called upon when the bees are examined, when they count more in the beehive and they keep the bee glue away from them.

---

15 Literally "to increase the teethless."

16 A reference to *krikštai*, traditional Lithuanian wooden grave markers. On *krikštai* see Greimas, *Of Gods and Men*, 197–99.

17 For an exegesis of this obscure passage see Greimas, *Of Gods and Men*, 53–55.

18 The reference is to Plutarch, *Life of Caesar*, xix.8.

19 Presumably a reference to the Poles.

Mellis copia.

Nusquam autem vel candidius mel est, vel minus caerae habet. Unde illae massae cae-
reae, quae in navibus in Belgium, Galliam, Hispaniam deportantur. Praeterea, sunt certis agris, quemadmodum nobilioribus familiis, singulares dei videlicet Devoitis agri
Poiurskii, Vetustis Retowskii, Guboi ac Twerticos Sarakowskii, Kirnis Plotelscii. Vielona
Deus animarum. Cui tum oblatio ofertur, cum mortui pascuntur. Dari autem illi solent
frixae placentulae, quatuor locis sibi oppositis, paullulum discissae. Eae Sikies Vielonia
pemixlos nominantur. Warpulis is esse p. 49 putatur, qui sonitum ante et post tonitru,
in aere facit. Caeterum quid agant Salaus, Szlotrazis, Tiklis, Birzulis, Siriczus, Dwargonth,
Klamals, Atlaibos aliique eius generis, non libenter id Christianis aperiunt. Opitulatores
illos hominum esse, ideoque invocandos persuasum habent.

Dii domestici.

Numeias, vocant domesticos. Ut est Ublanicza deus, cui curae est omnis supplex. Dugnai
dea, praeest farinae subactae. Pesseias, inter pullos omnis generis recens natos, post
focum latet. Tratitas Kirbixtu, deaster est, qui scintillas tugurii restinguit. Alabathis,
quem linum pexuri in auxilium vocant. Polengabia diva est, cui foci lucentis administra-
tio creditur. Aspelenie, angularis. Budintaia, hominem dormientem excitat. Matergabiae
deae a foemina ea placenta, quae prima e mactra sumta digitoque notata, in furno
coquitur. Hanc post, non alius quam paterfamilias, vel eius coniux comedit. Simili modo
Rauguzemapati offerunt, posteaque ebibunt, primum vel cerevisiae vel aquae mulsae,
e dolio haustum. Quem Nulaidimos, illum autem primum a massa exemtum panem,
Tawirzis cognominant. Eidem cervisiario deo offert, id est, praebibit paterfamilias cervisiae, post faeces acceptas intumescentis, spumantem pateram. Tum demum at alii hau-
riunt. Si is absit, mater id familias facit. Luibegeldas divas venerantes, ita compellant:
Luibegeldae per mare porire sekles gillie skaute. "Vos deae transmisistis ad nos omnia
semina siliginea, in putamine glandis."

The supply of honey

Nowhere is the honey clearer, or has less beeswax. From here cargoes of beeswax are carried in ships to the Low Countries, France, and Spain. Moreover, there are certain estates, just like the noble families, which belong particularly to a god; that is to say, Devoitis the god of the Poiurskii[20] estate; Vetustis the god of Rietavas; Guboi and Tvertikas the gods of the Sarakai estate; Kirnis the god of Plateliai. Veliona is the god of souls; they make offerings to him when the dead are fed. It is the custom for him to be given little fried pancakes, torn into small pieces and placed in four places. These are called *Sikies Vielonia pemixlos*. Varpelis is thought by these people to be the one who makes a sound in the sky before and after thunder. What others do—Salaus, Šluotražis, Tiklis, Biržulis, Siričius, Dvargantis, Klamals, Atlaibas, and others of this kind—they do not freely reveal to Christians. They are helpers of humankind, or thus those invoking them are so persuaded.

Household gods

The Numėjai they call household gods. Such is the god Ublanicza, whose care is every suppliant. The goddess Dugnai is foremost in grinding flour. Pesseias lurks behind the fire among recently born chicks. Kibirkščių Trotytojas is a godling who extinguishes sparks in the hut. Alabatis is the one they call upon for help when they are about to comb linen. Polengabija is a deity who is believed to govern the light from the hearth. Užpelenė is the deity of the corners. Budintoja wakes a sleeping person. A little cake is offered by women to the goddess Matergabija, which has first been taken from the kneading trough, marked with a finger, and cooked in the oven. After this not only the head of the family but also his wife eats it. In a similar way they offer to Raugų Žemėpatis (and afterwards drink) either beer or whey, drained from a vessel. They call him Nulaidimos and Tawirzis who is the first chunk taken from bread. The head of the family offers the same to the god of beer—that is, he drinks beer first of all, after the dregs rise up, spitting them onto a dish. Then at last the others drink. If he is away, the mother of the family does this. Venerating the deities called the Luibegeldas, they thus compel them: *Luibegeldae per mare porire sekles gillie skaute*: "You goddesses, send to us all wheat seeds, in the cup of an acorn."[21]

---

20 The location of the place-name is unknown, but Ališauskas (Łasicki, *Pasakojimas apie Žemaičių Dievus*, ed. Ališauskas, 61, 113) reads *Poiurskii* as a polonisation of Lithuanian *pajūris* ("seaside").

21 The Latin is not a translation of the Lithuanian, which should read "per marę perirė sėklas gilės kiaute" ("seeds cross the seas in a nutshell"). On this passage see Greimas, *Of Gods and Men*, 83.

Festum post collectas fruges.

Eadem turba agrestis, ut est auctor Alexander Gwagninus, in Sarmatia, sub finem mensis Octobris, frugibus plane collectis, solenne quoddam sacrificium, eo modo celebrat, nam omnes ad sacras epulas coacti, mensae foenum, postea panem, ac ex utraque parte duo vasa cervisiae plena imponunt. Deinde adducta utriusque sexus domestica animalia, sue, gallo, ansere, vitulo, et si quae sunt alia. hoc ritu mactant. primus augur, certa verba prolocutus, animalis caput caeteraque membra fuste verberat: quem turba idem agens, ac haec dicens sequitur. "Haec tibi o Zemiennik deus, gratias agentes offerimus: quod nos hoc anno incolumes conservaris, et omnia nobis abunde dederis. Idem ut et in posterum facias, te oramus."

Antequam vero ipsi comedant, uniuscuiusque ferculi portiunculam abscisam, in omnes domus angulos, ista dicentes abiiciunt: [p. 50] "Accipe o Zemiennik grato animo sacrificium: atque laetus comede." Tum demum ipsi quoque praelaute epulantur. Qui ritus etiam in nonnullis Lituaniae atque Russiae locis observatur, ac Ilgi dicitur. Fieri id sacrum Lascovius ait postridie festi omnium sanctorum. Qui dies est secundus Novembris.

Prussi trucidati.

Quo die Samagitae, Prussis, quibus erant oppignerati, quique in terra ipsorum fuere, excisis, Vitoldo duci Lituaniae, (qui diem obit 1430. 27. Octobris Wladislai Iagiellonis, patruelis frater) sese ultro subiecerunt. Tertio post Ilgas die, deum Waizganthos colunt virgines, ut illius beneficio, tam lini quam cannabis habeant copiam. Ubi altissima illarum, impleto placentulis, quas Sikies vocant, sinu, et stans pede uno in sedili, manuque sinistra sursum elata, librum prolixum, vel tiliae vel ulmo detractum (ex quo etiam calceos contexerunt) dextra vero craterem cervisiae, haec loquens tenet: *Waizganthos deuaite auging mani linus teip ilgies, ik mani, nie duok munus nogus eithi.* "Waizganthos," inquit, "produc nobis tam altum linum, quam ego nunc alta sum; neve nos nudos incedere permittas." Post haec craterem exhaurit (nam et foeminae bibaces sunt) impletumque rursum, deo in terram effundit, et placentas e sinu eiicit, a deastris, si qui sint Waizgantho, comedendas. Si haec peragens, firma perstet, bonum lini proventum anno sequenti futurum, in animum inducit. Si lapsa, pede altera nitatur, dubitat de futura copia, fidemque effectus sequitur.

The festival after the gathering of fruits

According to the author Alessandro Guagnini, in his *Sarmatia*,[22] the same rural crowd celebrates a certain solemn sacrifice in their way, having collected the harvest before the end of October. For all of them, having been gathered to the sacred feasting (the courses being hay, and afterwards bread), each one of them for their part places two vessels full of beer. Then they bring in two domestic animals of each sex—pigs, chickens, geese, calves, and whatever others. They slaughter them with this rite. First of all the augur, having spoken certain words, beats the animals' heads and other members with a club. The crowd does the same, saying the following:

> O Žemininkas, god! We offer these to you in thanks, since this year you
> have preserved us unharmed, and have given us all things abundantly;
> we pray you will do the same in the future.

Before they eat, with a portion having been set aside on the dish of each, they throw them into all the corners of the house, saying this: "Receive, o Žemininkas, the sacrifice with a grateful spirit, and eat it happily." Then at last they themselves eat heartily. The rite is also observed in many places in Lithuania and Rus', and is called Ilgės. Łaszkowski says that this rite is performed on the day after the feast of All Saints. That day is November 2.

The Prussians defeated

On that day the Samogitians, having defeated the Prussians—to whom they were allied—who were in their lands, subjected themselves voluntarily to Duke Vytautas of Lithuania (who died on October 27, 1430 and was the cousin of Władysław II Jagiełło). On the third day after Ilgės virgins worship the god Vaižgantas, so that by his beneficence they might have a good supply of linen as well as hemp. Then the tallest of them, having filled her lap with the pancakes they call *sikės*, and standing on one foot on a chair, with her left hand raised, and a long piece of bark either from a lime or elm tree stretched out (from which they make shoes), holds a cup of beer in her right hand, saying: *Waizganthos deuaite auging mani linus teip ilgies, ik mani, nie duok munus nogus eithi* ("Vaižgantas," she says, "produce for us a pile of linen as tall, as I am now tall; and do not allow us to fall into nakedness"). After this she drains the cup (for women are given to drink), and filling it up again she pours it on the ground for the god. And she throws the pancakes from her lap so they may be eaten by the godlings, if one of them is Vaižgantas. If in doing this she continues to stand stably, they think there will be good production of linen in the following year. If she falls, or leans upon the other foot, future plenty is doubtful, and from belief the effect follows.

---

22 The reference is to Guagnini, *Sarmatiae Europeae descriptio*, fol. 52v.

Parentalia.

Iisdem feriis, mortuos e tumulis a balneum et epulas invitant: totidemque sedilia, mantilia, indusia, quot invitati fuerint, in tugurio eam ad rem praeparato ponunt. Mensam cibo, potu onerant. Dehinc in sua mapalia reversi, triduum compotant. Quo exacto illa omnia in sepulcris, potu perfusis, relinquunt. tandem etiam manibus valedicunt. Interea haec ii auferunt, qui in silvis arbores cineris causa, quo fullones transmarini carere nequeunt, comburunt, et asseres faciunt, navium materiam, in Oceanum mittendam. Consimili huic errore, Christiani, seculo beati Augustini, in coemiteriis apud memorias defunctorum, ut idem epistola 64 ait, comessabuntur.

Livonum superstitio.

Veri quoque Livones hoc tempore, qui dura Germanorum servitute premuntur, monumentis mortuorum cibum, potum, securim, et nonnihil pecunie, hac cum naenia imponunt: "Transi" inquit [p. 51] "o miser ab hoc rerum statu, in mundum meliorem. Ubi non tibi Germani amplius, sed tu illis imperabis. habes arma, cibum, viaticum."

Cum autem nimia aestatis brevitas, fruges demessas, plane siccari non sinat, fit hoc sub tectis ad ignem. Tum vero precandus est illis hisce verbis "Gabie deus": *Gabie deu-aite pokielki, garanuleiski kirbixstu.* "Flammam" inquit "eleva, at ne dimittas scintillas."

Smik Smik Perlevenu. Hunc deum Lituani vere araturi, venerantur. Prima agri lyra vomere facta, huius ipsius est. Quam huic qui illam duxit, toto anno transgredi haud licet: alioquin divum sibi infensum haberet.

Skierstuwes festum est farciminum ad quod deum Ezagulis ita vocant: *Vielona velos atteik musmup vnd stala.* "Veni," inquit, "cum mortuis, farcimina nobiscum mandacaturus."

Aitwaros est incubus, qui post sepes habitat. Id enim verbum ipsum significat.

The *Parentalia*

In the same days of festivity they invite the dead from their tombs to bathe and feast; they put chairs, cloaks, and shirts in a cottage—as many as are invited—in preparation for the proceeding. They load the table with food and drink. Returning from thence to their huts, they drink together for three days. Having performed all this, they leave them in their tombs, having sprinkled them with drink. Eventually they say farewell to the spirits of the dead. In the meantime, while they carry out these things, they burn the trees of the forest for ashes (which foreign fullers do not want to be without) and they make beams—the material of ships—to send to the ocean. In a similar error, the Christians of the era of St. Augustine dined in cemeteries among the memorials of the dead, as the same says in *Letter* 64.[23]

The superstition of the Livonians

In this time the Livonians also (who are oppressed by the hard servitude of the Germans) put food, drink, an axe, and much money on the monuments of the dead, along with a funeral chant: "Pass on," he says, "o poor soul, from this state of things to a better world, where the Germans no longer command you, but you will command them; you have arms, food, and provisions for the journey."

But when the summer is too brief, and does not allow the gathered harvest to be dried out, they do this indoors before a fire. Then they must speak in these words to the deity Gabija: *Gabie deuaite pokielki, garanuleiski kirbixstu* ("Raise the flames high," he says, "and do not send out sparks").

Smik Smik Perlevenu. The Lithuanians venerate this god when they are about to plough. First they make song in the field with the ploughshare, which belongs to him. Then, for a whole year, they do not permit him who leads the plough to transgress; otherwise he will have the hostility of the god.

Skerstuvės is the feast of sausages, to which they summon the god Ežiagulis thus: *Vielona velos atteik musmup vnd stala* ("Come with the dead," he says, "to eat sausages with us").

Aitvaras is an incubus who lives behind hedges. The word itself means this.

---

23 This seems to be an error for Augustine, *Letter* 22, §6: "But since carnal and ignorant folk often regard these drinking bouts and dissolute banquets in the cemeteries as not merely honours paid to the martyrs, but also as consolations for the dead, it seems to me to be easier to dissuade them from this foul and shameful practice if it is already forbidden by the scriptures ..." *(Sed quoniam istae in coemeteriis ebrietates et luxuriosa convivia, non solum honores martyrum a carnali et imperita plebe credi solent, sed etiam solatia mortuorum; mihi videtur facilius illic dissuaderi posse istam foeditatem ac turpitudinem, si et de Scripturis prohibeatur)* (from Augustine, *Epistolae*, in *Opera omnia* 2, ed. Migne, Patrologia Latina 33, col. 92).

Lemures palmares.

Kaukie, sunt lemures, quos Russi Uboze appellant: barbatuli, altitudine unius palmi extensi: iis qui illos esse credunt conspicui: aliis minime. His cibi omnis edulii aponuntur. Quod nisi fiat, ea sunt opinione, ut ideo suas fortunas (id quod accidit) amittant: nutriunt etiam quasi deos penates, nigri coloris, obesos et quadrupedos, quosdam serpentes, Giuoitos vocatos. Hos timore perculsi, dum ex antris aedium ad pastum appositum prorepunt, seque pasti in ea recipiunt, aspiciunt et colunt. Si quid infortunii accidat cultori, serpentem male fuisse tractatum censent.

Srutis, et Miechutele, colorum dii sunt: quos in silvis, colores ad lanam tingendam quaerentes venerantur.

Isti sunt pluresque alii vulgi Samagitarum dii. quem admodum apostolus, "Sunt" inquit "dii et domini multi," 1. Corin. 8. At Christianorum Unus Deus est, Pater Filius et Spiritus Sanctus. In cuius nomine sacrum Baptisma sumitur. Et in quem, iuxta formulam symboli Apostolorum creditur. Qui personis discreti, essentia unum sunt. Omnia quae haec mundi machina continet, fecerunt, neque posthaec otiantur: "Pater" inquit "meus usque adhuc operatur et ego operor."

Dii falsorum Christianorum.

Et tamen permulti sunt Christiani, qui hoc unico omnipotenti numine minime contenti, et tam Samagitas quam veteres idolatras imitati, alios sibi ipsis adiutores finxerunt. Iohannes enim [p. 52] et Paulus superstitiosa opinione illorum, quaeque noxia a segetibus avertit. Ignis Agathae, ceu Vestae datus est curandus. Florianus miles, incendia restinguit. ut quidem haec liber de Origine erroris recenset Bullingerus. Nicolaus, quasi alter Neptunus, maris curam gerit. Idem a periclitantibus, iis vocibus excitantur: "O sancte Nicolae, nos ad portum maris trahe." Eidem sacella in littoribus consecrantur. Huius collega est, gigas Christoph[orus]. Canitur et B. Virgini, exortis procellis istud Carmen: "Ave maris stella, Dei alma mater." Et, "Salve Regina misericordiae, vita et spes nostra. Ad te clamamus."

Palm-sized spirits[24]

The Kaukai are the spirits whom the Rus'ians call *Uboze*; they have little beards, and are as tall as a single open palm. There are notable people who believe they exist; others not at all. They put out food and all kinds of edible things for them. Their opinion is that unless they do this they will thereby lose their good luck, whatever happens. They also feed like gods certain household gods—black in colour, fat, and four feet long, and certain snakes called Gyvatès. Overpowered by fear, while the snakes crawl from the entrances of the houses to the nearby pasture, they welcome them, look at them, and worship them. If something unfortunate befalls one of the worshippers, they consider that the person treated a snake badly.

Srutis and Mèletèlè are deities of colours, who are venerated by those who seek colours for dyeing wool in the woods.

And there are many more common gods of the Samogitians, for as the apostle says, "there be gods many, and lords many" (1 Corinthians 8:5). But the God of the Christians is one God, Father, Son, and Holy Spirit, in whose name holy baptism is received, and who is believed in according to the formula of the Apostles' Creed—who, while distinct in persons, are one in essence. They made everything that the machine of this world contains, nor did they afterwards remain idle: [Jesus] says, "My Father worketh hitherto, and I work" (John 5:17).

The gods of the false Christians

And there are also very many Christians who, not content with this one all-powerful spirit, and imitating the Samogitians as much as their old idolatries, fix on others as their helpers. For it is their superstitious opinion that John and Paul repel certain diseases from crops. Fire is given to the care of Agatha, as if she were Vesta. The soldier Florianus extinguishes fires, as Bullinger writes in a certain book on the origin of error.[25] Nicholas, like another Neptune, holds responsibility for the sea. The same is called upon by those in danger with these words, "O St. Nicholas, draw us to a seaport!" Chapels on the seashore are dedicated to him. His colleague is the giant Christopher. And this hymn is sung to the Blessed Virgin when storms spring up: "Hail, star of the sea," "Loving Mother of God," and "Hail, queen of mercy, our life, and our hope, to you we call …."[26]

---

24 *Lemures* has the sense of "spectres" or even "spirits of the dead," but in the context the more ambiguous term "spirits" seems a more suitable translation.

25 The reference is to Heinrich Bullinger, *De origine erroris libri duo* (1568), fol. 90v: "Others attribute these offices to John and Paul. Fire is assigned to Agatha, like a certain new Vesta; and Florianus is added for her who fears the terrifying energy of the fire less than all the others on account of the stupidity of her sex, entrusted with the equipment, who like a certain Inachus pours water from an urn into the fierce fire. To these is added Nicholas, the sea god, favourable to sailors—no doubt taking the place of Castor and Pollux; and his colleague next following is believed to be Christopher."

26 A reference to the three popular Marian hymns "Hail, star of the sea" (Ave maris stella), "Loving mother of our Saviour" (Alma redemptoris mater) and "Hail, holy queen" (Salve regina).

Vino praeest Urbanus. Rubigenem frumenti purgat Iodocus. Brucos depellit Magnus. Anseres curae sunt sancto Gallo, oves Vendelino, equi Eulogio, boves Pelagio, porci Antonio. alia nomina in aliis regionibus, harum similiumque rerum ficti curatores habent. Gertrudis mures a colis a colis mulierum abigit. Literarum studiosi Catharinam Virginem Alexandrinam, veluti alteram Minervam, alii vero Gregorium, quasi Mercurium colunt, ac huius die festo primum, suos natos, in scholas mittunt. Pictores Lucam, Medici Cosmam et Damianum, fabri Eulogium, calcearii Crispinum, Sarctores Gutmanum, figuli quendam Goarum, venatores Eustachium civem Romanum; scorta Aphram et Magdalenam invocant. Supplicant alii aliis, ac in periculis vitae constituti, vota illis nuncupant: in hos tutelam sui reiiciunt. Imploratur in pestilentia, ut olim Apollo, Sebastianus in morbo Gallico Rochus in febri Petronella, in dolore capitis Ita: dentium Apollonia, in partu Margarita, quemadmodum quondam Iuno ac Lucina. Iohannes Evangelista a veneno conservat. Wolphgangus contractorum Medicus est. Romanus Daemoniacos soluit. Marcus mortem repentinam avertit. Martinus miseriam. Quem et ego puer hisce verbis inclamabam: "Martine Sancte pontifex, sis miserorum opifex. Fer opem tuis famulis." Leonhardus vinctorum compedes rumpit. Vincentius amissa restituit. Valentinus comitiali morbo laborantes sanat. Quapropter nos epilepsiam, Valentini morbum vocamus. Susanna ignominiam arcet. Otilia oculis aegrotorum medetur. Collo praesidet Blasius, scapulis Laurentius. Erasmi venter est totus. Nicolao apud nos gregis est custodia iniuncta. Andreas, vigilia festi sui invocatur a ieiunis puellis, futuros illarum viros praemonstrat. Barbara a caedibus bellicis conservat. [p. 53] Quocirca tum a nostrae gentis hominibus in auxilium magnis clamoribus elicitur. Invocatur et virgo Maria, cuius Carmen, Deipara vocatum, ab iis qui in bellum proficiscuntur decantatur, legibus additum nostris. Adeo etiam periculosissimis temporibus, Deus servator omnium suo honore fraudatur.

Defensores provinciarum.

Praeterea sunt patroni terrarum constituti, non divina, sed humana voluntate. Stanislaus Polonorum, Albertis Prussorum, Nicolaus Moscorum, Martinus Germanorum, Iacobus Hispanorum, Dionysius Gallorum, Petrus, Paulus Romanorum, Marcus Venetorum, tres magi Coloniensium, Ambrosius Mediolanensium, virgo Maria et Ladislaus Hungarorum. Quod etiam aurei nummi testantur. At quis non videt, quomodo ii suas provincias tueantur?

Urban is in charge of wine. Judoc purifies grain from mildew. Magnus repels locusts. Geese are the special care of St. Gall, sheep of St. Wendelin, horses of St. Eulogius, cattle of St. Pelagius, and pigs of St. Anthony. In other regions these fictitious guardians of similar matters have other names. Gertrude drives away mice from women's affairs. Some learned in letters venerate the virgin Catharine of Alexandria, like another Minerva, and others Gregory, and first send their children to the schools on her feast day. Painters invoke Luke, physicians Cosmas and Damian, craftsmen Eulogius, shoemakers Crispin, tailors Homobonus, potters a certain Goar, hunters Eustachius, a Roman citizen; prostitutes invoke Afra and Magdalene.

Others pray to others, and make vows to them when they are in peril of their lives, giving themselves to their care. Sebastian is supplicated against plague, like Apollo of old; Roche against syphilis; Petronella against fever; Ita against headache; Apollonia for teeth, Margaret in childbirth, just like Juno and Lucina at one time. John the Evangelist preserves from poison. Wolfgang is the physician of the paralyzed. Romanus frees demoniacs. Mark averts sudden death, and Martin misery. And, as a boy, I used to call on him in these words, "O St. Martin the bishop, be an aid of the miserable; help your servants." Leonard breaks the manacles of the chained. Vincent restores what was lost; Valentine cures those labouring under the "disease of the assembly," for which reason we call epilepsy St. Valentine's disease. Susanna prevents ignominy. St. Odile cures the eyes of the sick. Blaise presides over the neck, Laurence over the shoulders. The whole stomach belongs to Erasmus. Among us, the protection of the flock is entrusted to Nicholas. Andrew is invoked on the eve of his feast day by fasting girls, and shows them their future husbands. Barbara preserves from death in war; on account of which great shouts for help are elicited from men of our nation.

And the Virgin Mary is invoked, whose hymn, called *Deipara*,[27] is sung by those who set out for war, and added to our laws. For thus, even in the most dangerous of times, God the Saviour of all is robbed of his honour.

Defenders of provinces

Furthermore, patrons of the earth are set up, not by divine but by human will. Stanislaus is the patron of the Poles, Albert of the Prussians, Nicholas of the Muscovites, Martin of the Germans, James of the Spanish, Denis of the French, Peter and Paul of the Romans, Mark of the Venetians, the three Magi of the citizens of Cologne, Ambrose of the Milanese, and the Virgin Mary and Ladislaus of the Hungarians. These are even attested on their gold coins. But who may not see in what way they guard their provinces?

---

27 Probably a reference to the hymn known as the "Hymn of St. Casimir," *In honorem Deiparae Virginis Mariae* ("In honour of the Virgin Mary, Mother of God"). On the Hymn of St. Casimir see Rigg, *St Anselm of Canterbury*, 96–103.

Ridet haec suaviter in *Naufragio* Erasmus Rot[terodamensis] minime Lutheranus. "Quamobrem tu, inquit, nullius divi praesidium implorasti?" "Quia spaciosum est coelum," respondit alter. "Si cui divo commendaro meam salutem, puta sancto Petro, qui fortasse primus audiet, quod adstet ostio, priusquam ille conveniat Deum, priusquam exponat causam ego iam periero. Recta adibam ipsum patrem, dicens: "Pater noster, qui es in coelis". Nemo divorum illo citius audit, aut libentius donat quod petitur."

Historia delectat.

Verum cum omnis historia quoquo modo scripta delectet, non pigebit lectoris causa de moribus nostrorum Sarmatarum plura adscribere. Haec igitur Iohannes Meletius Archipresbyter Ecclesiae Licensis in Prussia, Anno salutiferi partus 1553. ad Georgium Sabinum poëtam, litteris prodidit. Quae etiamnum multis in locis observantur.

Plura de diis Sarmaticis.

Die Georgii sacrificium faciunt Pergrubrio. Qui florum, plantarum omniumque germinum deus creditur. Sacrificulus enim, quem Wurschaiten appellant, tenet dextra obbam cervisiae plenam, invocatamque daemonii nomine, decantat illius laudes. "Tu," inquit, "abigis hyemem, tu reducis amoenitatem veris, per te agri et horti vigent, per te nemora et silvae frondent." Hac cantilena finita, dentibus apprehendens obbam, ebibit cervisiam nulla adhibita manu: ipsamque obbam, ita mordicus epotam, retro, supra caput iacit. Quae, cum e terra sublata, iterum impleta est: omnes quotquot adsunt, ex ea bibunt ordine, atque in laudem [p. 54] Pergrubii hymnum canunt. Postea epulantur tota die et choreas ducunt.

Similiter, quando iam segetes sunt maturae, rustici in agris ad sacrificium congregantur. Quod lingua Ruthenica Zazinek vocatur, id est, initium messis. Hoc sacro peracto, unus e multitudine electus, messem auspicatur, manipulo demesso, quem domum adfert. Postridie omnes, primo illius domestici, deinde caeteri quicunque volunt, messem faciunt. Facta autem messe, solenne sacrificium pro gratiarum actione conficiunt. Quod Ruthenica lingua Ozinek, id est, consummatio messis dicitur. In hoc sacrificio, Sudini Borussiae populi, apud quos succinum colligitur, capro litant, congregato namque populi coetu in horreo, adducitur caper.

Erasmus of Rotterdam, not at all a Lutheran, sweetly mocks this in his *Shipwreck*. "Why," he asks, "do you not seek the help of any saint?" "Because heaven is spacious," replies another. "If I should commend my welfare to some saint—think of St. Peter— who happens to be the first to hear, because he stands at the gate, he will meet God first; he will first expound the reason I am now perishing. I shall go straight to the same father, saying 'Our Father, who art in heaven ....' None of the saints hears faster than him, or gives more freely what is asked."[28]

The narrative delights

Since all of this narrative is written in a like manner to delight, it will not disgust anyone for us to write more about the customs of our Sarmatians on account of the reader. On this, therefore, Jan Malecki, archpriest of the church of Lyck in Prussia, produced letters to the poet George Sabinus in the year of salvation 1553,[29] which are seen even today in many places.[30]

More on Sarmatian gods

On St. George's Day they make a sacrifice to Pergrubris, who is believed to be the god of flowers, plants, and all growing things. The priestling, whom they call *Viršaitis*, holds in his right hand a beaker full of beer, and invoking the demon by name, chants these praises: "You drive winter away and bring back the comfort of spring; by you the fields and gardens flourish; by you the woods and groves come into leaf." Having finished this little chant, gripping the beaker with his teeth, he drinks the beer, with no use of hands allowed, and having gnawed it, he throws the same emptied beaker back over his head. When it has been picked up from the ground and filled again, everyone present drinks from it in order, and they sing a hymn in praise of Pergrubris. Afterwards they feast for the whole day, and take part in dances.

Similarly, when the crops are ready, the country people gather in the fields for the sacrifice which in the Ruthenian language is called *Zazinek*—that is, the beginning of harvest. When this rite has been performed, one chosen from the multitude divines the harvest from a cut handful which he takes home. The next day everyone—first those of that household, and then others who want to—gathers the harvest. When the harvest has been gathered in they perform a solemn sacrifice as an act of thanksgiving, which in the Ruthenian language is called *Ozinek* (that is, the end of harvest). In this sacrifice the Sudovian people of Prussia, among whom sap is collected, perform divination from the sacrifice of a goat. When the people are gathered together in a granary, the goat is led in.

---

28 The quotation is from the dialogue of the sailors Antony and Adolph in Erasmus's colloquy *Naufragium* ("The Shipwreck"); see Erasmus, *Colloquies*, trans. C. R. Thompson, Collected Works of Erasmus 29 (Toronto: University of Toronto Press, 1997), 356 (lines 26–30).

29 *Sic.* for 1551.

30 The remaining text is taken almost verbatim from Malecki, *Libellus de sacrificiis et idolatria*, ed. Schmidt-Lötzen, 185–96, with some small differences which are noted here in the footnotes.

Invocatio deorum.

Quem Wurschaites mactaturus, imponit victimae utramque manum, invocatque ordine daemones, quos ipsi deos esse credunt. Videlicet Occopiruum, deum coeli et terrae, Antrimpum maris, Gardoeten nautarum, Potrympum fluviorum ac fontium, Piluitum divitiarum, Pergrubrium veris, Pargruum tonitruum ac tempestatum, Pocclum inferni ac tenebrarum, Pocollum aëreorum spirituum, Putscetum sacrorum lucorum tutorem. Auscuntum incolumitatis et aegritudinis, Marcoppolum magnatum et nobilium, Barstuccas, quos Germani Erdmenlin, hoc est, subterraneos vocant. His invocatis, quotquot adsunt in horreo, omnes simul extollunt caprum, sublimemque tenent, donec canatur hymnus. quo finito, rursus eum sistunt in terra. Tum sacrificulus admonet populum ut solenne hoc sacrificium, a maioribus pie institutum, summa cum veneratione faciant, eiusque memoriam religiose ad posteros conservent.

Victima.

Post haec mactat victimam, sanguinemque patina exceptum dispergit; carnem vero tradit mulieribus, eodem in horreo coquendam. Quae interea dum caro coquitur, parant e farina siliginea placentas. Quas non imponunt in furnum, sed viri focum circumstantes, hinc illinc per focum iaciunt absque cessatione, quoad indurescant et coquantur. His peractis epulantur atque helluantur tota die ac nocte usque ad vomitum. Deinde summo mane extra villam progrediuntur. Ubi reliquias epularum certo in p. 55 loco terra operiunt, ne vel a volatilibus, vel a feris diripiantur. Postea suam quisque domum repetit.

Caeterum ex omnibus Sarmatiae gentibus, Borussis, Livonibus, Samagitis, Russis, multi adhuc singulari veneratione colunt Putscetum, qui sacris arboribus et lucis praeest. Is sub sambuco domicilium habere creditur. Cui passim homines litant, pane, cervisia aliisque cibis sub hac arbore positis, precantes eum ut placatum efficiat Marcoppolum, deum magnatum et nobilium, ne gravi servitute ad illis premantur. Utque sibi mittantur Barstuccae, quibus in domibus ipsorum viventibus, credunt se fieri fortunatiores.

Penates.

His ipsi collocant vesperi in horreo super mensam, mappa stratam, panes, caseos, butyrum et cervisiam. Nec dubitant de fortunarum accessione, si mane hos cibos absumptos reperiant. Quod si aliquando intactus cibus in mensa remanet, magna anguntur cura, nihil non adversi intuentes. Eaedem gentes colunt spiritus quosdam visibiles, qui lingua Ruthenica Coltki, Graeca Cobili, Germanica Coboldi vocantur.

Invocation of the gods

The *Viršaitis* who is about to slaughter it places each hand on the victim and invokes in order the demons whom they believe to be gods. That is to say, Ukapirmas, the god of heaven and earth; Antrimpas the god of the sea; Gardaitis the god of sailors; Patrimpas the god of rivers and springs; Pilvytis the god of riches; Pergrubris the god of spring; Perkūnas the god of thunder and storms; Poklius the god of hell and shadows; Pokulas the god of spirits of the air; Puškaitis[31] the guardian of the sacred groves; Aušautas the god of health and illness; Markopolas the god of magnates and nobles; and the Barstukai, whom the Germans call *Erdmenlein*. Having invoked these, as many as are present in the granary lift up the goat at the same time, and hold it aloft while a hymn is sung. When this is finished they put it down again on the ground. Then the priestling admonishes the people that they should perform the solemn sacrifice devoutly instituted by their ancestors with the utmost veneration, and preserve the memory religiously for posterity.

The victim

After this he slaughters the victim, and having caught the blood in a dish, he scatters it. He gives the flesh to the women to be cooked in that same granary. In the meantime, while the flesh is cooked, they prepare pancakes of wheat. They do not put these in an oven, but the men, standing around fires, throw them here and there through the fire without stopping, until they harden and are cooked. Having done these things, they feast and overindulge all day and all night, to the point of vomiting. Then, on the last morning, they process outside the village. Here, in a certain place, they bury the remains of the feast in the ground lest it be taken away by birds or by wild animals. Afterwards each returns to his house.

Of all the other Sarmatian peoples—the Prussians, Livonians, Samogitians, and Rus'ians—many still worship Puškaitis, who is in charge of sacred trees and groves. He is believed to have his dwelling beneath the elder. Everywhere people offer him sacrifice, putting bread, beer, and other foods beneath this tree, beseeching him to placate Markopolas, the god of magnates and nobles, lest they should be oppressed by heavy servitude to them. And the Barstukai are sent from him, who, living in their homes, they believe make them more fortunate.

Household spirits

For these they put out bread, cheese, butter, and beer in the evening on a table draped with a cloth. And they do not doubt the arrival of good fortune if, in the morning, they discover the food consumed. But if any food remains untouched on the table, they are greatly troubled with anxiety, perceiving nothing as not unlucky. The same peoples worship certain visible spirits who are called *koboldy* in the Ruthenian language, *kobaloi* in Greek, and *Kobolde* in German.

---

31 The Lithuanian version of this theonym was reconstructed by Greimas, *Of Gods and Men*, 22–23.

Cultus spirituum.

Hos habitare credunt in occultis etiam aedium locis, vel in congerie lignorum. Nutriuntque eos laute omni ciborum genere, eo quod afferre soleant altoribus suis frumentum, ex alienis horreis furto ablatum. Cum vero hi spiritus alicubi habitare atque ali cupiunt, hoc modo suam erga patremfamilias voluntatem declarant: in domo congerunt noctu segmenta lignorum, et mulctris lacte plenis imponunt varia animalium stercora. Quod ubi paterfamilias animadvertit, nec segmenta dissipaverit, nec stercora e mulctris eiecerit, sed de inquinato lacte cum omni sua familia comederit, tunc illi apparere permanereque dicuntur.

Serpentum.

Praeterea Lituani et Samagitae in domibus sub fornace, vel in angulo vaporarii ubi mensa stat, serpentes fovent. quos numinis instar colentes, certo anni tempore precibus sacrificuli, evocant ad mensam. Hi vero exeuntes per mundum linteolum conscendunt, et super mensam morantur. Ubi delibatis singulis ferculis, rursus discedunt, aeque abdunt in cavernis. Serpentibus digressis, homines laeti fercula praegustata comedunt, ac sperant illo anno omnia [p. 56] prospere sibi eventura. Quod si ad preces sacrificuli, non exierunt serpentes, aut fercula apposita non delibaverint: tum credunt se anno illo subituros magnam calamitatem. Adhaec eaedem gentes habent inter se sortilegos, qui lingua Ruthenica Burti vocantur. Ii Potrimpum invocantes, caerem in aquam fundunt, atque ex imaginibus inter fundendum expressis, pronuntiant et vaticinantur, de quibuscunque rebus interrogati fuerint. Novi ipse mulierculam, quae cum diu reditum filii absentis expectasset, ex Borussia in Daniam profecti, consuluit super eo sortilegum. a quo edocta est, naufragio illum periisse. Caera enim in aquam fusa, expressit formam fractae navis, effigiem resupini hominis iuxta navim fluitantis. Apud Samagitas est mons ad fluvium Newassam situs, in cuius vertice olim perpetuus ignis a sacerdote conservabatur, in honorem Pargni, qui tonitruum et tempestatum potens esse, a superstitiosa gente adhuc creditur.

Ritus nuptiales.

Hactenus de sacrificiis. nunc de ritibus nuptiarum ac funerum, non minus ridicula quam superstitiosa narrabo.

Apud Sudinos, Curonenses, Samagitas et Lituanos nubiles puellae multis in locis gestant tintinnabulum. Quod funiculo alligatum, e cingulo dependet usque ad genua. Nec ducuntur, sed rapiuntur in matrimonium, veteri Lacedemoniorum more a Lycurgo instituto. rapiuntur autem non ab ipso sponso, sed a duobus eius cognatis. Ac postquam raptae sunt, tunc primum requisito parentum consensus, matrimonium contrahitur. Cum nuptiae celebrantur; sponsa ter ducitur circa focum: deinde ibidem in sella collocatur. Super quam sedenti, pedes lavantur aqua.

The cult of the spirits

They believe that these live in hidden places of buildings, or in the crossing of beams. And they feed them sumptuously with all kinds of food, so much so that they are accustomed to bring grain to their nourishers, stolen by theft from other granaries. When these spirits wish to live and be fed elsewhere, they declare their will to the head of the family in this way; they gather pieces of beams in the house at night, and put the dung of various animals in pails full of milk. When the head of the family notices this, he will neither break up the pieces, nor empty the dung from the milk pails, but will drink the contaminated milk with all his family; then [the Barstukai] are said to appear and remain.

The cult of snakes

Furthermore, the Lithuanians and Samogitians keep snakes warm underneath the stove, or in the chimney corner where the table stands. At a certain time of year the priestlings, worshipping them as the image of a deity, call them by prayers to the table. Coming up by a clean linen cloth they crawl up, and remain on the table. Having tried several dishes, they depart again, and likewise hide themselves in caves. When the snakes have gone, the people joyfully eat the pre-tasted dishes, and hope that everything will turn out prosperously that year. But if the snakes do not come out at the prayers of the priestlings, or they do not taste the dishes that have been put out, they believe a great calamity will befall them that year. And those same people have sorcerers still among them who are called *burti[ninkai]* in the Ruthenian [*sic.*] language. These people, invoking Potrimpus, pour wax into water, and expound and divine from the images made during the pouring on whatever matters they are asked about. I myself knew a little woman who had long awaited the return of her absent son who had set out from Prussia to Denmark. She consulted a sorcerer about him, from whom she learnt that he had perished in a shipwreck. For the wax, poured into the water, took the form of a broken ship, with the effigy of a man lying on his back floating next to the ship. Among the Samogitians there is a hill situated by the River Nevėžis, on whose summit at one time a perpetual fire was kept burning by a priest in honour of Perkūnas, who is still believed by this superstitious people to be powerful in thunder and tempests.

Nuptial rites

So much for sacrifices. Now I will tell about nuptial and funerary rites, which are no less ridiculous than they are superstitious.

Among the Sudovians, Couronians, Samogitians, and Lithuanians young women of marriageable age wear a bell in many places. Tied to a cord, it hangs from her girdle to her knees. And they are not taken in marriage but carried off, after the ancient Spartan fashion instituted by Lycurgus. But they are not carried off by the groom himself, but by two of his relatives. And after they are carried off, then the parents' consent is first sought, and a marriage is contracted. When the marriage is celebrated the bride is led three times around the hearth; then she is set in a seat. As she sits on it her feet are washed with water.

Qua lectus nuptialis, tota supellex domestica, et invitati ad nuptias hospites consperguntur. Postea sponsae os oblinitur melle et oculi teguntur velamine, quibus sic velatis, ducta ad omnes edium fores, iubetur eas attingere dextroque pulsare pede. Ad singulas fores circumspergitur tritico, siligine, avena, hordeo, pisis, fabis, papavere, sequente uno sponsam cum sacco pleno omnis generis frugum. Cumque eam hic circumspergit, inquit, nihil defuturum sponsae si religionem coluerit, remque domesticam ea qua debet diligentia curaverit. His actis aufertur sponsae velamen ab oculis, et convivium celebratur. Similis olim obnubendi ratio ▓p. 57▓ capitis apud Latinos, nuptae nuptiarumque nomen dedit. Vesperi sponsae ad lectum deducendae, abscinduntur inter saltandum crines. tum ei a mulieribus imponitur sertum, albo linteolo obvolutum. Quod uxoribus gestare licet donec filium pepererint. Tamdiu enim se pro virginibus gerunt. Ad extremum introducitur in cubiculum: pulsataque et verberata aliarum pugnis, non iratarum, sed nimia quadam laeticia gestientium, in lectum iniicitur sponsoque traditur. Tum pro bellariis afferuntur testiculi caprini vel ursini. Quibus illo nuptiali tempore manducatis, creduntur coniuges fieri foecundi. Eandem ob causam nullum animal castratum ad nuptias mactatur.

Parentalia.

Contra in funeribus hic servatur a rusticanis ritus: Defunctorum enim cadavera vestibus et calceis induuntur et erecta super sellam locantur. Quibus assidentes propinqui perpotant ac helluantur. Epota vero cervisia, fit hisce verbis lingua Ruthenica funebris lamentatio: *Ha lele i procz ti mene vmari? i za ti nie miel szto iesti, abo piti? i procz ti vmari? Ha le le, i za ti nie miel Krasnoie mlodzice? I procz ti vmari?* Id est, "Hei hei quare tu mihi mortuus es? An non quod comederes vel biberes habuisti? Quare mortem obiisti? Hei hei mihi, num formosa coniuge caruisti? Cur diem obiisti?" Hoc modo lamentantes enumerant ordine omnia externa mortui bona, liberos, oves, boves, equos, anseres, gallinas. Ad quae singula respondentes, occinunt hanc naeniam: "Cum haec habueris, quamobrem mortuus es?" Lamentatione absoluta, dantur cadaveri munuscula. Mulieri fila cum acu: viro linteolum collo eius implicatum.

With this water the nuptial bed, all the household goods, and those invited to the wedding are sprinkled. Afterwards the bride's mouth is smeared with honey and her eyes covered with a veil. Thus veiled, she is led to all the doors of the building and ordered to touch and kick them with her right foot. Each door is sprinkled with corn, wheat, reeds, barley, peas, beans, and poppy seeds, since someone follows the bride with a sack full of all kinds of produce. And as she thus sprinkles around her, she says there will be nothing wanting for the bride if she cultivates religion and carries out all her domestic duties as she should. When these things have been done the bride's veil is lifted from her eyes and a feast is celebrated (A similar method of marrying the head among the Latins, gave the name of nuptials to the bride[32]). In the evening the bride is led to the bed, and her hair is let down amid dancing. Then a scarf made of folded white linen is placed on her by the women,[33] which wives are permitted to wear until they bear a son. Until then they bear themselves as if virgins. At last she is led into the bedroom, pushed and pummelled by the fists of others, not out of anger but from the excessive joy of those who are eager,[34] and she is thrown into bed and given to her husband. Then the testicles of a goat or bear are brought as sweetmeats; these, they believe, if eaten at the time of marriage, make the spouses fertile. For the same reason no castrated animal is slaughtered at the feast.

The *Parentalia*

By contrast, at funerals this serves as a rite for the country people: for the bodies of the dead are dressed in clothes and shoes, and placed upright in chairs, and their relatives drink and make merry with them sitting down. When the beer has been drunk, this lamentation is sung in the words of the Ruthenian language: *Ha lele i procz ti mene vmari? i za ti nie miel szto iesti, abo piti? i procz ti vmari? ha le le, i za ti nie miel Krasnoie mlodzice? i procz ti vmari?* That is, "Alas, alas, why are you dead to me? Do you not have food to eat or drink to drink? Why have you fallen into death? Alas, alas for me, did you lack a handsome wife? Why did you die that day?" Lamenting in this way, they enumerate in order all of the deceased's external goods, children, sheep, cattle, horses, geese, and chickens; and each replying to this, they chant this dirge: "Since you had all this, why did you die?" When the lamentation is finished, gifts are given to the body: to a woman, a needle and thread; to a man, a strip of linen wrapped around his neck.

---

32 An obscure passage thatAlišauskas (Łasicki, *Pasakojimas apie Žemaičių Dievus*, ed.Ališauskas, 128n24) suggests may be an annotation by Łasicki, perhaps included in error in the printed text.

33 Łasicki's text here differs from Malecki, *Libellus de sacrificiis et idolatria*, ed. Schmidt-Lötzen, 192, since Malecki describes the bride's hair being cut before the headcovering is put on (as well as describing the headcovering as *adornatum* ("decorated"). This suggests that Łasicki may have been aware of slight changes in customs between his era and when Malecki was writing.

34 Łasicki's explanation of why the bride is pushed and pummelled is an addition to Malecki's text.

Daemones fugantur.

Cum ad sepulturam effertur cadaver, plerique equis funus prosequuntur, et ad currum obequitant, quo cadaver vehitur. Strictisque gladiis verberant auras, vociferantes,
Geigeite begaite pekelle. "Eia fugite daemones in Orcum." Qui funus mortuo faciunt, nummos proiiciunt in sepulchrum futurum mortui viaticum. Panem quoque et lagenam cer-
visie plenam, ad caput cadaveris in sepulchrum illati, ne anima vel sitiat vel esuriat, collocant. Uxor vero tam oriente quam occidente sole, super extincti coniugis sepulchrum
sedens vel iacens, lamentatur diebus triginta. Caeterum cognati celebrant convivia die a
funere tertio, sexto, nono et quadragesimo. Ad quae animam defuncti invitant, precantes
ante ianuam. Ubi tacite assident mensae, tanquam muti, nec utuntur cultris: ministran-
tibus [p. 58] duabus mulieribus, sed absque cultris, cibumque hospitibus apponentibus.
Singuli vero de unoquoque ferculo aliquid infra mensam abiiciunt, quo animam pasci
credunt, eique potum effundunt. Si quid forte decidat in terram de mensa, id non tollunt: sed desertis, ut ipsi loquuntur animis, quae nullos habent vel cognatos vel amicos
vivos, a quibus excipiantur convivio, relinquunt manducandum. Peracto prandio, surgit
a mensa sacrificulus, et scopis domum verrens, animas mortuorum cum pulvere, tanquam pulices, haec dicens eiicit. *Jeli, pili, duszice, nu ven, nu ven.* "Edistis," inquit, "bibistis, animae, ite foras, ite foras." Posthaec incipiunt convivae inter se colloqui et certare
poculis, mulieribus viris praebibentibus, et viris vicissim illis, sequentur invicem oscu-
lantibus. Haec de parentalibus paganorum, quorum et sanctus Augustinus sermone 15.
de sanctis meminit: "Miror" inquit "cur apud quosdam infideles hodie tam perniciosus
error increverit, ut super tumulos defunctorum cibos et vina conferant. Quasi egressae
de corporibus animae, carnales cibos requirant. epulas enim et refectiones, caro tantum
requirit, spiritus autem et anima iis non indigent. Parare aliquis suis charis dicit, quod
ipse devorat. Quod enim et refectiones, caro tantum requirit, spiritus autem et anima iis
non indigent. Parare aliquis suis charis dicit, quod ipse devorat. quod praestat ventri,
imputat pietati."

The demons put to flight

When the body is being borne to the tomb, many horses follow the funeral procession and ride up to the cart on which the body is carried. With drawn swords they beat the air, shouting: *Geigeite begaite pekelle*, "Demons! Flee now to Orcus!"[35] When they perform the funeral rites for the dead, they throw coins into the tomb to be provision for the journey for the dead; also bread and a bottle full of beer laid at the head of the body in the tomb—lest their soul should either be hungry or thirsty. The wife, sitting or lying on the tomb of her dead husband from sunrise to sunset, laments for thirty days. The other relatives celebrate feasts on the third, sixth, ninth, and fortieth days after the funeral, to which they invite the soul of the deceased, praying before the doorway. They sit down in silence at the table like mutes, and do not use knives, serving the food to the guests.[36] Each one of them discards a dish under the table, from which they believe the soul feeds, and they pour out drink for it. If anything happens to fall to the floor from the table they do not pick it up; but they say that they leave it to be eaten by the lonely souls who have neither relatives nor friends alive, for whom it is taken from the feast. When the meal is finished, the priestling rises from the table and, sweeping the house with a broom, ejects the souls of the dead with the dust like fleas, saying: *Jeli, pili, duszice, nu ven, nu ven*: "You have eaten, you have drunk, o souls; go outside! Go outside!" Afterwards the dinner guests begin to talk among themselves and compete in drinking, the women outdrinking the men, and going on to kiss each of the men in turn.[37] St. Augustine, in his Sermon 15 [*sic*] on the saints, recalls this about the *Parentalia* of the pagans: "I marvel," he says, "how among certain unbelievers such a pernicious error has grown, that they bestow food and wine on the tombs of the dead. As if, once souls have left the body, they require fleshly food. For the soul and spirit do not need feasts and refreshment, even though flesh requires it. Someone says he prepares edible roots for them, which he himself devours. That which supplies the stomach, he imputes to piety."[38]

---

35 Malecki, *Libellus de sacrificiis et idolatria*, ed. Schmidt-Lötzen, 192 has *in infernum*.

36 Łasicki here omits a sentence from Malecki, *Libellus de sacrificiis et idolatria*, ed. Schmidt-Lötzen, 193: "Two women serve at the table, who put the food before the guests, using no knife at all."

37 Łasicki omits Malecki's reference to the men kissing one another.

38 Augustine, Sermon 190 (from Augustine, *Sermones*, in *Opera omnia* 5, part 2, ed. Migne, Patrologia Latina 39, col. 2101).

BIBLIOGRAPHY

Primary Texts

Ališauskas, Vytautas, ed. *Baltų Religijos ir Mitologijos Reliktai Lietuvos Didžioje Kunigaikštystejė (XIV–XVIII a.): Šaltinių Rinkinys* [abbrev. *BRMR*]. Vilnius: Lietuvių Katalikų Mokslo Akademija, 2016.

Augustine. *The City of God against the Pagans*. Edited and translated by R. W. Dyson. Cambridge: Cambridge University Press, 1998.

Bullinger, Heinrich. *De origine erroris libri duo*. Zurich: Froschauer, 1568.

Buonaccorsi, Filippo. *Vita et mores Sbignei cardinalis*. Edited by Ludwik Finkel. Lviv: Academia Scientiarum Cracoviensis, 1891.

Dantyszek, Jan [Johannes Dantiscus]. *Victoria serenissimi Poloniae regis contra Vayevodam Muldaviae, Turcae tributarium et subditum, 22. Augusti parta*. Rome: Blado, 1531.

——, *Ioannes Dantiscus' Correspondence with Alfonso de Valdés*. Edited by Anna Skolimowska. Warsaw: Polska Akademia Umiejętności, 2013.

Długosz, Jan [Johannes Dlugossus]. *Historiae Polonicae libri XII*, 2 vols. Leipzig: Gleditsch and Weidmann, 1711–1712.

——. *The Annals of Jan Długosz: A History of Eastern Europe from A.D. 965 to A.D. 1480*. Translated by Maurice Michael. Chichester: IM, 1997.

Erasmus, Desiderius. *Collected Works of Erasmus*. Various translators. 89 vols. Toronto: University of Toronto Press, 1974–2019.

Grunau, Simon. *Preussische Chronik*. Edited by M. Perlbach. 3 vols. Leipzig: Duncker und Humblot, 1875–1896.

Guagnini, Alessandro. *Sarmatiae Europeae descriptio, quae regnum Poloniae, Lituaniam, Samogitiam, Russiam, Masoviam, Prussiam, Pomeraniam, Livoniam, et Moschoviae, Tartariaeque partem complectitur*. Speyer: Albin, 1581.

Hemming, Nicolaus [Niels Hemmingsen]. *Admonitio de superstitonibus magicis vitandis*. Copenhagen: Stockelman and Gutterwitz, 1575.

Hussovianus, Nicolaus. *Song of the Bison: Text and Translation of Nicolaus Hussovianus's "Carmen de statura, feritate ac venatione bisontis."* Edited and translated by Frederick J. Booth. Leeds: Arc Humanities Press, 2019.

Kromer, Martin. *De origine et rebus gestis Polonorum libri XXX*. Basel: Oporinus 1555.

Łasicki, Jan. *De diis Samagitarum caeterorumque Sarmatarum, et falsorum Christianorum*. In *De moribus Tartarorum, Lituanorum et Moschorum, fragmina X multiplici Historia referta, et Iohanni Lasicii Poloni de diis Samagitarum, caeterorumque Sarmatarum, et falsorum Christianorum, item de religione Armeniorum*. Edited by Johann Grasser, 42–58. Basel: Waldkirch, 1615. Available online at http://www5.kb.dk/e-mat/dod/120700017250_color.pdf.

——. *Jono Lasickio Pasakojimas apie Žemaičių Dievus*. Edited and translated by Vytautas Ališauskas. Vilnius: Aidai, 2012.

Lituanus, Michalo. *De moribus Tartarorum, Lituanorum et Moschorum, fragmina X*. In *De moribus Tartarorum, Lituanorum et Moschorum, fragmina X multiplici Historia referta, et Iohanni Lasicii Poloni de diis Samagitarum, caeterorumque Sarmatarum, et falsorum Christianorum, item de religione Armeniorum*. Edited by Johann Grasser, 1–41. Basel: Waldkirch, 1615. Available online at http://www5.kb.dk/e-mat/dod/120700017250_color.pdf.

Malecki, Hieronim. *De sacrificiis et idolatria veterorum Borussorum, Livonum, et aliarum vicinarum gentium.* In *Livoniae historia in compendium ex annalibus contracta a Thoma Hornero Egrano; de sacrificiis et idolatria veterum Livonum et Borussorum libellus Ioannis Menecii.* Edited by Thomas Horner, sigs F ıJr–(G ıııJr). Königsberg [Kaliningrad/ Królewiec]: Lufft, 1551.

——. "Libellus de sacrificiis et idolatria veterum Borussorum, Livonum, aliarumque vicinarum gentium." Edited by K. E. Schmidt-Lötzen. *Mitteilungen der Litterarischen Gesellschaft Masovia* 8 (1902): 177–96.

Mažvydas, Martinas. *Catechismusa prasty szadei.* Königsberg [Kaliningrad/Królewiec], 1547.

Miechowa, Maciej z. *Tractatus de duabus Sarmatiis Asiana et Europiana et de contentis in eis.* 2nd ed. Augsburg: Grimm and Wirsung, 1518.

Münster, Sebastian, *Cosmographiae universalis libri VI.* Basel: Petri, 1554.

Patrologia Latina cursus completus. Edited by J.-P. Migne. 221 vols. Paris: Migne, 1844–64.

Piccolomini, Enea Silvio. *Cosmographia Pii Papae in Asiae et Europae eleganti descriptione.* Paris: Estienne, 1509.

Rostowski, Stanisław. *Lituanicarum Societatis Iesu historiarum libri decem.* Vilnius, 1768.

Rotundus, Augustine. *Epitome principum Lituaniae.* In *Studya nad stosunkami narodowościowemi na Litwie przed Unią Lubelską.* Edited by Jan Jakubowski, 94–104. Warsaw: Nakładem Towarzystwa Naukowego Warszawskiego, 1912.

Sarnicki, Stanisław. *Annales, sive de origine et rebus gestis Polonorum et Lituanorum, libri octo.* Kraków, 1587.

Stryjkowski, Maciej. *Kronika Polska.* Königsberg [Kaliningrad/Królewiec]: [Osterberg], 1582.

Stüler, Johannes [Erasmus Stella]. *De Borussiae antiquitatibus libri duo.* Basel: Froben, 1518.

Vėlius, Norbertas, ed. *Baltų Religijos ir Mitologijos Šaltiniai* [abbrev. *BRMŠ*]. 4 vols. Vilnius: Mokslo ir Enciclopedijų Leidykla, 1996–2005.

Secondary Sources

Ališauskas, Vytautas and Pranas Vildžiūnas. *Dingęs Šventybės Pasaulis: Dievai ir Šventieji XVI a. Žemaitijoje: Jono Lasickio Knygos Interpretacija.* Vilnius: Aidai, 2009.

Allen, Nick J. "Debating Dumézil: Recent Studies in Comparative Mythology." *Journal of the Oxford Society of Anthropology* 24 (1993): 119–31.

Almagor, Eran and Joseph Skinner, eds. *Ancient Ethnography: New Approaches.* London: Bloomsbury, 2013.

Amato, Loredana Serafini. "Morfologia dei composti nominali de Prussiano antico." *Europa Orientalis* 11 (1992): 197–222.

Ando, Clifford. "Interpretatio Romana." In *The Impact of Imperial Rome on Religions, Ritual and Religious Life in the Roman Empire,* edited by Lukas de Blois, Peter Funke, and Johannes Hahn, 51–65. Leiden: Brill, 2006.

Antonov, Dmitriy. "Between Fallen Angels and Nature Spirits: Russian Demonology of the Early Modern Period." In *Fairies, Demons, and Nature Spirits: "Small Gods" at the Margins of Christendom,* edited by Michael Ostling, 123–44. London: Palgrave MacMillan, 2018.

Barisitz, Stephan. *Central Asia and the Silk Road: Economic Rise and Decline over Several Millennia.* Cham: Springer, 2017.

Baronas, Darius. "Christians in Late Pagan, and Pagans in Early Christian Lithuania: The Fourteenth and Fifteenth Centuries." *Lithuanian Historical Studies* 19 (2014): 51–81.

Baronas, Darius and S. C. Rowell. *The Conversion of Lithuania: From Pagan Barbarians to Late Medieval Christians.* Vilnius: Institute of Lithuanian Literature and Folklore, 2015.

Beard, Mary, John North, and Simon Price. *Religions of Rome*. 2 vols. Cambridge: Cambridge University Press, 1998.

Belier, Wouter W. *Decayed Gods: Origin and Development of Georges Dumézil's* Idéologie Tripartie. Leiden: Brill, 1991.

Berend, Nora, ed. *Christianization and the Rise of Christian Monarchy: Scandinavia, Central Europe and Rus' c. 900–1200*. Cambridge: Cambridge University Press, 2007.

Beresnevičius, Gintaras. "Rickoyotto šventykla: Simono Grunau aprašymas ir kultinis Šiaurės Europos kontekstas ankstyvaisiais Viduramžiais." *Naujasis Židinys-Aidai* 10 (1996): 621–29.

——. *Lietuvių Religija ir Mitologija: Sisteminė Studija*. Vilnius: Tyto Alba, 2004.

——. "Prūsijos amfiktionijos steigtis prūsų legendose ir germaniškasis kontekstas." *Baltų Mitologos Fragmentai* 31 (2006): 190–200.

Bojtár, Endre. *Foreword to the Past: A Cultural History of the Baltic People*. Budapest: Central European University Press, 1999.

Bonda, Moreno. *History of Lithuanian Historiography: Didactical Guidelines*. Kaunas: Vytautas Magnus University, 2013.

Boureau, Alain. *Satan the Heretic: The Birth of Demonology in the Medieval West*. Chicago: University of Chicago Press, 2006.

Brienen, Rebecca Parker. *Visions of Savage Paradise: Albert Eckhout, Court Painter in Colonial Dutch Brazil*. Amsterdam: Amsterdam University Press, 2006.

Brummett, Palmira. "The Myth of Shah Ismail Safavi: Political Rhetoric and 'Divine' Kingship." In *Medieval Christian Perceptions of Islam*, edited by John V. Tolan, 331–60. London: Routledge, 1996.

Cameron, Euan. *Enchanted Europe: Superstition, Reason, and Religion, 1250–1750*. Oxford: Oxford University Press, 2010.

Carver, Martin, ed. *The Cross Goes North: Processes of Conversion in Northern Europe, AD 300–1300*. Woodbridge: York Medieval Press, 2003.

Cervantes, Fernando. *The Devil in the New World: The Impact of Diabolism in New Spain*. New Haven: Yale University Press, 1994.

Chauvin, Pierre. *A Chronicle of the Last Pagans*. Translated by B. A. Archer. Cambridge, MA: Harvard University Press, 1990.

Classen, Albrecht, ed. *Meeting the Foreign in the Middle Ages*. London: Routledge, 2002.

Davies, Owen. *Paganism: A Very Short Introduction*. Oxford: Oxford University Press, 2011.

Davies, Surekha. *Renaissance Ethnography and the Invention of the Human: New Worlds, Maps and Monsters*. Cambridge: Cambridge University Press, 2016.

Dini, Pietro U. *Prelude to Baltic Linguistics: Earliest Theories about Baltic Languages (16th Century)*. Leiden: Brill, 2014.

Frost, Robert. *The Oxford History of Poland-Lithuania: The Making of the Polish-Lithuanian Union, 1385–1569*. Oxford: Oxford University Press, 2015.

Fonnesberg-Schmidt, Iben. *The Popes and the Baltic Crusades, 1147–1254*. Leiden: Brill, 2007.

Frick, David A. *Polish Sacred Philology in the Reformation and the Counter-Reformation: Chapters in the History of Controversies*. Berkeley: University of California Press, 1989.

Gimbutas, Marija. *The Balts*. New York: Praeger, 1963.

Green, Richard Firth. *Elf Queens and Holy Friars: Fairy Beliefs and the Medieval Church*. Philadelphia: University of Pennsylvania Press, 2016.

Gładysz, Mikolaj. *The Forgotten Crusaders: Poland and the Crusader Movement in the Twelfth and Thirteenth Centuries*. Leiden: Brill, 2012.

Greimas, Algirdas J. *Of Gods and Men: Studies in Lithuanian Mythology*. Bloomington: Indiana University Press, 1992.

Hoggett, Richard. *The Archaeology of the East Anglian Conversion*. Woodbridge: Boydell and Brewer, 2010.

Hutton, Ronald. "How Pagan Were Medieval English Peasants?" *Folklore* 122 (2011): 235–49.

———. *Pagan Britain*. New Haven: Yale University Press, 2013.

Hyland, William P. "John-Jerome of Prague (1368–1440): A Norbertine missionary in Lithuania," *Analecta Praemonstratensia* 78 (2002): 228–54.

Insoll, Timothy. "Introduction." In *Archaeology and World Religion*, edited by Timothy Insoll, 1–32. London: Routledge, 2001.

Jaskiewicz, W. C. "A Study in Lithuanian Mythology: Jan Łasicki's Samogitian Gods." *Studi Baltici* 1, no. 9 (1952): 65–106.

Kahk, Juhan. "Estonia II: The Crusade against Idolatry." In *Early Modern European Witchcraft: Centres and Peripheries*, edited by Bengt Ankarloo and Gustav Henningsen, 273–84. Oxford: Clarendon, 1990.

Kaushik, Roy. *Military Transition in Early Modern Asia, 1400–1750: Cavalry, Guns, Government and Ships*. London: Bloomsbury, 2014.

Khanmohamadi, Shirin A. *In Light of Another's Word: European Ethnography in the Middle Ages*. Philadelphia: University of Pennsylvania Press, 2014.

Klussis, Mikkels, ed. *Old Prussian Written Monuments: Text and Comments*. Kaunas: Lithuanians' World Center for Advancement of Culture, Science and Education, 2007.

Knoll, Paul W. *"A Pearl of Powerful Learning": The University of Cracow in the Fifteenth Century*. Leiden: Brill, 2016.

Koczerska, Maria. "L'amour de la patrie et l'aversion pour la dynastie: exemple de Jan Dlugosz, historiographe des Jagellon." *Pariser Historische Studien* 47 (1998): 171–80.

Kregždys, Rolandas. "Sūduvių knygelės nuorašų formalioji analizė bei analitinė eksplikacija." *Archivium Lithuanicum* 20 (2018): 89–124.

———. "On the Origin of the Mythonyms OPruss. *Worskaito / Borsskayto* (S. Grunau) // Yatv. *Wourschkaite* (*Yatvigian Book*)." *Komunikaty Mazursko-Warmińskie* 4 (2019): 780–807.

Krollmann, Christian. *Das Religionswesen der alten Preußen*. Königsberg [Kaliningrad/Królewiec]: Altpreußische Forschungen, 1927.

Lepschy, Giulio C., ed. *History of Linguistics, Volume III: Renaissance and Early Modern Linguistics*. 2nd ed. London: Routledge, 2014.

Louthan, Howard. "A Model of Christendom? Erasmus, Poland, and the Reformation." *Church History* 83 (2014): 18–37.

Lupher, David A. *Romans in a New World: Classical Models in Sixteenth-Century Spanish America*. Ann Arbor: University of Michigan Press, 2003.

MacCormack, Sabine. *On the Wings of Time: Rome, the Incas, Spain, and Peru*. Princeton: Princeton University Press, 2007.

McLean, Matthew. *The Cosmographia of Sebastian Münster: Describing the World in the Reformation*. London: Routledge, 2007.

Malcolm, Noel. *Useful Enemies: Islam and the Ottoman Empire in Western Political Thought, 1450–1750*. Oxford: Oxford University Press, 2019.

Mänd, Anu and Marek Tamm, eds. *Making Livonia: Actors and Networks in the Medieval and Early Modern Baltic Sea Region*. London: Routledge, 2020.

Mažeika, Rasa "Granting Power to Enemy Gods in Chronicles of the Baltic Crusades." In *Medieval Frontiers: Concepts and Practices*, edited by David Abulafia and Nora Berend, 153–71. London: Routledge, 2002.

Meltzer, Françoise. "Reviving the Fairy Tree: Tales of European Sanctity." *Critical Enquiry* 35 (2009): 493–520.

Meserve, Margaret. *Empires of Islam in Renaissance Historical Thought*. Cambridge, MA: Harvard University Press, 2008.

Mierzyński, Antoni. "Jan Łasicki. Źródła do mytologii litewskiej." *Rocznik towarzystwa naukowego z uniwersytetem Krakowskim połączonego*, ser. 3, 18 [cum. 41] (1870): 1–102. Available online at http://hint.org.pl/hid=a5001.

Miller, Dean A. "Georges Dumézil: Theories, Critiques and Theoretical Extensions." *Religion* 30 (2000): 27–40.

Mishima, Kenichi. "The 'Disenchantment of the World' or Why We Can No Longer Use the Formula as Max Weber Might Have Intended." In *The Oxford Handbook of Max Weber*, edited by Edith Hanke, Lawrence Scaff and Sam Whimster, 353–74. Oxford: Oxford University Press, 2020.

Mullett, Michael. *Historical Dictionary of the Reformation and Counter-Reformation*. Plymouth: Scarecrow, 2010.

Murray, Alan V., ed. *Crusade and Conversion on the Baltic Frontier, 1150–1500*. London: Routledge, 2001.

——, ed. *The Clash of Cultures on the Medieval Baltic Frontier*. Farnham: Ashgate, 2009.

——. "The Saracens of the Baltic: Pagan and Christian Lithuanians in the Perception of English and French Crusaders to Medieval Prussia." *Journal of Baltic Studies* 41 (2010): 413–29.

Nagy, Gregory. *Greek Mythology and Poetics*. Ithaca: Cornell University Press, 1990.

Narbutas, Sigitas. "Latinitas in the Grand Duchy of Lithuania: Chronology, Specifics and Forms of Reception." In *Latinitas in the Polish Crown and the Grand Duchy of Lithuania: Its Impact on the Development of Identities*, edited by Giovanna Siedina, 145–60. Florence: Firenze University Press, 2014.

Niedźwiedź, Jakub. "How Did Virgil Help Forge Lithuanian Identity in the Sixteenth Century?" In *Latinitas in the Polish Crown and the Grand Duchy of Lithuania: Its Impact on the Development of Identities*, edited by Giovanna Siedina, 35–48. Florence: Firenze University Press, 2014.

Noyes, Dorothy. "The Social Base of Folklore." In *A Companion to Folklore*, edited by Regina F. Bendix and Galit Hassan-Rokem, 13–39. Chichester: Wiley, 2012.

Ostling, Michael. "Introduction: Where've all the Good People Gone?" In *Fairies, Demons, and Nature Spirits: "Small Gods" at the Margins of Christendom*, edited by Michael Ostling, 1–53. London: Palgrave MacMillan, 2018.

Palmer, James T. "Defining Paganism in the Carolingian World." *Early Medieval Europe* 15 (2007): 402–25.

Pluskowski, Aleksander. *The Archaeology of the Prussian Crusade: Holy War and Colonisation*. London, Routledge, 2013.

Pócs, Éva. "Small Gods, Small Demons: Remnants of an Archaic Fairy Cult in Central and South-Eastern Europe." In *Fairies, Demons, and Nature Spirits: "Small Gods" at the Margins of Christendom*, edited by Michael Ostling, 255–76. London: Palgrave MacMillan, 2018.

Pompeo, Lorenzo. "Etnografia umanistica ne *L'epistola sulla religione ed i sacrifici degli antichi prussiani* di Jan Sandecki Malecki (Meletius)." *Studia Mythologica Slavica* 3 (2000): 63–74.

Rasmussen, Siv. "The Protracted Sámi Reformation—or the Protracted Christianising Process." In *The Protracted Reformation in Northern Norway: Introductory Studies*, edited by Lars Ivar Hansen, Rognald Heiseldal Bergesen and Ingebjørg Hage, 165–84. Stamsund: Orkana, 2016.

Reynold, Burnam W. *The Prehistory of the Crusades: Missionary War and the Baltic Crusades*. London: Bloomsbury, 2016.

Rigg, James M. *St Anselm of Canterbury: A Chapter in the History of Religion*. London: Methuen, 1896.

Robbins, Joel. "Crypto-Religion and the Study of Cultural Mixtures: Anthropology, Value, and the Nature of Syncretism." *Journal of the American Academy of Religion* 79 (2011): 408–24.

Rowell, S. C. *Lithuania Ascending: A Pagan Empire within East-Central Europe, 1295–1345.* Cambridge: Cambridge University Press, 1994.

———. "Unexpected Contacts: Lithuanians at Western Courts, c. 1316–c. 1400." *English Historical Review* 111 (1996): 557–77.

Rubiés, Joan Pau. *Travel and Ethnology in the Renaissance: South India through European Eyes, 1250–1625.* Cambridge: Cambridge University Press, 2000.

Russell, Frederick. "Paulus Vladimiri's Attack on the Just War: A Case Study in Legal Polemics." In *Authority and Power. Studies on Medieval Law and Government Presented to Walter Ullmann*, edited by Brian Tierney and Peter Linehan, 237–54. Cambridge: Cambridge University Press, 1980.

Segal, Robert A., ed. *Structuralism in Myth: Lévi-Strauss, Barthes, Dumézil, and Propp.* London: Routledge, 1996.

Selart, Anti. *Livonia, Rus' and the Baltic Crusades in the Thirteenth Century.* Leiden: Brill, 2015.

Tamm, Marek, Linda Kaljundi, and Carsten Selch Jensen, eds. *Crusading and Chronicle Writing on the Medieval Baltic Frontier: A Companion to the Chronicle of Henry of Livonia.* Farnham: Ashgate, 2011.

Tasbir, Janusz. "La conquête de l'Amérique à la lumière de l'opinion polonaise." *Acta Poloniae Historica* 17 (1968): 5–22.

Torres, Mónica Domínguez. *Military Ethos and Visual Culture in Post-Conquest Mexico.* Farnham: Ashgate, 2013.

Trinkūnas, Jonas, ed. *Of Gods and Holidays: The Baltic Heritage.* Vilnius: Tvermė, 1999.

Usačiovaitė, Elvyra. "Motiejus Strijkovskis apie lietuvių pagonybę: aukojimas dievams." *Kultūrologija* 18 (2010): 107–39.

Vaitkevičius, Vykintas. "The Main Features of the State Religion in Thirteenth-Century Lithuania." *Balto-Slavic Studies* 16 (2004): 331–56.

Valk, Heidi. "Christianisation in Estonia: A Process of Dual-Faith and Syncretism." In *The Cross Goes North: Processes of Conversion in Northern Europe, AD 300–1300*, edited by Martin Carver, 571–80. Woodbridge: York Medieval Press, 2003.

Vėlius, Norbertas. *The World Outlook of the Ancient Balts.* Vilnius: Mintis, 1989.

Watson, Christine. *Tradition and Translation: Maciej Stryjkowski's Polish Chronicle in Seventeenth-Century Russian Manuscripts.* Uppsala: Acta Universitatis Upsalensis, 2012.

Weber, David J. "Conquistadores of the Spirit." In *Colonial America: Essays in Politics and Social Development*, edited by Stanley N. Katz, John M. Murrin, and Douglas Greenberg, 127–56. New York: McGraw Hill, 2001.

Young, Francis. *A History of Exorcism in Catholic Christianity.* London: Palgrave MacMillan, 2016.

———. "Lingua semilatina: de fabulata origine linguae Lituanicae apud auctores saeculi sexti decimi." *Vox Latina* 56 (2020): 57–61.

———. "Authorities and Control." In *A Cultural History of Magic in the Age of Enlightenment*, edited by Andrew Sneddon. London: Bloomsbury, forthcoming.

Zinkevičius, Zigmas. *The History of the Lithuanian Language.* Vilnius: Mokslo ir Enciklopedijų Leidybos Institutas, 1998.

LITHUANIAN SUMMARY / SANTRAUKA

Baltai priėmė krikščionybę vieni paskutiniųjų Europoje, o protėvių ikikrikščioniškos religinės praktikos išliko dar ne vieną amžių po oficialaus krikšto. Pagonys (ir neseniai tokiais buvę) lietuviai ir prūsai žavėjo Renesanso humanistus, kurie svetimą religinę sistemą siekė suprasti pasitelkdami naujausius istoriografinius ir etnografinius metodus. XIV a. pab., iškilus Jogailaičių dinastijai ir Lietuvos Didžiajai Kunigaikštystei tapus viena iš didžiųjų krikščioniškojo pasaulio jėgų, europiečiams tapo itin svarbu suprasti lietuvių kilmę. Priešingai nei ankstyvaisiais Viduramžiais, kai pagonybė krikščionių buvo smerkiama, ankstyvuoju Naujųjų laikų periodu lietuvių religija buvo nuodugniai tyrinėjama, tikintis atrasti bet kokių įrodymų apie tariamą romėnišką lietuvių kilmę. Tuo pačiu Reformacija paskatino iš naujo stengtis atversti baltus į krikščionybę. Su šiomis pastangomis įsivyravo ir suvokimas, kad tikslas bus pasiektas tik perpratus baltų kalbas ir kultūrą.

Į šią knygą įtraukti 11 autorių tekstai parašyti tarp 1450 ir 1590 m. lotynų kalba, universalia mokslinės komunikacijos kalba krikščioniškajame Vakarų pasaulyje. Kartu šie tekstai suteikia vienus iš detaliausių, bet kuriai ikikrikščioniškai Europos religijai tinkančius aprašymus. Vis dėlto skaitant šiuos tekstus privalu atsižvelgti į kontekstą. Be atidžios analizės jie negali būti pasitelkiami baltų religinės pasaulėžiūros ar praktikų rekonstravimui. Autoriai rašė atsižvelgdami į interpretavimo ir literatūros tradicijas. Kai kurios jų menė Senovės pasaulį, taigi atskirti literatūros apie pagonybę ypatumus nuo faktinių detalių gali būti nemenkas iššūkis. Vis dėlto daugumą šių tekstų būtų galima pavadinti smalsumo pergale prieš akstiną pasmerkti netikinčiuosius. Šie humanistiniai baltų pagonybės aprašymai tiek atitiko senuosius, tiek nuspėjo būsimus nepažįstamų Naujojo pasaulio religinių sistemų aprašymus. Būdami tokie jie yra labai svarbūs siekiant suvokti, kaip Europos krikščionys XV ir XVI a. bandė pažinti vietines religijas. Dėl šios priežasties ankstyvojo Naujųjų laikų periodo baltų pagonybės aprašymai yra svarbūs pasauliui tiek pat, kiek jie yra svarbūs Europai ar nacionaliniu lygmeniu Baltijos šalims.

Vertė Saulė Kubiliūtė

INDEX

The index refers to the Introduction and English translations. Place names are given in the modern country where they are located, in the language of that country.

Printed in the United States
by Baker & Taylor Publisher Services